WELCOME TO THE ERA OF GEORGE M. STEINBRENNER . . .

1973: George M. Steinbrenner III takes over ownership of the New York Yankees. Two Yankees pitchers make headlines by swapping wives, houses, kids, and pets.

1976: Billy Martin takes over as Yankees manager. Yanks win pennant, lose to Reds in World Series. George brings Reggie Jackson to New York.

1977: Martin and Jackson brawl in dugout. Jackson hits three home runs in a row. Yanks win World Series!

1978: Jackson calls Martin and Steinbrenner "liars." Martin quits. Yankees win Series again.

1979: Steinbrenner fires championship manager Bob Lemon. Rehires Martin. Thurman Munson dies in plane crash. Martin fights marshmallow salesman in Minneapolis. Steinbrenner fires him again.

1983: Steinbrenner fires manager Clyde King. Hires Billy Martin. George Brett in infamous pine-tar incident. Winfield arrested for beaning a seagull in Toronto. Yanks make headlines, not Series.

1984: Martin fired again. Yogi Berra hired. Yankees stumble. Yogi fired.

1987: Yanks finish fourth. Steinbrenner fires almost everyone. Hires Billy Martin as manager again.

1990: Steinbrenner suspended from baseball for contacts with gambler. Yanks finish seventh.

1995: Yanks play first postseason game in fourteen years—and the glory years begin!

. . . NEW YORK HAS NEVER BEEN THE SAME!

ALSO BY MAURY ALLEN

ALL ROADS LEAD TO OCTOBER

BOSS STEINBRENNER'S 25-YEAR REIGN OVER THE NEW YORK YANKEES

MAURY ALLEN

St. Martin's Paperbacks

For Amanda and Matthew,
both great

ALL ROADS LEAD TO OCTOBER

Copyright © 2000 by Maury Allen.

Jacket Photographs of Reggie Jackson and Derek Jeter by AP/Wideworld Photos

Jacket Photograph of Yankee Stadium © Rich Pilling/Major League Baseball

Inside cover photos courtesy of the Associated Press

Library of Congress Catalog Card Number: 00-027850

ISBN: 0-312-97868-5

Printed in the United States of America

St. Martin's Press hardcover edition / July 2000
St. Martin's Paperbacks edition / April 2001

St. Martin's Paperbacks are published by St. Martin's Press, 175 Fifth Avenue, New York, NY 10010.

10 9 8 7 6 5 4 3 2 1

ACKNOWLEDGMENTS

The heart of this book is the joy of the game. Baseball has been a vital part of my life for more than six decades as a boyish fan, a schoolyard player, a caring observer. It began at a historic place called Ebbets Field where my parents paid for the bleacher seats and sent me off on a Brooklyn subway with older friends. In 1947, I spend a night on a Bedford Avenue and Sullivan Place corner at World Series time for a glimpse of a game between the Brooklyn Dodgers and the New York Yankees. Joe DiMaggio homered off Rex Barney.

Soon I was traveling north to Yankee Stadium where they let us walk on that historic grass after games in those days, the same field where Babe Ruth, Lou Gehrig, and Joe DiMaggio played; where Mickey Mantle would soon play; and Reggie Jackson, Goose Gossage, Thurman Munson, and Lou Piniella would bring the Yankees back to their former glory.

I was writing sports by then and being paid, really, for sitting above the field at Yankee Stadium, at Shea Stadium, at Wrigley Field and Fenway Park, at Tiger Stadium and Forbes Field, at a wonder of creation called the Houston Astrodome and a fantasy field called Dodger Stadium.

Each day was an adventure. Each game was unique. Each player was a challenge. I admired them all for the skills they showed in hitting, fielding, running, and throwing and devoted my professional energies to bringing readers a taste of those times.

This work is a celebration of more than a quarter of a century of exciting Yankee baseball years on and off the field as I witnessed them, recorded them, and enjoyed them.

My wondrous wife, Janet Allen, edited each and every word before anything could escape my computer. If the Yankees are famous for winning as a Team with that large *T*, Janet and Maury Allen live, work, and love as a Team.

Our kids, daughter Jennifer Blazkiewicz and husband Tom with their children, Amanda and Matthew, our so grand grandchildren, and son Ted and wife Sheryl were supportive and encouraging during the grinding process of concept to book.

My Hall of Fame agent, Doris Michaels, thrust the idea at me for this work. She is the Joe Torre of agents, a creative leader who has a wonderful sense of timing and tact.

Joe Veltre, associate editor at St. Martin's Press, was patient and considerate from title to text.

A huge amount of thanks goes to all my sportswriting colleagues, dead and alive, for contributions at any past moment. This work is partly the sum total of all those memories from press boxes, airplane rises, bus trips, and dimly lit bars.

Finally, appreciation goes to all the players who wore the Yankee uniform with honor, all the managers and coaches, and all the executives from George M. Steinbrenner III on down who understood the tradition of this Team of the Century.

PROLOGUE

Boss.

There could never be a nickname enjoyed more. Everyone calls George M. Steinbrenner III, principal owner of the New York Yankees, winners of three World Series titles in the last four years of the twentieth century, the Boss.

They may call him other things behind his back. He simply laughs, wiggles his fingers showing off World Series rings, and moves through life with entitled arrogance.

George Herman Ruth was the Babe. Lou Gehrig was the Iron Horse. Joe DiMaggio was the Yankee Clipper. Mickey Mantle was the given Mickey. Ted Williams was the Splendid Splinter. Bob Feller was Rapid Robert. Stan Musial was the Man. Nolan Ryan piloted the Ryan Express. William Ellsworth Hoy was Dummy. Who said all nicknames are wonderful?

Steinbrenner was the Boss of all bosses, the dominant figure in baseball, a significant American icon or villain depending on the point of view, a power in the national social scene of the last quarter of the twentieth century.

On a crisp, late September evening of 1999, as the Yankees moved closer to their third World Series title in four years, Steinbrenner arrived by limousine at the entrance of Tavern on the Green, one of New York's swankiest restaurants on the west side of Central Park.

This was an A-list party given by public relations magnate Howard Rubenstein, celebrating his forty-five years in the business of getting the names of important people into the newspapers and seen on television, or keeping them out as the case might be.

The Boss showed up early. He wore his familiar white

turtleneck shirt, a dark sports jacket, light trousers, glistening, black shoes, perfectly groomed hair, and that good old boy smile of his.

There were 3,500 guests spread around in the dozen Tavern on the Green dining rooms filled with outrageously colorful Tiffany-style chandeliers, gleaming gilded mirrors, and a glitteringly wrapped tree sparkling with miniature Christmas lights at the center of the restaurant.

The Boss stood in the middle of the largest dining room as photographers begged for photos of the Yankee leader with A-list guests. He posed with Diane Sawyer, the television anchor lady, and her husband, producer/director Mike Nichols; with New York City Mayor Rudolph Giuliani; with The Donald (not a bad nickname but no Boss), building magnate Donald Trump and that evening's hand-picked supermodel; New York City Police Commissioner Howard Safir, the man who made NYC safer. Also in attendance were psychological love specialist Dr. Ruth Westheimer in all her four-feet-nine-inch glory, and the former Duchess of York, Sarah Ferguson, an ex-royal and Weight Watchers ingenue.

As lightbulbs flashed and the media hordes moved closer to the Boss and friends, even Rubenstein had to notice who was the star of his anniversary party.

Sarah Ferguson, who has been in the United States long enough to know better, admitted she did not know who Steinbrenner was, but was pleased to pose for pictures with him. She turned to the Boss and said, "I don't know who you are but you must be very successful."

She probably asked him for World Series tickets a few weeks later.

Steinbrenner worked the room carefully, shaking hands, signing autographs, chatting with Randy Levine, former baseball executive and now an aide to the New York City mayor.

I caught the Boss in the corner of the largest dining room, congratulated him on the 1999 pennant the Yankees were about to clinch and asked about the impending merger of the Yankees with the New Jersey Nets NBA basketball team for cable television income purposes. I told him we were probably the only two people in the room who remembered his time in basketball more than a quarter of a century earlier with the Cleveland Pipers.

"Yeah," he said, "and we won."

A few days later Steinbrenner was sitting in his Stadium office, high above the historic field where Babe Ruth, Lou Gehrig, Joe DiMaggio, Mickey Mantle, Yogi Berra, and Whitey Ford created the Yankees dynasty—the most famous sports team in the world.

Fans drove along the Major Deegan highway, emptied out of the Bronx subway stop on 161st Street, walked across the Third Avenue Bridge, and sauntered through Macombs Dam Park on their way to the House That Ruth Built.

There was a crowd of 57, 545 in the Stadium as the Yankees opened the 1999 Division series against the Texas Rangers. They beat the Rangers 8-0 in the first game behind Cuban exile Orlando Hernandez. The man known as El Duque allowed the Rangers only two hits, Bernie Williams had six RBIs and made a sliding catch of a fly ball hit by Juan Gonzalez. The Yankees coasted to their seventh straight Division series win over Texas.

The only dramatic moment of the game came in the fifth inning when Yankee second baseman Chuck Knoblauch hit a foul ball into the Yankee dugout. The baseball crashed into the left side of coach Don Zimmer's face, bruising his jaw and cutting his ear. Trainer Steve Donohue treated Zimmer on the dugout floor as worried manager Joe Torre watched. Zimmer was taken back into the clubhouse for further treatment. He quickly reappeared on the bench with an ice bag held against his jaw.

The next day Zimmer sat on the Yankee bench wearing an old army helmet with the Yankee logo letters *NY* painted on the front.

Andy Pettitte, a left-hander born in Baton Rouge, Louisiana, and raised in Deer Park, Texas, set the Rangers down over 71/3 innings in the second game, got relief help from Jeff Nelson and the ever-present Mariano Rivera, and won 3-1.

After the game the Yankees flew by chartered jet to Texas for the third game of the series. George Steinbrenner sat in the front of the plane. Joe Torre sat a couple of rows behind him. Coach Don Zimmer, now recovered from his foul-ball attack, was at his side.

Zimmer had started his baseball career fifty years earlier riding battered old school buses to out-of-town games. He lived in dollar-a-night rooming houses, walked to wooden ballparks, lived on hot dogs and sodas, and was paid $125 a month. He loved every minute of it.

Now he rode with Steinbrenner, Torre, and the players of the Yankees on sleek, chartered jets; stayed in huge rooms in luxury hotels; dined in the finest restaurants; was carried back and forth to ballparks in luxury buses; and was paid a quarter of a million dollars a year. He loved every minute of it.

The Texas series ended in Arlington at The Ballpark in Arlington (What a great name for a ballpark in Arlington) with a 3-0 Yankees win. Roger Clemens allowed only three hits in seven innings, Darryl Strawberry hit a three-run homer, and the Yankees sent Texas home again after three games.

Clemens had purchased more than thirty tickets for family members and friends with his wife, Debra, and their four sons cheering him on. Clemens had been a power pitcher for over fifteen years in Boston, Toronto, and now New York; had struck out over 3,100 batters; and had once struck out 20 batters in a single game. Baseball score sheets mark strike-outs with the letter K. Clemens had marked his legacy with his sons—Koby, Kory, Kacy, and Kody—all having names starting with the letter K.

The Yankees win over the Rangers was expected. What was *not* expected in New York was the Mets win over the Arizona Diamondbacks.

If the Mets could get past Atlanta in the next series and the Yankees were to win the American League Championship Series against Boston, a Subway series, the first in New York since 1956, would thrill New Yorkers and probably aggravate the rest of the country.

The Yankees did their part by beating Boston four games to one.

The Mets made it exciting by threatening Atlanta after losing the first three games of that series. Reminded that no team in baseball history had ever come back to win from three games down, the Mets continued their dream season with two wins at Shea Stadium and a final 10-9 loss in Atlanta in the last game when left-hander Kenny Rogers walked home the winning run. He should have stuck to his singing.

The Mets had lost seven in a row and seemed out of the wild-card race in the final days of the season. Then they won three in a row over Pittsburgh, finished the regular season in a wild card tie with Cincinnati, and beat the Reds for a chance at the playoffs on their own home field.

Joel Martin, a lifelong friend of mine and a fifty-year baseball fan, said the Mets reminded him of his dead alcoholic uncle.

"When my uncle died, of causes unrelated to drinking, it took them two days to beat his liver to death after the rest of him had already quit breathing," Martin said at the end of the Mets' unsuccessful run for the pennant. "The Mets were like that. They died three weeks ago but the Braves had to beat up on their liver to finally put them away."

The Red Sox, surprisingly, beat Cleveland in the other Division playoff. It cost Mike Hargrove—the guy known as the Walking Rain Delay during his playing days because he took so much time getting ready to hit at home plate—his managerial job.

Boston really thought they could beat the Yankees. They had done well all year against them and they had the best pitcher in baseball, Pedro Martinez, on their side. How foolish of them. This was October.

Boston fans know that for them October is all about agony and anguish. Yankee fans know October is all about trial and triumph.

Bernie Williams hit a leadoff homer in the tenth inning of game one of the ALCS for a 4-3 Yankees win. Boston cops were carefully watching the Charles River for possible jumpers. It had happened before.

The Yankees went up two games to none after David Cone pitched a gritty seven innings in a Stadium chill; Chuck Knoblauch and Paul O'Neill got key hits and the Yankees won 3-2.

Examine the Curse of the Bambino for an instant. Babe Ruth was traded from Boston to the Yankees in 1920. Not many good things have happened in Boston baseball since. Consider a Series loss in 1946 to the Cardinals, a bitter defeat to the Reds in 1975, the blown fourteen-game lead and playoff loss to the Yankees in 1978, and the agonizing loss to the Mets in 1986.

Are Boston fans just gluttons for punishment? Why don't they stay home in October and read books?

Instead they filled Fenway Park again, with 33,871 people shoe-horned inside the charming old park first opened in 1912. Roger Clemens, the Rocket who provided so much hope for so many years in the Back Bay, was awful. Martinez, despite back problems, allowed only two hits. The Red Sox won 13-1.

Could this be the year? Could the Red Sox shake the disasters of seventy-nine years and thrust the haughty Yankees out on their ears in this ALCS battle? Could those banners in the stands demanding an end to the Curse by the likes of Boston's Nomar Garciaparra; John Valentin; the Martinez brothers, Pedro and Ramon; former Yankee Mike Stanley; and manager Jimy Williams, a guy who can't even spell his own first name, be realized?

Not in this fading twentieth century.

The Yankees beat the Red Sox 9-2 the next day for a 3-1 lead. Manager Williams was tossed out of the game for arguing a call. Red Sox fans, giving in to a lifetime of frustration, threw batteries, soda and water bottles, and half-eaten fruit onto the field. The Yankees just wanted to get out of town.

George Steinbrenner sat through it all in a box seat next to the Yankees dugout. He wore a heavy Yankees jacket over his suit and turtleneck shirt against the Massachusetts chill.

Scout Frank Dolson, a former newspaper columnist in Philadelphia, sat next to him.

When the game ended Steinbrenner walked onto the field into a waiting television camera.

"This is a disgrace," he said of the Boston fans' conduct.

The Yankees closed out their thirty-sixth pennant triumph the next night with an easy 6-1 win. Derek Jeter and Jorge Posada hit two-run homers, Orlando Hernandez was splendid on the mound, and the Red Sox knew they would add another year to their run of no Series triumphs since 1918. Just keep cursing, Bambino.

The possibility of an all New York World Series ended the next night. Atlanta beat the Mets 10-9 in the second thriller of the set after New York's fifteenth-inning win on Robin Ventura's grand-slam single, a ball that went over the wall with three on but was converted into a single by onrushing Mets well-wishers around second base.

Orlando "El Duque" Hernandez opened the Series for the Yankees in Atlanta on October 23, 1999, the last Series in the twentieth century, the second for the Cuban exile and the seventh for The Boss in twenty-seven seasons as Yankee leader.

Luis Tiant, a Cuban right-hander who pitched a couple of years with the Yankees in 1979 and 1980 after a noble career with Boston, turned completely around on the mound as he looked at the center field wall before he whirled back to let go of his pitch.

Fernando Valenzuela, a chubby Mexican left-hander who starred with the Los Angeles Dodgers in the 1980s, looked skyward with closed eyes before he released a pitch, as if he was imploring an outside force for help on his screwball.

There must be something in the water that Hispanic pitchers drink that sets them in strange motion on the mound. Hernandez turned, twisted, kicked, bent, coiled, and uncoiled before he let the baseball rush forward to challenge confused hitters.

Hernandez was brilliant against the Braves in the Series opener. He allowed only one run and one hit, a Chipper

Jones fourth-inning homer. Jones had crushed the Mets most of the season but Mets fans got back at him with a banner attack. His given name is Larry Wayne Jones. He despises his first name and never uses it. Mets fans picked up on the Larry part and unfurled banners reading, HEY, LARRY, WHERE'S MOE? in mock memory of the Three Stooges, Larry (the original—not Jones), Moe, and Curly.

Left-hander Tom Glavine, the Cy Young Award winner, was supposed to start the first Series game but came down with the flu. Greg Maddux, a four-time Cy Young winner, got the ball and held the Yankees scoreless through seven innings. Then Scott Brosius singled, Darryl Strawberry walked as a pinch hitter for El Duque, and the Braves first baseman Brian Hunter messed up Chuck Knoblauch's bunt. Derek Jeter singled and New Reliable Paul O'Neill, not to be confused with Old Reliable Tommy Henrich of another Yankee generation, singled for two more runs.

With Mariano Rivera warming up in the bullpen as the Yankees pulled ahead 3-1 on their way to a 4-1 win, the cry in the press box was heard, "This game—over!" It was an expression created by several young sportswriters in the early days of the expansion Mets. As soon as the opposition scored on Casey Stengel's Mets, one of us would shout, "This game—over!" We were right 120 times in the first 1962 season of the New York Mets.

David Cone set the Braves down with one hit through seven innings of the second game at Ted Turner Field at 755 Hank Aaron Drive in Atlanta. Ramiro Mendoza and Jeff Nelson finished up, and the slumbering Braves, still shell-shocked from their grueling series in the NLCS against the Mets, managed all of five hits.

This Series—over!

Tom Glavine recovered in time for his Series start in the third game. No matter. He couldn't hold a 5-1 lead. Home runs by Chad Curtis, Tino Martinez, and a two-run tying shot by Chuck Knoblauch after manager Bobby Cox allowed a weary Glavine to pitch to him, tied the score.

Bob Gibson, the St. Louis Cardinals Hall of Fame right-hander, got in trouble in the final game of the 1964 Series against the Yankees. Manager Johnny Keane allowed a tired Gibson to finish his own game. When questioned after it was over by me and other young reporters about why he didn't go to the bull pen, Keane quietly replied, "I had a commitment to his heart."

It was simply the most touching managerial line I could ever remember. Cox clearly had a commitment to Glavine's heart, not to say the clever pitcher's head. It just didn't work against the Yankees. Curtis hit his second homer of the game leading off the tenth inning against reliever Mike Remlinger for a 6-5 victory and a 3-0 lead.

The Braves knew they should catch a Wednesday matinee in the Broadway theater, have a fine lunch at the All Star Café, Gallagher's Steak House, Mickey Mantle's, or The Palm. It made sense to take their wives for a Central Park horse and carriage ride and shop for toys for the kids at FAO Schwarz. They would be going home after the Wednesday night game. They wouldn't be back to New York until the next century.

George Steinbrenner gambled on an aging Roger Clemens in February. He got a great return on his investment on October 27, 1999, as Clemens locked up the final Series game of the twentieth century.

Was there any pressure on Clemens with his team ahead 3-0? Only the most, maybe, he had ever experienced in his incredible career. He had won everything but a Series game. He had been brought to New York and had agreed to come for only one reason—a World Series ring. Now was his chance to solidify his baseball legend with a Series win. He did it in style.

Clemens allowed only four hits in $7\frac{2}{3}$ innings, beat another Cy Young Award winner in John Smoltz, and walked off the field to the standing cheers of 56,752 fans in Yankee Stadium. Jeff Nelson and Mariano Rivera, named the Series MVP, finished up. The Yankees won 4-1.

The fans cheered lustily as Keith Lockhart hit a whimpering, simpering fly ball to Chad Curtis in left for the final out of the final Series game of the final year of the century. The players hugged and kissed each other on the field. The lusty sounds of Frank Sinatra's rendition of "New York, New York," filled the air in the cavernous park, the most sacred in all of American sports history. The electric clock read 11:06 on a joyous October evening in the Bronx, New York.

The Yankees, under manager Joe Torre, once called Clueless Joe when he first came on as Yankee field underboss under the Boss, had now recorded his second Series sweep in a row and the third Yankee Series victory in the last four seasons of the century.

The Yankees were clearly the team of the Decade, the Team of the Century, the Team of the Millennium.

The Yankee clubhouse afterward was more subdued than it had been in 1996 and 1998. Three Yankee players had lost their fathers within seven weeks, third baseman Scott Brosius, backup infielder Luis Sojo and outfielder Paul O'Neill, only hours before the final game. O'Neill had chosen to play as he said his father, who had manufactured him as a player, clearly would have wanted him to do. He allowed himself one moment of grief at the end of the game. As his teammates swirled around him, hugging and backslapping in the ecstasy of victory, O'Neill doubled up. The celebrating went on around him. He recovered his taciturn expression by the time the TV cameras caught him coming into the clubhouse.

Torre was still being monitored by doctors after his March cancer surgery for removal of his prostate.

Darryl Strawberry was still having regular checkups after his colon cancer surgery the previous October. He was also regularly attending meetings of Alcoholics Anonymous, a lifelong chore if he wanted to save his career and his family.

There were overtones of reality in that winning clubhouse. There was a sense of sadness amidst the joy. These were talented athletes and sports executives under that New York State champagne. These were also men with families, with personal heartache, with illnesses they had to handle and injuries they had to cure.

Steinbrenner was there, of course, once again accepting the World Series trophy from Commissioner Bud Selig, congratulating all his players and coaches, thanking the fans and singling out the manager for enormous praise.

"He has a touch of genius to him," Steinbrenner said, in a steamy Yankee clubhouse. "He just knows what to do. The relationship with him is the best I've ever had. Billy [Martin] was a great manager. Lem [Bob Lemon] was a great manager. But for one reason or another those things came to an end. But this guy is just tremendous. You can't say enough good about him."

The benefits began the next day for the heroes of the Series. David Letterman is always on the top of his game when it comes to inviting sports heroes onto his show after big triumphs. He had five Yankees—Jim Leyritz, Jeff Nelson, Clay Bellinger, Jason Grimsley and winner Roger Clemens—reading the night's Top Ten list along with coach Mel Stottlemyre and manager Joe Torre. Their subject: The Top Ten Things the Yankees Have Always Wanted to Say.

Clemens read number three on the Letterman list, "I don't play for the money. I play because I like having guys pat me on the ass."

Mel Stottlemyre, the pitching coach, read number four on the list, "Man, oh man, do I love betting on baseball."

Torre, of course, read the number one thing the Yankees Have Always Wanted to Say. "I was rooting for the Braves."

After the show was taped Torre said he enjoyed it tremendously. "It's great when you win the World Series. You get two phone calls—one from the President and one from Letterman."

Then he added, "We finished the century out right. Hopefully we can start the next century out on the right foot."

On the final Friday of October in 1999, more than a million people clogged lower Manhattan to cheer the Yankees on in a celebratory parade organized by super Yankee fan, Mayor Rudolph Giuliani of New York City.

On the Canyon of Heroes, lower Broadway in Manhattan, where Charles Lindbergh, General Dwight Eisenhower, General Douglas MacArthur, the 1969 New York World Series Mets, and the 1969 astronaut moon walkers had also been honored, where two time space traveler John Glenn was honored for his second ride at age seventy-seven, where World War II soldiers, sailors, and marines paraded and Gulf War veterans were cheered, the 1999 Yankees came through in open wagons.

George Steinbrenner was cheered under a sea of ticker tape as he waved a broom for the team's sweet sweep for the joy of delirious fans. Teenage girls exhausted themselves yelling for Golden Boy Derek Jeter, his eyes hidden by sunglasses, begging him to marry them. Signs in Spanish greeted Orlando Hernandez and Jorge Posada. Darryl Strawberry was greeted with no-longer mocking howls of "Darryl, Darryl, Darryl," and David Cone laughed when a Hasidic Jewish youngster held up a sign reading, "We don't care if you are not a Jewish Cone."

The players were feted at City Hall on taxpayer lunch money, awarded keys to the city (the second of the year for Cone who earned one with his perfect game), fawned over by every city staffer on hand, and smothered in love.

Strawberry was asked to talk to the packed crowd outside the steps of City Hall where many of the players sat in their Yankee warm-up jackets and new World Series championship caps.

"I would like to say to Joe Torre, thank you for caring for me. You are like a father figure to me," said the son of a single mother. He turned to his teammates behind him and simply said, "I love you guys." Then he exploded in tears with many of his teammates choking on their own emotions. After one day of spring training in 2000, Strawberry was suspended for the year for failing a drug test.

Cone spoke next. He laughed and said, "I want to thank George Steinbrenner, my grandfather figure."

It was a wonderful end to a wondrous season, maybe the best ever in Yankee history.

Team of the Decade? Positively. Team of the Century? For sure. Team of the Boss's?

You can bet your mortgage on that one.

CHAPTER

ONE

Don Larsen pitched a perfect game the last time two New York baseball teams got together in the 20th century for the 1956 World Series.

Yogi Berra was the catcher for the New York Yankees that day and historic icon Jackie Robinson was an aging third baseman for the Brooklyn Dodgers.

Johnny Kucks of the Yankees allowed the Dodgers only three hits, Moose Skowron hit a grand slam home run and Don Newcombe failed for the fifth time to win a Series start as the Yankees won the 13th all-New York Subway Series in the seventh game on October 10, 1956.

Tickets in the bleachers cost a dollar, hot dogs were a quarter and a subway ride from Coney Island in Brooklyn to the 161st Street and River Avenue stop at Yankee Stadium in the Bronx was 15 cents.

Tourists strolling along Pennsylvania Avenue in Washington, D.C. could often see President Dwight Eisenhower as he putted golf balls on the White House lawn. Not one American in a hundred could locate North or South Vietnam on a world map. John F. Kennedy offered himself up as a Democratic candidate for vice president that year. Adlai Stevenson was about to lose his second straight run at the presidency.

Forty-four years later, in the Millennium World Series of 2000, the New York Yankees and the New York Mets met for the first time in the October Classic. Hot dogs cost seven dollars, grandstand seats were $110, the subway ride was $1.50 and the MTA offered a free subway ride back from the games for anyone who cared.

The Yankees won four games to one and owner George

Steinbrenner, dressed in champagne-stained jacket and turtleneck white sweater, choked up as he accepted the triumph and the trophy from Baseball Commissioner Bud Selig in a steamy Shea Stadium clubhouse.

"I can't say enough about these guys," he stammered into network microphones, nodding towards manager Joe Torre and the partying Yankee players. "They showed me as much heart as any team I've ever had."

Steinbrenner had experienced this joy five previous times, 1977, 1978, 1996, 1998 and 1999 with World Series winners but showed a greater abundance of emotion with the third straight Yankee championship and the fourth in five years. It was all about the Subway Series, the first time Steinbrenner had enjoyed a neighborhood victory.

The Yankees were the defending world champions, the big brother to the over-achieving Mets, and still the most famous sports team in American history. It made the victory so much sweeter for the owner of the Yankees.

"We beat a great team," Steinbrenner said. "The Mets gave us everything we could want. It was the battle of New York."

Manager Joe Torre hugged New York City Mayor Rudolph Giuliani, an unabashed, unashamed, demonstrative Yankee fan. Torre and Giuliani, two guys from the New York City borough of Brooklyn, were sharing the glory of the team from the Bronx in the Queens Shea Stadium locker room.

"What is this—an Italian coalition?" kiddingly asked Steinbrenner, a once and former shipping executive son of German immigrants in Cleveland.

Details would be worked out by Giuliani and Steinbrenner for another parade down Lower Broadway in Manhattan, down city streets now called the Canyon of Heroes. Frolicking fans could almost reach out to touch Yankee players wearing team jackets and World Champion baseball caps.

On Monday, October 30, 2000, Yankee players and families, team executives and baseball officials rolled through Manhattan streets for two hours to a City Hall reception.

The event ended with stars Paul O'Neill and David Cone, maybe for the last time, standing before thousands in the City Hall plaza thanking fans for unbridled affection.

"This never gets old," Steinbrenner said quietly to a beaming Giuliani.

It was the first Subway Series of the new millennium and may well be remembered a dozen years from now or a half century from now not for four Yankee wins in five marvelous games but for Mike Piazza's broken bat and the heave of shattered wood by Roger Clemens, the efficient $50,000 fine on Clemens and resulting peace treaty offered up by commissioner assistant Frank Robinson. People may recall Piazza's long, final batted fly ball out as the last play of 2000. As Bernie Williams caught Piazza's deep fly and Torre and Yankee players on their bench breathed free finally after five mysteriously grinding games, the Millennium Subway Series took its perfect place in baseball lore.

If the Mets and Yankees meet again in October a dozen times in the next two decades it could not possibly equal the emotion, the tension or the attention of this first Series meeting of these teams in the opening year of the 21st century.

The 1927 Yankees are considered by many devotees as baseball's best team ever with an outside challenge from the 1961 Yankees of Roger Maris and Mickey Mantle in their pursuit of the Babe Ruth home run record. Even the 1998 Yankees are now mentioned as the game's best. That team of Torre's won 114 games in the regular season and 11 more in October for an astounding 125 victories from one end of the season until the other.

Will the 2000 Yankees linger in the game's glory role for 87 victories and a meager two and a half game lead over Boston when the schedule was played out?

Distinguished Pulitzer Prize columnist Dave Anderson of the *New York Times* wrote on the first Monday of October, "Only a month ago the chance of a Subway Series seemed feasible. Now that chance seems feeble. About the only way the Yankees will get to the World Series is if they are mercifully granted a bye through the American league playoffs."

Steinbrenner was asked in the champagne-covered clubhouse after the last triumph about a comparison with the Yankees of 1949–1953, the only team in the game's history to win five titles in a row.

"This team had to go through three separate playoffs to make it here," he said, referring to the Division Series against Oakland, the League Championship Series against Seattle and the World Series against the Mets. "This was much harder."

The miracle wasn't that the Yankees won the World Series again in 2000—their third in a row and fourth in five years under Torre's leadership. The miracle was that they were still standing there so late in October.

There wasn't much competition in the Eastern Division and the Yankees stumbled, stammered and slept through most of the later weeks of the season. Doubt filled the minds of the players and all observers. Pitcher David Cone, a future Hall of Fame candidate, couldn't get anybody out and seemed finished. Paul O'Neill, fighting himself harder than Mike Tyson used to fight an opponent, had a weary body and a slow bat.

Chuck Knoblauch was a second baseman more dangerous in the field than at bat. The highlight of his season seemed to be an errant throw into the stands that almost beaned the mother of sportscaster Keith Olbermann. Knoblauch was fast becoming the Steve Blass of second basemen, a head case who couldn't hit first baseman Tino Martinez's glove on a fly. Blass, a Pittsburgh pitcher, couldn't find home plate with a radar gun after World Series heroics more than a quarter of a century ago.

Derek Jeter was his brilliant self again, the best young player the Yankees had since Mickey Mantle electrified Stadium fans in the early 1950s. Mariano Rivera was as certain as ever as Torre's late inning anchor. Jorge Posada had become a confident catcher and solid switch hitter with the absence of scholarly catcher Joe Girardi. Bernie Williams erased all doubts about his superstardom. Andy Pettitte, who seemed to own the most eerie staring eyes in baseball, was reliable most of his starts as a lefthanded ace. Orlando Hernandez, Cuba's El Duque, showed signs of wear and true aging but was competitive in any start. Roger Clemens, the hired gun from the Red Sox and Blue Jays, finally fit in comfortably with the Yankees in his second season. He'll certainly be dressed in a Red Sox cap when his bust is built in Cooperstown.

Still, as the Yankees won the division title, losing their last seven games in a row and 15 games of their last 18, it was the Mets more New York fans talked about and forecast for October thrills.

Ahh, c'mon. These were the *Yankees*. This was October. If there was to be a Subway Series, the first ever between the Mets and Yankees in the 39th chance at that, no real student of the game could dismiss the Yankees.

What made the team picture of the Yankees far different in October than it had been in April, was the addition of so many new faces for the October fun. David Justice was now a Yankee instead of a member of the Braves or Indians. Dwight Gooden was actually back with the team after being released by the lowly Tampa Bay Devil Rays. Amazingly, Jose Canseco was added to the roster. Glenallen Hill was busting up games with home runs. Jose Vizcaino added a needed glove. Luis Sojo, with a roster age of 34, a face indicating 54 and an enthusiasm showing 24, was a useful utility man. Luis Polonia, once banished for off-the-field conduct by the Yankees, came back with professional poise. Denny Neagle, who could imitate a train whistle with a cheeky breath, added depth from the mound.

Torre had maneuvered through the final days of the season, played everybody wearing pinstripes, never once showed doubt about the ultimate success and calmed Steinbrenner's nerves. There was much talk that Steinbrenner, who had turned 70 years old on July 4, 2000, was losing his fast ball. The bite wasn't there. The explosions were hardly heard. The absences exceeded the appearances by far. Where have you gone, George Steinbrenner?

It was all about trust. Steinbrenner recognized the skills

of his general manager, Brian Cashman, in bringing Torre the needed players and he recognized Torre's' managerial genius. It had worked well in 1996, 1998 and 1999. Steinbrenner, in a spectacular change in his usual style, allowed his field leaders to lead.

Days before the opener against Oakland I walked into the Yankee offices to purchase playoff tickets made available to members of the press. George was at the reception desk, surrounded by several aides, the driver of his car, his security man and a team executive. His eyes were bright.

He bellowed at all of the help at one time, carried on several conversations, talked on the phone and reminded his driver what time he was expected to have the car ready for the evening trip. Then he spotted me.

"You look great, Maury. You look like you're ready," he said in a cheerful voice.

Good luck," I said.

"We'll need it," he laughed.

Then he was gone behind the glass doors in the Stadium offices marked New York Yankees. I could see just see his back as he moved away rapidly. I knew someone inside those offices would pay the price if they were not at their desk.

The Division series opened in Oakland. The A's were a young team that had battled down to the last day with Seattle and Cleveland for the two spots in the playoffs not controlled by the Yankees and the Chicago White Sox.

Oakland, Seattle and Cleveland all won on the final day of the regular season. That made Oakland the West winner to be matched against the Yankees, and Seattle the Wild Card winner to be matched against the White Sox.

The A's beat the Yankees 5-3 in the Division opener. It was the Yankees' eighth straight loss. Roger Clemens was not a Hall of Fame pitcher in that game. Oakland brothers Jason and Jeremy Giambi had important hits and manager Art Howe, a calm man with a shiny, bald head, was up on Torre with only a split needed in the last four games for a knockout punch.

The Yankees won the second game in Oakland 4-0 behind Andy Pettitte's impressive performance with a little routine help from Mariano Rivera. Glenallen Hill as the DH, knocked in a run instead of good-hit, no-field Chuck Knoblauch. Luis Sojo knocked in two runs with a double and the Yankees showed there was life left in the Bronx Bombers.

The best entertainment of the Oakland night occurred in the eighth inning. Terrence Long of the A's hit a routine grounder to second base. A Little Leaguer could have played it. Luis Sojo couldn't. He caught the ball, moved his right foot across his left to make the soft throw to first base and fell down. Long was safe at first. The Yankees got out of the inning without a score and about half a dozen Yankees came up to Sojo as he reached the bench as the inning ended inquiring about his physical health. Ball players find almost as much pleasure in a sharp needle to a teammate as they get from a game winning homer.

With 57,545 people screaming their heads off at the Stadium, Orlando Hernandez twisted, turned, tossed and topped the A's 4-2 in the third game of the set. Rivera, of course, got another save. El Duque ran his post season record to 6-0.

The A's tied the five game series with an 11-1 pounding of Clemens, reliever Mike Stanton and a bad facsimile of Dwight Gooden, once considered the best pitcher in baseball at the age of 19 some 15 years earlier.

The Yankees flew 3,000 miles across the country and scored six runs in the first inning of the fifth game at the Oakland Coliseum. A's manager Art Howe didn't have a hair on his head to tear out as the Yankees hung on with Rivera out of the bullpen after no other Yankee pitcher from Pettitte to El Duque seemed serious about winning. The Yankees ended the nightmare scenario with a 7-5 nail biter.

The Yankees were back in the League Championship again with the Seattle Mariners, a team that shocked them in 1995 because David Cone couldn't throw a strike on a 3-2 pitch.

Lou Piniella, the Seattle manager and former anchor man

for the winning Yankees of 1977–1978, led his team to a 2-0 victory in the first game behind the strong pitching of starter Freddy Garcia and the anemic bats of the Yankees. It was Oakland all over again as the Yankees were looking up again at their opponents.

This time it would be easier. The championship series is the best of seven and there is more reliance on depth of pitching than on a single lucky win as might happen in the five game division title.

A seven run eighth inning, another quality performance by El Duque and the enthusiastic support of a sellout Stadium crowd gave the Yankees a 7-1 victory and evened the series at a game apiece.

The Yankees won the next two games in the ALCS with 8-2 and 5-0 victories. Roger Clemens pitched his best game as a Yankee in that shutout, allowing only a single hit, a double to right by Al Martin of Seattle and struck out 15 Mariners. The Yankees then lost the fifth game 6-2 in Seattle with Neagle and reliever Jeff Nelson failing to end things.

David Justice, who couldn't make a steady marriage out of it with actress Halle Berry, crushed a line drive into the right field stands at Yankee Stadium for three runs in the seventh inning of a come-from-behind 9-7 win in game six.

It gave the Yankees pennant number 37 from Babe Ruth's first as a Yankee in 1921 to Justice's first as a Yankee in 2000. Can't anybody else ever win an American league pennant? It only happened once since Joe Torre signed on for the 1996 season.

Now it was on to the World Series for the Yankees. Beginning in 1921, this would be the 37th Series in 80 baseball seasons. For the Mets, it was their fourth time at their October Classic in the 39 seasons they had played in the National League. The Mets had beaten San Francisco in the Division Series and defeated St. Louis in the League Championship series for a shot at the World Series.

The two teams were playing their games about ten miles apart, the Yankees in the borough of the Bronx, north of Manhattan and South of the rest of New York state and the

Mets in the borough of Queens, just across the East River.

Mets fans had come alive in 1962 when the team first took the field in a National league game. They promptly set a losing record with 120 defeats. Casey Stengel had won 10 pennants in 12 seasons as manager of the Yankees from 1949 through 1960. He was named manager of the Mets for the opening 1962 season. Maybe the difference between winning and losing really was the players.

Mets fans, in those first days, were mostly old Brooklyn Dodgers fans, angry at the loss of their team to owner Walter O'Malley's greed when he moved the club to Los Angeles. Some New York Giant fans came to the Polo Grounds and later to Shea in those early days, especially when Willie Mays came back with the San Francisco Giants. Even a few Yankee fans could be spotted with their NY caps at Mets games. Mostly for laughs.

The Yankees were way down in 1969 when the Mets first won. The intensity of the rivalry between the teams never really took off until after 1973 with the arrival of George Steinbrenner as new owner. The rivalry deepened after 1980 when Nelson Doubleday and Fred Wilpon bought the Mets.

The Yankees began winning seriously again in 1995, only to lose the Division series to Seattle. They won the World Series in 1996, 1998, and 1999 as the Mets failed to get into Series play. The Mets just missed out in 1999 when they couldn't come back from a 3-0 deficit against Atlanta.

They finally made it to the October classic in 2000 with a wonderful finish in post-season play. The Yankees were there with them and the City of New York became the center of the baseball universe as it had not been since 1956.

Would anybody outside of New York care? The fans of the Mets and Yankees cared not a bit about that.

All of it started in glorious fashion with a 12 inning game that lasted four hours and 51 minutes, the longest World Series game in history. A single to left field by backup second baseman Jose Vizcaino, starting only because he had been successful against Mets starter Al Leiter over his career, won the 4-3 game.

The Yankees celebrated with the hugging and lifting of Vizcaino after he came back from hitting the winning single the way teams sometimes celebrate the seventh game Series win. No surprise. This was the Mets they had defeated. They knew what this all meant to George Steinbrenner. If they wanted to stay Yankees they had better excel against the Mets. Vizcaino knew the theory well.

The Yankees won the second game 6-5 after almost blowing a 6-0 lead. Mike Piazza hit a two run homer in the ninth and Jay Payton hit a three run homer. Rivera struck out utility shortstop Kurt Abbott to end the game.

What mattered most, what will be talked about and viewed in Series films for years, was a strange act by Roger Clemens. The hard throwing right hander had struck Mike Piazza in the batting helmet in a July 8 game between the two teams in interleague play. Piazza lay motionless at home plate as Clemens asked the umpire for another ball.

The Mets catcher recovered well enough to walk off the field. Baseball historians reminded fans about the fatal beaning of Cleveland shortstop Ray Chapman by underhand pitcher Carl Mays in 1920, the only baseball death caused by a play on the field.

Piazza believed he was hit intentionally. Clemens, notorious for throwing hard inside, denied it. The controversy lasted all season and was revived during the World Series. Clemens faced Piazza for the first time since the incident. He threw a fastball inside. Piazza swung hard. The pitch shattered his bat. The handle stayed in Piazza's hand as he jogged toward first. The barrel of the bat bounced out towards Clemens on the mound.

Roger the Rocket bent down, picked up the bat and flung it angrily toward the foul line just before Piazza reached that point. He later explained that he thought it was a ball.

There were 57,545 people at the game with about 57,000 opinions of what really happened. Newspaper columnists and reporters, television interviewers and talk show hosts filled their outlets with descriptions, analysis and psychological examination of the event. After half a century of watching baseball games, this is what happened. A broken bat came tumbling back at an intense pitcher. He hurled it off his territory. Ball players, trained to defend their teammates and their turf, filled the field in front of the pitcher's mound. No punches were thrown. A few dirty words were exchanged. In July, it would have been worth a few clubhouse laughs. In October, it became Hamlet, Macbeth and King Lear all squeezed on to one stage.

The scene shifted to Shea Stadium in Queens for the third game of the Series. The Mets, with a strong performance by Rick Reed and their bullpen, beat El Duque and the Yankees 4-2 with a key double by Hawaiian outfielder Benny Agbayani.

For the first time in 14 years and for the first time in a Subway Series, Mets fans could root for their team in the October classic, showing off their enthusiasm, revealing their clever signs and standing equal to the triumphant Yankee fans.

"I went to a game at Yankee Stadium and the stands seemed filled only with Yankee fans," said Yankee fan and the author's son, Ted Allen. "At Shea it was different. The stands were more Mets fans than Yankee fans but certainly enough Yankee rooters to make the cheering louder and more interesting."

The Yankees won game four of the Series 3-2 for a 3-1 lead. The moment of highest drama occurred in the fifth inning with the Yankees ahead by a run. Denny Neagle, a left-handed pitcher, left with a lead. With two outs the hitter was Mike Piazza, another sure Hall of Famer on the field along with Derek Jeter and Roger Clemens. A home run would tie the game.

Torre walked to the mound and Neagle walked off. The new pitcher was David Cone. He jogged in from the left field bullpen, took the baseball from Torre, tugged at his cap, said a couple of words to Jorge Posada and went to the back of the mound. Now Piazza was ready. Cone took the sign and threw an inside strike. Then another strike. Then a foul ball. Then another inside pitch that Piazza swung mightily on and popped up for the final out of the inning.

"Coney was surprisingly calm," said Torre later about using a struggling starter in such a deadly middle game role.

In the annals of World Series history, this was no home run by Bill Mazeroski or Kirk Gibson, no perfect game by Don Larsen, no strikeout masterpiece by Carl Erskine, Bob Gibson or Sandy Koufax.

It was one batter, one popup, one out in the fourth game of the 2000 World Series won by the Yankees. Cone, at 37, was coming off a 4-14 season knowing this might be his final act in a Major League game. It was one beautiful moment.

"I can never forget it," Cone said later. "I can never forget the trust Joe showed in me by letting me face Piazza in that spot."

The fifth game was another thriller. The Yankees closed out the Series with a 4-2 win on Luis Sojo's routine ground single up the middle in the top of the ninth inning of a 2-2 game. Jorge Posada raced around from second, roared past third, charged home and slid hard in front of Piazza at the plate. Posada used his body to block the play as he reached the plate and Jay Payton's throw clipped his backside. Scott Brosius also scored as the ball rolled away.

Mariano Rivera struck out pinch hitter Darryl Hamilton leading off the Mets ninth. He walked Benny Agbayani, a homerun threat, and put him on first as the tying run. Edgardo Alfonzo flied short to right. Two out. Piazza up.

Rivera threw a strike to the Mets catcher. Shea Stadium fans roared and howled and prayed. The next pitch seemed over the middle of the plate, belt high, about 92 miles an hour. Piazza swung hard. The ball disappeared into the dark night.

"Everytime Piazza hits a ball into the air I think 'home run'," Torre said later.

It headed for the Shea Stadium fence. Maybe a tie game. Maybe the end of the winning World Series streak of the Yankees. Maybe no 20th century dynasty gliding gracefully into the 21st century.

Then the ball reappeared from wherever it had been in the

outer reaches of Shea in that dark night sky. Bernie Williams was a step from the track, a half dozen steps from the wall, holding his glove at shoulder level. The ball was dropped into it by some magical force of baseball history. Last out. It was a Yankee World Series victory. Again.

Williams bent down on that Shea grass with one knee, looked at the baseball in his glove, came up for air and began the joyous journey into the dugout and clubhouse.

Soon there were Yankees on the mound pounding at Rivera, pushing him down, piling on top of him in this youthful ritual, now as much a part of the October wins as emotional tears.

The Yankees had their World Series again, number 26 in 37 tries, number four in five tries for Torre's Yankees, number three in a row, number one in the new century, the new Millennium, the new decade.

There would be a raucous clubhouse with cheers and tears. There would be the Monday ride down the Canyon of Heroes. There would be winter awards and realistic agony. Darryl Strawberry, who had brought so many tears only a year before, would be facing the law instead of facing fawning fans as 2000 wound down.

In some few days the win would be history. Spring training for another season was only a hundred days away. Decisions were to be made. Players were to be signed and released and traded. Glory lasts only through the next calendar change.

Bernie Williams, David Cone, Paul O'Neill, Mariano Rivera and Derek Jeter were the only Yankees to share the significance of all four Series wins in the 1996–2000 run.

Joe Torre had established himself as one of the game's most successful leaders.

New players came and went. New executives filled the Stadium offices. The Yankees showed quickly on November 30, 2000 that they were driving hard on baseball's most elegant feat, the five straight Series triumphs of Casey Stengel's Yankees from 1949 to 1953. They signed Baltimore free agent pitcher Mike Mussina to a six-year contract for $88.5 million.

One man was a constant around this team, a life force, *the* central figure of the organization as few persons have ever been in or out of baseball. He could be admired. He could be hated. He could be criticized. He could be praised.

If the Yankees had to be summed up in the last quarter of the 20th century and the first year of the 21st, it would not be with tales of Torre or the wondrous deeds of Jeter, Williams, Cone, O'Neill, and Rivera.

The Yankees from 1973–2001 could be summed up easily. George Martin Steinbrenner III, reigning king of the greatest baseball team of all time.

CHAPTER

TWO

The telephone rang in my home early on the morning of January 3, 1973. It was old pal Bob Fishel, publicity director of the New York Yankees. He was calling me to a press conference at New York's fashionable "21" club.

Fishel had worked for many years as the publicity director for Bill Veeck with the old St. Louis Browns. He was the guy who hid Eddie Gaedel, baseball's most famous midget, while the 1951 crowd in Sportsman's Park anticipated another exciting Veeck event.

Gaedel appeared in all his three-feet-seven-inch glory. The number [E] could clearly be seen on the back of his fine-fitting St. Louis Browns uniform. Surprisingly, he walked.

It was one of the most memorable moments in baseball history. Gaedel's name and fame would be enshrined in baseball record books forever. You could look him up on page 916 of *The Baseball Register* just between Len Gabrielson and Gary Gaetti. Veeck, a Hall of Famer in the game's Cooperstown Valhalla, would talk merrily about the day and event until his death.

Fishel, as decent, intelligent, and gentle a man as the game had ever seen, was forever connected to the incident. Nothing again could give Fishel that sense of the game's history throughout his brilliant career with the Indians, Browns, Yankees, and the American League.

Then came George M. Steinbrenner III.

This man would change Fishel's life, the life of general manager Lee MacPhail, the life of manager Ralph Houk, the life of every Yankee player for the next generation, and the lives of so many dedicated, devoted, determined fans of the New York Yankees.

I drove my car from my home in suburban New York City to the famed restaurant in midtown Manhattan. As I moved closer to the midtown restaurant I wondered, who was this guy named Steinbrenner.

I would spend a good part of the next quarter of a century trying to find out and trying hard to explain that to the readers of the *New York Post*.

Steinbrenner had been a Cleveland industrialist and had run the American Shipbuilding Co., mostly a carrier of iron ore on the Great Lakes, after his tyrannical father had turned over the director's chair to him.

No matter how well young George ran it, and he ran it quite well, it was never good enough for his father. A lot of Freudian stuff here better left for the hundred-dollar-an-hour shrinks.

This young Steinbrenner, an athlete of sorts at Williams College—not an athletic bastion—and later a football coach at Northwestern, always kept his finger close to the sports scene as fan, player, and then owner of something called the Cleveland Pipers, a professional basketball team of no small distinction. No large distinction, either.

Steinbrenner thought this sports connection allowed him to sit in the main room of the legendary "21" restaurant where the sports bosses, television types and top jocks , the elite, would meet to eat. The "21" Club was not about food. It was about being there. Newspaper columnists, dating back to speakeasy days, led off their stories quite often with, "While I was sitting at the "21" Club . . ."

Steinbrenner knew a lot of this history and when he made it big in shipping his secretary would call the "21" Club just almost every time he came to New York on business. Just about every time he did that the answer was the same. The snooty reservationist would tell this big Cleveland boss that a reservation could be made at the "21" Club at four o'clock in the afternoon upstairs or a bit later downstairs. Nobody important would be there. Steinbrenner fumed. And dreamed. He would get that lunch in the main, important room of the "21" Club even if he had to buy the Yankees to do it.

For a paltry 10.3 million dollars, the Columbia Broadcasting System got out of the baseball team ownership business and turned it over to a limited partnership led by George Steinbrenner.

"There is nothing as limiting as being a limited partner with George Steinbrenner," fellow magnate John McMullen, later to own the Houston Astros baseball team and the New Jersey Devils hockey team, would subsequently say.

Old Cleveland pals and show business buddies, the Nederlanders, who allowed Steinbrenner in on their production of *Applause,* starring Lauren Bacall on Broadway, would be among the limited group.

Steinbrenner met the New York press that January day in 1973. His hair was smoothed down. His suit fit beautifully. He looked slightly overweight. He actually did very little talking. The front man was baseball executive Gabe Paul, who had led the Reds and the Indians.

Paul had started out his career as a traveling secretary of the Cincinnati Reds. He was known as a cliché expert when questioned by the press and he was known as a guy tight with a dollar.

As he watched a rainstorm from an open press box, while the crowd froze in a chill, he would always say, "It will stop raining. It always has."

It always did, especially when it was early enough to keep the receipts.

He was the traveling secretary when a morose player named Willard Hershberger, a backup catcher to the future Hall of Famer Ernie Lombardi, failed to show for a game one day in 1940 in Boston.

Paul was dispatched to the hotel room. He saw Hershberger in the bathtub of his hotel room, blood all around him, the thirty-year-old catcher from Lemon Grove, California, dead of self-inflicted knife wounds. Paul knew what to do.

He moved to Hershberger's clothes closet, took out the rest of his meal money for the trip, and saved the Reds about twenty bucks. Then he bragged about it. That's how some guys move up in baseball.

Paul became instrumental in Steinbrenner's purchase of the Yankees through his longtime contacts. He told an old story about how a sportswriter could decide if someone was a good general manager or not.

"If you can wake up another general manager at three in the morning and he asks what he can do for you instead of screaming about the hour, you know he is a good general manager," he said.

Through the contacts with the CBS ownership of the Yankees, especially through operating head Michael Burke, Paul discovered the Yankees were for sale. They had finished fourth in 1972 for the second year in a row, had fallen under a million in attendance for the first time since 1945, the last year of World War II, and seemed to have lost fans to the exciting Mets, a World Champion in 1969.

CBS knew a lot about broadcasting. It knew nothing about baseball. Burke had been a dashing football player at the University of Pennsylvania, a World War II OSS agent, a dapper dresser, and a major attraction for the ladies. It did not qualify him to outslick Paul or any other general manager in a baseball trade.

Steinbrenner really suggested that day that he would be sort of a behind-the-scenes boss, that Paul would assist Burke in the operation of the team, and that things would move forward as before with a deep sense of regard for the Yankees tradition. After all, this was the team of Babe Ruth, Lou Gehrig, Joe DiMaggio, Mickey Mantle, Yogi Berra, Whitey Ford, and the rest. Nobody tampers with that tradition.

Burke had always been a charmer. He dressed in English tweed jackets, discussed intellectual books he had read with interested sportswriters, talked easily about his war exploits, and conversed daily with CBS executives.

None of this helped the Yankees win any games.

By late 1972, CBS was ready to go back to broadcasting and get away from baseball. Paul, who had a nose for news, mentioned this fact to his Cleveland pal, George Steinbrenner. The idea intrigued Steinbrenner. This would be high profile baseball instead of laboring (pre-Michael Jordan) basketball. This would be the most famous sports team in history. This would be New York, New York—a helluva town.

Steinbrenner put together the limited partnership, purchased the Yankees from CBS, and announced at the "21" Club press conference that Burke, a part owner in the new deal, would have a significant role. That lasted about as long as it took Steinbrenner to get out of the door of the "21" Club that day. This was a new day, a new boss—later to be Boss—a new era of New York Yankees history.

There were two dominant media personalities around at the time. Dick Young was the feisty, outspoken hard-hitting columnist of the *Daily News*. Howard Cosell was ABC's Young.

Young was a New York kid who came from the Washington Heights area of Manhattan, a street kid, slight in build but gigantic in status. He could destroy a player with his pen—a team, too. He wrote critically of the fading Brooklyn Dodgers. Some Dodgers and some Dodger fans never forgave him.

Cosell was from Brooklyn, well educated, a former practicing attorney who got into broadcasting through the back door. He had represented a Brooklyn Little League, which led him to Ebbets Field games. He saw the vacuum in broadcasting and immediately filled it. He was a comical sight in his earliest days, when he lugged a huge broadcasting power pack on his back while he interviewed players for ABC radio.

This was still before Monday Night Football, which brought Cosell to national attention, but he had already made a significant impact on the sports scene around New York. He had gained much air time with his advocacy of the cause of a young fighter named Cassius Clay, later remade as Muhammad Ali.

Young and Cosell were bitter enemies, each jealous of the attention the other always got, constantly fighting for the lead spot at any sports event, often making biting remarks about each other to neutral sportswriters. Each had an ego the size of Montana. I was competitive with Young. I was amused by Cosell. Young hated me. Cosell lectured me.

If this new guy Steinbrenner was going to be a big shot in the big town he had to romance these two powerful media types. It didn't take him very long. Young got an exclusive interview the first day, while the rest of us wrote off the press conference.

Cosell put that press conference on the air but upped Young by one lunch. He invited Steinbrenner to join him at the same "21" Club the next afternoon for lunch on ABC. Cosell could hardly have known what this meant to Steinbrenner. After all these years, after all those emotional disappointments of not being important enough to gain entrance to the inner sanctum of the place to be at Manhattan lunchtime, Steinbrenner would be there.

Cosell put together a small lunch table with himself at the head, Steinbrenner facing the crowded room, National Football League Commissioner Pete Rozelle on one side, and New York Giants glamorous great, Frank Gifford, on the other. This was a power lunch before the power lunches of the 1980s, when billions were talked about over lunch were ever invented.

The Cosell table at high noon was in the center of the room. That spot, that lunch, that ego-stroking afternoon only cost Steinbrenner $10.3 million. Oh yeah, he also got the Yankees for that money—to go with the lunch.

A few years later Steinbrenner took Barbara Walters to lunch at the "21" Club. It was a beautiful spring day and Steinbrenner ordered his limousine driver to stop a couple of blocks away from the famous restaurant on Manhattan's Fifty-second Street. They talked and chatted for a while as fans nodded to them or called out their names. Steinbrenner, feeling his Boss power, decided to start counting the greetings from his fans against the greetings Walters received. It was about two to one for Walters (even before she'd mingled with Monica), and that destroyed the joy of the lunch for Steinbrenner.

Steinbrenner knew he needed more attention in the papers, more controversy, more exposure in media-mad Manhattan if he was going to have the impact he wanted and needed.

The Yankees prepared for spring training in 1973 under the leadership of general manager Lee MacPhail and field manager Ralph Houk. MacPhail was the soft-spoken, painfully shy son of flamboyant baseball personality Larry MacPhail. Larry MacPhail had run the Cincinnati Reds, the Brooklyn Dodgers, and the Yankees before self-destructing in a drunken rage after the team's 1947 World Series triumph over the Brooklyn Dodgers. Larry MacPhail may not have been baseball's most famous drinker, an honor probably shared by Babe Ruth, Paul Waner, and Grover Cleveland Alexander. But MacPhail was certainly one of the top drinkers in the game's history, and his fights with other owners, executives, and especially his favorite punching bag, Leo Durocher, were legendary.

Lee MacPhail could have a pop now and then but never lost his calm or his cool. One day at a wonderful spring training dinner in Fort Lauderdale, with all the sportswriters and their wives as guests, Lee MacPhail called on my wife, pregnant with our son, Ted, for a few words of greeting. Janet was a little weary from the pregnancy, which she described as going on as long as an elephant's, a little tired from the long night, and a little bored by the endless baseball conversation.

She stammered a few words and sat down. MacPhail moved the program along and said nothing further about it. As we left, Janet said to MacPhail, "Next year, I'll do better."

"Next year," MacPhail said, "I won't call on you."

MacPhail was soon swallowed up by Steinbrenner's dominance. He would move into the office of the baseball commissioner and ended his Hall of Fame baseball career as president of the American League.

Ralph Houk, a World War II army ranger, a cigar smoker of note, an intimidating figure for players and press, was the field boss. I had my run-ins with Houk. Houk, a backup catcher to Berra in the late 1940s and 1950s, managed at Denver and coached under Casey Stengel before taking over the team in 1961. Stengel had lost the seventh game of the World Series to Pittsburgh. Then he got fired. He was seventy years old.

Houk took over, managed the 1961 home run season of Roger Maris (sixty-one) and Mickey Mantle (fifty-four) with great care for their psyches, won the World Series easily over Cincinnati and won again in 1962. The Dodgers beat the Yankees in the 1963 World Series and Houk turned over the field job to Berra as he became the general manager. It allowed him to smoke more cigars.

When Berra was fired after failing to win the 1964 World Series, St. Louis Cardinals manager Johnny Keane, a baseball fish out of water in New York, was named Yankees manager. He lasted a year and a bit, until his players quit on him. Houk came back on the field.

He seemed different this time around, less angry, less combative. Maybe the war experiences were fading further into his psyche. I wrote a column about him in the *New York Post,* about how he was a softer guy, how some of his younger players—Joe Pepitone, Jim Bouton, Phil Linz—were running away from Houk. It was mostly a complimentary column about his past successes, but a little hard on his present operation. I remember using the word, *marshmallow* next to his name.

When George complained that 17 (Gene Michael), 1 (Bobby Murcer), and 28 (Sparky Lyle) had hair that was too long, Houk knew the interference would be too much. MacPhail also sensed this, during the first game of spring training. Murcer, who had hit 33 home runs and had 96 RBIs in 1972, won a big contract for his performance. He popped up in his first training at bat.

"Is that the bum we are paying a hundred thousand dollars?" Steinbrenner howled.

No matter. He paid. Then he fell in love with Murcer and kept him around for many years as a broadcaster.

All of this was typical Steinbrenner, as Yankee employees, players, and fans would find out in the next quarter of a century or so. He could embarrass a player publicly one day and hire him the next for a key Stadium job. He could trade away a player in anger and bring him back. He could fire a manager one, two, three, four, five times (read: Billy Martin) and bring him back. He could even be thinking about bringing him back again when Martin died in 1989.

Steinbrenner's first season in baseball was definitely my strangest. A couple of flaky Yankee pitchers named Fritz Peterson, thirty-one, and Mike Kekich, twenty-eight, were the catalysts.

Peterson was a forever-smiling left-handed pitcher as interested in a practical joke as he was in a Yankee win. He loved to give sportswriters and teammates a hot foot before, during, or just after games. He often put moldy hot dogs into the gloves of sensitive teammates, especially shortstop Gene Michael, who would howl wildly when he ran out to his position and placed his left index finger into a squishy wiener instead of baseball leather.

He called up teammates and imitated sportswriters over hotel phones asking for exclusive interviews. He called Mickey Mantle's room once and pretended he was a beautiful girl sent to visit Mickey as a going-away present. He was a fanatic hockey fan and later a hockey broadcaster. He often printed up phony newspaper headlines, proclaiming crashes of Yankee chartered airplanes with himself as lone survivor. He had a bachelor's degree in physical education from Northern Illinois, University, near his Mount Prospect, Illinois home and later earned a master's degree in physical education from Morehead State University in Kentucky.

With a good fastball, much guile, and a great pickoff move to first, he was 12-11 in his rookie 1966 Yankee year. The team finished in tenth place but Peterson laughed his way through a successful season.

"This is a lot better than teaching," he said.

In 1970 he won twenty games, the cherished amount every pitcher since Cy Young has always dreamed of achieving as the standard for pitching success. After being relieved Peterson went into fetal position under a clubhouse table with a towel pulled tight over his head against the clubhouse din of the radio broadcast of the game. His teammates stormed into the locker room to tell him he was the winning pitcher for the twentieth time in 1970.

After Peterson joined the Yankees in 1966, he quickly became friendly with pitcher Jim Bouton, the witty, wacky, wonderful, iconoclastic, right-handed pitcher who would later pen the muckraking baseball book, *Ball Four* with my former *New York Post* colleague Leonard Shecter. Bouton and I and our wives—Bobbie Bouton, Jim's first wife, and my one and only, Janet Allen—became pals through spring-training dinners, an occasional road-restaurant visit, and a barbecue once in a while at each other's homes. The test of a relationship between a baseball player and a sportswriter is whether or not they make it to the other guy's home. Lots of sportswriters, me included, drank lots of beers with players in lots of hotel bars for lots of years but never met the little lady at home or visited the other guy's backyard. Casey Stengel was my favorite manager. I was invited to his Glendale, California, home many times for interviews and baseball parties. I never invited him to mine. I'm sorry about that. Casey would have been big in my neighborhood.

Bouton and Peterson became very close. After a twenty-one game winning season in 1963 and two dramatic World Series wins over the Cardinals in 1964, Bouton was losing it as an effective pitcher when Peterson joined the team. He was having arm trouble, the curse of the pitching profession. My friendship soured with Bouton when I wrote a story in the *Post* about his failing wing. He thought what he had told me about his arm was off the record. I thought it was a great story about a great guy losing his fastball, the overachieving fastball that saw him lose his oversized hat as he exploded off the mound but could still outmuscle the Cardinals in the Series. (Willie Mays always wore a bigger hat than necessary so his hatless outfield catches would be more dramatic.)

A dinner in Fort Lauderdale with the Boutons and the Petersons was about as much fun as Janet and I could have in Florida spring training. These players were very bright, interesting, articulate, and warm. Bobbie Bouton and Marilyn Peterson—Fritz called her Chip because her maiden name was Marilyn Monks and Chip Monks was too funny for him to pass up—got along well with my wife, who always appreciates humor, intelligence, and warmth.

The wives of most ballplayers I have met were adjuncts of the player—glowing, pretty cheerleader types silently worshiping at the shrine of the big leaguer. Bobbie Bouton and Marilyn Peterson—I could never call her Chip—were exceptional in that scene. They were pretty, all right, but they could think, talk, and disagree when necessary.

Bouton left the Yankees after the 1968 season to finish his career in Seattle, Houston, and Atlanta. He filled his notebook steadily and shocked baseball when he wrote of Mickey Mantle's drinking habits. He exposed the secrets of ballplayers when he wrote of beaver shooting from a Washington hotel rooftop (looking for pretty girls scantily dressed at the pool) and Joe Pepitone's love life. His greatest truism was expressed in the final line of his book, "You spend a good piece of your life gripping a baseball and in the end it turns out that it was the other way around all the time."

Peterson now became my closest friend on the team.

Mike Kekich joined the Yankees in 1969 after being traded over to the team from the Los Angeles Dodgers.

I was never close to him. He seemed too loud, too much of a self-promoter, too anxious for attention he could not earn on the field. The Dodgers thought they had another Sandy Koufax when they signed him for a then whopping 1964 bonus of $50,000. About all he had in common with Koufax was throwing a baseball from the left side of the mound.

Kekich was a hippie type after the hippie era had about faded. He wore blue jeans, tight-fitting sports shirts, loved high-speed motorcycle rides, flew gliders, scuba dived, and did some parachute jumping. He threw very hard but most games were adventures when he pitched because he was so often behind hitters in the count. He had good stuff, as all his managers agreed, but he somehow never realized his pitching potential. He never won more than ten games in any big league season.

On the evening of July 15, 1972, my wife, Janet, and I hosted a little party at home. Fritz and his wife, the former Marilyn Monks, thirty-one, who we were friendly with after his many years with the Yankees, were among our guests. He asked if we could include Kekich and his wife, Susanne, twenty-eight. Why not? Throw another hamburger on the grill and buy another six-pack. Done. Ron Swoboda, a pal from Mets days and wife Cecilia and Dick Kaplan, editor of the *Ladies' Home Journal,* and wife Julie filled out the happy crowd.

Marilyn Peterson shocked us all when she arrived with long, light brown hair hanging halfway down her back. Although no one in baseball knew it, Marilyn had always worn a blond wig, referred to privately by Peterson, we found out that evening, as "Marilyn's helmet." The blond wig was chic and glamorous, and she looked very sophisticated whenever we had dinner together. She was a beautiful woman so none of this really mattered, but for Marilyn, the wig had represented security. This evening, somehow, Fritz had convinced her to come as the "real" Marilyn. She looked startlingly different. The "new" Marilyn Peterson, sweet and shy and looking much more innocent and girlish than the Marilyn we had all known, would be the center of the evening's attention. As she came in the door, my wife and I stared at her. "Please," she said nervously, "don't look at me." The Petersons and Kekichs had arrived at the same time.

Susanne Kekich stood on the stairs together with Marilyn. They made quite a contrast. Where Marilyn was petite and shy, Susanne was a tall brunette—athletic looking and aggressive. As my wife was trying to accustom herself to the new Marilyn, Susanne saw me approaching. Her husband had just pitched a few days ago, and I had written about him. She looked at me and said, "Why aren't you writing about *me*? I just ran a mini-marathon." I just smiled and shrugged.

Throughout the evening, Susanne seemed to be competing for attention with the new Marilyn every chance she got. There were conversations over beers and burgers, the empty cans piled high on a dining room table, the burgers filling empty stomachs.

Ron Swoboda remembered the evening vividly when he visited in New York again in 1999 as part of the 30th anniversary celebration of the 1969 World Champion New York Mets. He had starred for that team with a memorable diving catch in right field that is shown almost every year as part of the World Series broadcast introduction.

"I couldn't believe it when Marilyn walked in the door of your house," Swoboda said during a 1999 conversation. "She looked so different, so dramatically different. I could barely believe it was the same girl. I think that change in her hair style set the tone for that incredible evening and the later events."

This all took place in July during an off day on the Yankees schedule, and with a game the following night the party broke up by 2:00 A.M. or so. Janet and I got the last dish into the dishwasher, the last pot scrubbed, the last chair back put under the table (where no player remained) somewhere after 3:00 A.M. Hey, all you detectives out there. This wasn't a homicide. Don't hold me to the times. I had a couple of pops myself.

Now we moved to shut the curtains on our front windows. Early summer sun, remember. So when we looked out and saw two Petersons and two Kekiches standing in front of one car in front of our house about an hour after they had left, we were puzzled. We remarked about it and went to bed. These are ballplayers, remember, different than you and me.

Fast forward to January. I was working on my musical rendition of a new baseball song for the annual Baseball Writers Dinner when I got a message at the hotel to call Fritz Peterson. January was traditionally the slowest of news times in baseball in those days, so I was happy to drop my potential singing career and call Fritz back. I could always use a good off-season story.

"Maury," Fritz said with great enthusiasm, "I have a story for you."

Nothing gets the juices of a reporter flowing faster than those wonderful words. I could see my byline on the back page of the *Post* again, my competitors jealous as hell and my wonderful boss, Ike Gellis, rolling in the glory as he lit another cigar when he went for lunch.

Then Peterson unloaded the facts of the story he wanted me to write. On that evening back in July at our home, he and Kekich had made the original plans for exchanging wives. Also kids, houses, furniture, dogs, and cats. The new families had been in operation for several months, everything was still going well, and he wanted to share his wonderful news with the world. He had chosen me as the conduit.

"Are you crazy?" I asked.

"No, we'd been thinking about this for many months," he said. "We wanted you to write it because you won't make it sound dirty."

Peterson insisted and I resisted. I didn't want anything to do with it. It wasn't that the final terms of the deal were made in front of my house. It was that I thought this was private stuff, best if it had never been done, but certainly better left unsaid. Hey, this was 1973. Presidents didn't even talk about their sex lives in those days.

My wife, Janet, remembered an evening we had spent at the Peterson's home, late in June. While Fritz and I were talking baseball in the living room, Marilyn shyly asked my wife a personal question. "How many times a week do you think is normal to have sex?" It was obviously very important to her. Back in those days, women didn't discuss the subject as freely as they do today. My wife was embarrassed about answering, and she recalled laughing and saying to Marilyn that there was no answer to that question. Normal was whatever felt normal to you—whether it was three times a day or once a month. She knew it wasn't what Marilyn was hoping to hear and later blamed herself for not having been more open about the subject. As we found out later,

it was Marilyn who was more interested in sex than Fr
Perhaps that may have contributed to the wife swapping.

Peterson and Kekich decided, despite my protests, th
they would spell it all out in public during spring training.
ducked the story by choosing to go to spring training with
the Mets in St. Petersburg, instead of with the Yankees in
Fort Lauderdale (that was the only one ever, Ike, I swear). A
new young female reporter, Sheila Moran, was sent to the
Yankee camp for the *Post*. I eventually told Peterson to give
the story to Milton Richman, UPI columnist. He was a fair
guy, a baseball devotee, and very well read.

The story exploded on the national scene. Hey, the Vietnam War was winding down. Where was a good news organization to go?

Dick Young set himself up as the moral conscience of the
game. He ripped the two pitchers apart. Commissioner
Bowie Kuhn jumped on the wagon just before it left the station. He called the two pitchers in to discuss it.

Why? Nobody knew. Maybe he considered it public adultery, and baseball, of course, had never had any experience
with adultery.

Kuhn, as far as anybody around baseball might know,
was always loyal to his lovely Luisa. Young, as far as sportswriters knew, was a great columnist. Young and Kuhn damaged both players irreparably with their public outcry.

Kekich was the first to tell Yankee general manager Lee
MacPhail about the wife swap. "It wasn't a wife swap," he
later said, "it was a life swap. We're not saying we're right
and everyone else who thinks we are wrong are wrong. It's
just the way we felt."

"It wasn't a sex thing," Peterson later said, knowing full
well it *was* a sex thing, mostly. "It was not a cheap swap."

The story of the wife swapping—really husband swapping because the players had handled all the logistics for the
previous months—was now being whispered about around
the Yankee training camp. The two muddled couples had
even visited teammate Mel Stottlemyre and his wife, Sally
Jean, close to both pitchers, at their Washington home over

the winter. It only added to the confusion and widened the circle of those who knew the secret. Ball clubs feast on gossip. It moves faster than a speeding bullet, a Koufax fastball, or the Internet.

While I sat in St. Petersburg, where the Mets trained, and ducked phone calls about my personal involvement, Peterson and Kekich spelled out their feelings to voracious sportswriters. Hey this was the ultimate story, public Yankee sex. Sure, Babe Ruth filled a room with hookers. Sure, Joe DiMaggio had some luscious lovelies visit his hotel room long before Marilyn. Sure Mickey Mantle arrived late to the ballpark after entertaining several women in his suite. These stories stayed within the tight circle of players and sportswriters, never printed, never offered up to hungry fans. Now it was all, public stuff. Fritz and Mike. Wife swapping. Would the game survive?

One of the wisest reactions came from manager Ralph Houk, a World War II army ranger hero, a guy as tough as anybody around, a strong drinker who never showed it, and a cigar smoker without competition.

"It doesn't bother me other than what effect it might have on their pitching," Houk said. "Their personal lives are their own business. They live their own lives and they've got a lot of years to live. If you are not happy, you have to remember you only go through the world once. Why go through it unhappy?"

What might have been the ultimate measure of the exchange was the simple fact that the children stayed with their mothers. Marilyn Peterson kept her children, Gregg, six, and Eric, two and a half, with her when Mike moved in to her New Jersey home.

Susanne Kekich kept her children, Kristen, six and Reagan Leigh, two and a half, with her when Fritz Peterson moved in. Permanently, as it turned out.

Shortly after the story broke publicly, my pal Dick Kaplan, editor of *The Ladies' Home Journal*, called and asked me to write an article about the events for his magazine. All four participants were willing to talk to me about their feelings. It proved to be just about the most difficult article I had ever written. Fritz was an old pal and Mike wasn't. Marilyn was a lady my wife and I knew well, cared for a lot, and respected. Susanne was relatively unknown to me, seemed competitive and ambitious and a little too eager for publicity.

In a long, detailed article all four were able to make their valid points about what Kaplan had called a trade of mates in the headlines. Susanne Kekich proved to be the most incisive. She said her marriage to Mike Kekich was crumbling long before the trade started.

"I always believed I had married for better or for worse," Susanne Kekich said, "for richer or for poorer, till death do us part. I worried about that for a long while. I never could seem to live up to Mike's standards. No matter what I did, he wanted me to do it a little better. I always felt unsure about him, uncertain about myself, a little insecure. Fritz accepted me as I was."

Fritz Peterson was terribly concerned about his sons.

"If Marilyn and Mike don't make it, what happens to my kids?" Peterson asked me. "It's hard to think of them with no father, no family. It eats me up. But I simply can't go back. I'll never go back."

The romance quickly went out of the relationship between Mike and Marilyn.

"I thought Marilyn and I were perfectly suited," Kekich said. "But things developed and we began to butt heads. She worried about being divorced and it became too much for her."

Marilyn Peterson expressed the most emotion at the time. She was clearly the one reluctant swapper. She insisted she wanted to save her marriage with Fritz after all that had happened in the previous months.

"Fritz wouldn't have me," she said. "I tried but he wouldn't have me. He wanted Susanne."

Fritz and Marilyn and Mike and Susan had often been asked through the years to authorize books on their experiences. They were never interested.

Finally, in early 2000 several film projects were in the works about the players and their past and present wives. I didn't care who would play them. I cared who would play Janet and Maury Allen. Where were William Powell and Myrna Loy now that I needed them?

Peterson and Susanne Kekich actually married and are still married. Kekich and Marilyn Peterson, basing their attraction on her physical beauty, lasted just a few months past the horrible spotlight of that spring training fiasco. For her, the swap was never comfortable. She agonized over public opinion and at one point admitted that she had begged Fritz to take her back, but that he wouldn't do it.

"I can't go back. I'll never go back," Fritz later said.

It took several years of living alone with her boys before Marilyn found a man who could appreciate who she was. She is married to a physician and is living comfortably in New Jersey.

Kekich was traded to Cleveland later in 1973. He went alone. He pitched for the Indians, Texas and Seattle before his baseball life ended in 1977. I never saw him again.

Peterson was also traded to the Indians, after Kekich had left that team, won 14 games for them in 1975 and ended his career with a stint in Texas in 1976.

Fritz would show up occasionally in ball parks through the years, selling insurance, working for a religious group, selling bibles, later teaching school again in Illinois as he had in the off seasons while he played. There was a strain in our relationship now. We knew too much about the past. I asked about Susanne and he always said they were doing fine.

Well, this was all part of George Steinbrenner's first year with the Yankees. It would not get any less entertaining over the next quarter of a century or so.

CHAPTER

THREE

George Steinbrenner had always been active in Cleveland politics. He was a strong supporter of Cleveland's first black mayor, Carl Stokes. He was a personal friend of Senator Edward Kennedy. He had been a contributor to Democratic politicians across the country. Like many corporate executives, he hedged his bets by contributing to Republican politicians as well.

In 1972 he had made substantial contributions to the re-election campaign of President Richard Nixon. In 1974 it caught up with him. When Watergate exploded and investigators began snooping around Cleveland and examining his books, he went to old political pal Tip O'Neill, Speaker of the House, for help.

"Get Ed Williams," suggested O'Neill.

He immediately hired famed Washington attorney Edward Bennett Williams as his counsel. Williams had been a longtime power with politics and knew everybody in Washington. He hosted card games at home with such players as David Brinkley, Art Buchwald, assorted senators, and dozens of lobbyists as regular sit-ins.

Williams had also been a great pal of Joe DiMaggio. For more than a dozen years DiMaggio spent Christmas at Williams's Washington home, playing with the Williams kids, opening toys with them, enjoying a raucous family dinner, and telling baseball stories far into the night.

It was Williams, when I interviewed him for my biography on DiMaggio, *Where Have You Gone, Joe DiMaggio?* in 1974 who best explained the Yankee Clipper's dedication and determination.

"Joe always said that the reason he played so hard all the

time," Williams explained, "was because some kid might be seeing him for the first time. Or the only time. He felt he owed him his best."

Now Williams owed Steinbrenner his best. He accomplished that.

As dozens of us media types waited outside the Federal Court Building in Washington on a sweltering August afternoon for Williams to plead Steinbrenner's case on charges of illegal campaign contributions, all bets were off. This was Edward Bennett Williams. He could make magic in a courtroom. He did that day.

Steinbrenner was fined $15,000, about the cost of a backup utility infielder.

When Steinbrenner and Williams walked down from the last step of the ornate Washington building, a TV type yelled out, "Are you going to appeal?"

Steinbrenner, who looked an awful lot like a kid who had been caught with his hand in the cookie jar, only better coiffed and dressed, said nothing. Williams moved to the microphones and said, "Appeal what?"

He had succeeded in keeping his client out of jail for a pittance and wasn't about to make waves on the matter. Columnist Red Smith of the *New York Times* would insist on calling him "convicted felon George Steinbrenner," and Billy Martin, his once and future manager, in one of his more emotional outbursts against Reggie Jackson and Steinbrenner, mumble drunkedly, "One's a born liar (Jackson), the other's convicted." Very cute, especially from a guy who didn't know the truth when he fell over it.

Commissioner Bowie Kuhn, a paper shuffler as a lawyer, later suspended Steinbrenner for two years, trying to look like Judge Kenesaw Mountain Landis, and commuted it some eighteen months later, March 1, 1976.

Kuhn kept Steinbrenner out of the ballpark, which happened to be Shea Stadium that year, as Yankee Stadium was being remodeled, but didn't keep him off the telephone. Steinbrenner was in constant contact with the club through his calls, especially with Gabe Paul, so he ran the Yankees as well that year as he had in the years he was not under suspension. Alexander Graham Bell hardly knew what he was doing for Steinbrenner when he invented that contraption.

After a fuss over trying to hire Oakland's successful skipper Dick Williams, whose contract really wasn't clear, fell in a heap, Steinbrenner made Bill Virdon the new Yankee manager.

Virdon was the guy who put Tony Kubek in the hospital and really made Mickey Mantle cry in the 1960 World Series. Virdon was the Pittsburgh center fielder who hit a hard ground ball to shortstop. As Kubek moved to field it, the ball hit a rock and jumped into Kubek's throat. It was a hell of a knockout punch.

When the game was over, manager Casey Stengel's Yankee career was over, and Kubek was being attended to on a training table in the steamy, crowded Yankee clubhouse. Mantle entered the room. He burst into tears when he saw blood running from Kubek's neck.

The Pirates won the World Series. Bobby Richardson, the Yankee second baseman, was named the Series MVP, driving Bill Mazeroski, who hit the famed winning homer, a little nuts. Winning wasn't everything. Winning was nothing for Mazeroski if he couldn't have that World Series trophy in his living room.

Virdon was a dedicated baseball guy, an overachiever as a player with fine defensive skills but not much power as a hitter. He stressed defense and conditioning in his first Yankee camp and had guys like Lou Piniella and Sparky Lyle running until they could barely breathe. Neither was famous for loving exercise. That didn't stop Piniella from being one of the game's best hitters or Lyle from being one of the game's best relief pitchers.

Virdon had been a Yankee farmhand in the Houk image as a manager. Never a talkative guy, he was tough, smart about the game, and straight with the players. He had the team in top condition when the 1974 season opened.

Early in the season, Virdon made a dramatic change in the outfield defense. He moved Elliott Maddox, a smooth outfielder, from right field to center field and moved Bobby Murcer from center field to right field. It helped the defense. It ruined Murcer's Yankee career.

There was an old saying around the Yankees: "tradition by position."

Every first baseman was compared to Lou Gehrig. Every catcher was compared to Bill Dickey and Yogi Berra. Every shortstop had to measure up to Phil Rizzuto. Every center fielder had to walk in the image of DiMaggio and Mantle.

Murcer handled it well. He was only nineteen years old when he joined the team in 1965, a teammate of the fading Mantle. Mantle adopted Murcer, a fellow Oklahoma kid, showed him the hot spots around the league, taught him how to carry himself as a Yankee, and encouraged him in every way possible.

At five feet eleven inches and 180 pounds, with a cherubic smile and a delightful drawl, Murcer was popular and successful in Mantle's last years. He assumed the starring role on bad Yankee teams after Mantle retired before the 1969 season. His ego was severely bruised when Maddox took over his spot.

Murcer didn't care that Babe Ruth was a right fielder. He only cared that Mickey Mantle was the center fielder; he was Mantle's pal and he wanted that position. Virdon only cared about somebody catching the ball.

Several players—Piniella, Thurman Munson, Graig Nettles and Sparky Lyle—agitated Murcer about not being the center fielder. Agitating was one of the most entertaining parts of being a baseball player. Most guys on a team, especially a team not winning a pennant, loved to agitate.

Somehow, Virdon was able to survive all this inner nonsense. The team played well most of the season and actually had a decent chance at winning the pennant well into September.

With Steinbrenner hiding behind the scenes, with Paul making some good field moves, including trading away my loving pals Fritz Peterson and Mike Kekich in a deal for first baseman Chris Chambliss, the Yankees seemed capable of regaining their long lost glory. After all, they hadn't won anything since 1964. The Cardinals beat them in the World Series that year and Yogi Berra was fired after it all ended.

It was all downhill in the 1960s after that. With Steinbrenner's time, it was up, up, and almost away in 1974.

It all ended in 1974 inside a revolving door.

The Baltimore Orioles were a game ahead of the Yankees with just two games to go. The Yankees were delayed in the Cleveland airport as they awaited their final flight of the season into Milwaukee.

A lot of these big, strong, athletic guys need help getting on an airplane—even the comfortable charters they fly most often with the best meals, the most drinks, and the best looking stewardesses. They get that help at the airport bar.

Thurman Munson was the Yankees star catcher and Rick Dempsey, later to be the 1983 World Series MVP for Baltimore, was his backup. Bill Sudakis, called Sudsy by the players for his name and his drinking habits, was the third string catcher, and first string agitator.

After some serious drinking in the airport bar and some serious drinking on the plane, as they actually ignored the stews, the needling got heavier. The conversation grew nastier. Sudakis, a professionl backup, was telling Dempsey that he would be in his league, a lifelong backup with no career to care about. Mix that kind of conversation and a few beers with a dozen competitive professional athletes and you have a very volatile situation.

We moved closer to the Pfister Hotel on Milwaukee's main street. The sounds from the back of the bus grew louder. I had been around the Yankees long enough by then to know that I'd better have my pencil ready. Some of the players were about to blow up.

The revolving door in the Pfister hotel served as the loaded gun. Sudakis and Dempsey got off the bus at about the same time. They moved toward the revolving door together. They each tried to get into the hotel first, never a very smart idea. Actually manager Bill Virdon had long been in the hotel first, because he sat up front on the bus, jumped off when it parked, and moved quickly to his hotel suite. His wife, whom he hadn't seen for several months, had flown in from St. Louis home to greet him.

I was a few feet behind the two catchers as they crunched in one section of the revolving door. The door stopped. The cursing began. A bellboy pulled from inside and Sudakis swung free. Dempsey was a step behind as the revolving door turned again. As Dempsey was launched into the lobby by the sudden swing of the door he landed on Sudakis. Dempsey, a distant relative of famed fighter Jack Dempsey, put on his best performance (he had studied as an actor in school) and smashed into Sudakis with a hard right. Sudakis weighed about 225 pounds and Dempsey could hit 175 pounds on the scale. No matter. Dempsey was the aggressor.

Soon they were rolling on the floor. Tables were turned over, and the lamps, probably purchased by the hotel back in the 1920s, were knocked all over the lobby. Guests registering at the front desk moved back to avoid a flying Yankee. Except for the fact that there was no bar close to the lobby and no card table, it could easily have been a John Wayne film on the back lot of Paramount. Bobby Murcer jumped on the pile of Yankee bodies as a peacemaker.

Traveling secretary Bill Kane, called "Killer" Kane by the Yankees for his sweet personality, immediately moved to the phone.

"Bill," he said. "Killer here. You better come down."

"What's up?" asked the manager.

When Kane described the havoc in the hotel lobby, the manager told him to take care of it himself. The players had scattered by now—Sudakis was no longer bleeding, the battered tables were being picked up by hotel employees, the guests at a nearby dance party had gotten over the shock and returned to their 1940s music, and most of us reporters had enough information for a good front page story.

The *Post* played the fight on page one and I got a kick out of seeing Sudakis and Dempsey in boxing position in a funny picture that superimposed their heads over the bodies of real fighters.

It was good pregame conversation the next night as Sudakis and Dempsey walked past each other gingerly, each suffering more from serious hangovers than from the variety of blows inflicted on each other in the battle.

Virdon, who never mentioned the fight to the press and denied any knowledge of it when questioned by those of us who saw it, said he was trying to win that night's game. He posted his lineup and Murcer's name was not there. Murcer had damaged his hand as he wrestled the two battling bruisers away from each other. Maddox was in center field as usual, Roy White was in left field, and Lou Piniella was in right field. Murcer was nursing his injured hand on the bench.

Doc Medich pitched a strong game into the seventh inning. Then Piniella, with Maddox coming toward him from the opposite side, shied way from a fly ball dancing in the Milwaukee wind. The ball fell behind him for a double, a couple of runs scored, Milwaukee tied the game, and the Yankees were in trouble. The Brewers won the game with a run in the tenth, and the dream of an upset title went up in flames.

Baltimore won to clinch the pennant. Earl Weaver, a Piniella antagonist ever since he'd managed Lou in the minors, sent a telegram to the Yankee clubhouse.

"Thanks, Lou," it read. "I knew you would screw up some way."

As the players were dressing for the final game of the year, owner George Steinbrenner and general manager Gabe Paul walked into the clubhouse. Each seemed in a pleasant mood.

"You all played well," Steinbrenner told his troops. "I'm very proud of you. Nobody expected us to go the whole way and we almost did. I admire your guts and this is just an example of what we can do if we all play hard and pull together."

It was probably something he pulled directly out of the speech book of his hero General George S. Patton after he'd watched the film on the World War II hero's life for the tenth

or twelfth time. Steinbrenner knew that it was too late to berate, but just right to set the tone for the following season.

Yogi Berra had often said that 95 percent of hitting was
75 percent in your head. Under that mathematical formula,
95 percent of winning in professional sports is about 100
percent in your head.

Before free agency helped teams collect all the talent in
one locale, the difference between winning and losing teams
was quite small. Confidence was probably as significant a
factor in triumph as a good second baseman, a slugging outfielder, or a strikeout pitcher.

Steinbrenner had played and coached enough in sports to
understand that building a player's confidence was as much
a factor in success as physical skills.

Lee MacPhail, who had spent a year working for Steinbrenner before The Boss's interference ran him off, was a
baseball lifer. He believed that the toughest thing in baseball
was to size up young talent. About the second hardest thing
was to get that talent to reach its maximum potential.
MacPhail believed that only one signed player out of one
hundred would ever make it to the big leagues. He cited factors such as size, growth rate, romances, change in lifestyle,
and financial conditions as important in indicating whether a
player succeeded or not as baseball talent.

There was one more major change in the Yankee picture
at the end of 1974, before Steinbrenner's exciting quarter of
a century from 1975—2000 would fall into place. Jim (Catfish) Hunter would become a Yankee.

Marty Appel, Bob Fishel's assistant, called my home late
on New Year's Eve, December 31, 1974. The Yankees had a
signing to announce.

This was no surprise. For several weeks owners and general managers of most clubs had gathered in the tiny town of
Hertford, North Carolina, to await the word of Hunter and
his country lawyers. Clyde Klutz was Yankee scouting director and he and Jim Hunter, the baseball player known everywhere but at home as Catfish, were hunting pals. That tipped
the scale almost more than the three million dollars Stein-

brenner was willing to pay the Oakland star for his free agent services.

Oakland owner Charles O. Finley had neglected to make an insurance payment on Hunter's contract. The seventeen-year-old boy he had gambled on despite a hunting accident that resulted in a toe being shot off, had become baseball's best pitcher.

After Oakland won its third World Series in a row, Hunter chose to exercise his option for free agency. He sat back on his tobacco and soybean farm and allowed baseball owners to throw huge numbers at his representatives. On New Year's Eve he made his decision to accept Steinbrenner's offer.

We sportswriters gathered in a large, cold Parks Department room in Flushing, while the Stadium was still undergoing repairs, to hear the final word. Hunter would be a Yankee starting in 1975.

He was a wonderful pitcher, a humorous fellow, and a great pal to all his teammates. It was with much sadness in 1998 that players, fans, and press heard the news that Hunter was suffering from Lou Gehrig's disease, amyotrophic lateral sclerosis.

He was a Hall of Fame pitcher and a Hall of Fame wit. I remember the day he was defeated in a close game by Milwaukee. The winning hit was delivered by Sixto Lezcano of the Brewers.

Not a sound was heard in the somber clubhouse until Hunter looked up at the chagrined press waiting for someone to talk to them so they could get a revealing story.

"Well," he drawled, "I guess that's the first time in baseball history a guy named Sixto beat nine toe."

Hunter would show up at most spring trainings of the Yankees, kid with the players he knew, help a young pitcher with his slider or curve, and tell funny stories about the old days. He showed up for the last time in the Yankee camp in Tampa, Florida, in March 1999 while, the disease was sapping his strength.

"I get teary-eyed quicker than I used to," Hunter told reporter John Delcos of the *Gannett Journal News* on March 4 in the press box at Legends Field, spring home of the Yankees. "You only live one day at a time. Sometimes you want to cry, and other times you look around and are thankful you are living."

Hunter joked around that day with former teammates of the Yankees, Willie Randolph and Chris Chambliss, Yankee coaches Ron Guidry and Goose Gossage, special instructors, and many of the younger players who sought his wisdom.

After two weeks in camp he went home with his wife, Helen, watched over his farm, spent time with his children, and lived quietly without complaints.

He suffered a serious fall at home in early August, spent a month in a hospital, and returned home September 4, 1999. He died September 9, 1999. He was fifty-three years old.

"I remember one night when I was in the Fort Lauderdale hotel room with my wife," recalled former Yankees public relations director Marty Appel. "About midnight I could hear Catfish and Lou Piniella walking to the room they shared next to mine. They were screaming at each other and obviously had had a few drinks.

"I thought I was in for a tough night. For the next several hours they argued with much profanity. About baseball. 'This is how you pitch to this guy. This is how you bat against that guy.' It was funny, wonderful, and educational," Appel said.

CHAPTER

FOUR

Billy Martin was born on the mean streets of West Berkeley, California, on May 16, 1928, in a small upstairs bedroom at 1632 Seventh Street.

His mother was Joan Amelia Salvini Pisani Martin Downey. His father was a Berkeley fisherman named Alfred Manuel Martin.

Martin père had slick black hair, sharp features, Rudolph Valentino eyes, and a long pointed nose he would pass on to his new son. He played guitar and sang in neighborhood clubs. Shortly after Joan Salvini became pregnant with the child who would grow up to be Billy Martin, she discovered she had married a bum.

"I don't even like to talk about him," Joan Downey told me when I visited with her in her Oakland, California, home in 1979. "He was no good. He told everybody he left me. I threw *him* out. He was sleeping with the girls from the university. When I found out about it I busted up his car with a hammer. Then I threw all his clothes out on the street. I don't even like to mention his name. He's still alive around here someplace. He showed up once or twice after Billy made it to the big leagues. I'll spit on his grave. I promised him that. He can count on it. I don't ever want his name mentioned."

There was one small picture of Martin, the biological father of Billy Martin, in Joan Downey's family album. He was playing a guitar with a small group behind him.

"Nobody's ever seen this picture. Nobody ever will. I won't let it out of the house. I don't know why I keep it. Billy don't want it. That ain't his father. Jack Downey is his father. Jack raised him and took care of him," Joan Downey said.

"I consider Jack Downey my father," Billy Martin once told me, about his mother's third husband. "He is the only father I have ever known. I don't know anything about my natural father."

According to Mrs. Downey in the 1979 interview, Billy Martin's name was listed erroneously and duplicitously on his 1928 birth certificate as Alfred Manuel Pisani, the last name taken from her first husband and father of her first child, Francis (Toto) Pisani. The elder Pisani had broken up with Joan, traveled back to Italy, come back to the United States, was taking a cross-country train from New York back to San Francisco, had stopped overnight in Kansas City, gotten into a heated card game and been shot dead.

"He had this habit of flashing big money," recalled Billy Martin's mother. "He flashed it one time too often and somebody wanted to take it from him. It didn't bother me none when I heard about it. Like I said, we were already divorced and he was a bum."

She soon met and married Martin, a Berkeley fisherman, in a relationship that lasted just long enough for future baseball figure Billy Martin to be conceived. When that relationship ended on the heels of the University of California gals, Billy Martin's home environment was fixed.

He was raised by his strong, feisty, tiny mother and her mother, Raefella Salvina, who would be credited with turning young Alfred Martin into baseball player Billy Martin.

Grandmother Salvini, called Nona (Italian for *grandmother*) by the family, always referred to young Alfred as *bellis,* or *belissimo,* a beautiful boy, and the name was called out often on the streets in front of 1632 Seventh Street. It was not long before the name Alfred was forgotten and Billy had become the name of the pugnacious kid.

The family was soon enlarged again when Joan married John Thomas Downey, a Berkeley truck driver and lumper, a man who loads cargo on large trucks. He was a quiet fellow who enjoyed cooking and singing on vacation boats. Joan and Jack would add three more children to the household—Jack, Patsy, and Joannie—none of whom would have a meaningful relationship with Billy Martin through the years.

The Great Depression impacted on the Downey home as severely as it did on millions of others. There had not been much money around to support five children before the Depression and even less after it hit.

When Billy Martin was four, five, and six years old there was barely enough food on the table to feed the family.

"We were always poor when I was a kid," Martin once told me. "There wasn't much to eat. I remember I ate stale bread dipped in coffee for breakfast most of my early life. I ate a hot lunch in school and had spaghetti or lasagna for dinner. In the summer I didn't eat much lunch. I was too busy playing ball."

As the three smaller Downey children came along in the early 1930s, Billy and his older brother, Toto, were dispossessed. The younger children stayed in the larger home at 1632, and Billy and Toto moved in with their grandmother at 1634.

Billy Martin said that he slept in the same bed with his grandmother until he was fifteen years old, not an uncommon Depression ritual for poor families. The psychological result of such a relationship is better explained by the hundred-dollar-an-hour shrinks, none too available around baseball circles.

"I had to get out at fifteen because I was kicking too much," Billy Martin once laughed.

Martin grew up in a matriarchal society built around his mother, his grandmother, and his half sisters. Jack Downey, though kind and sympathetic, was rarely available for parental duties in economic times that demanded endless hours of employment for survival.

Billy Martin was a high school boy of eighteen when his grandmother died in 1946. She was probably the most significant female influence in his life, perhaps even more loving than his three wives—Lois Berndt, Gretchen Winkler, and Jilluan Guiver.

While his home influences were predominantly female, his male influences were ethnically mixed. His poor neighborhood consisted of a mixture of working-class Italians, Irish, Mexicans, Portuguese, and even a few Blacks. His best boyhood friends from the Berkeley neighborhood were Howard Noble, a Portuguese; Ruben Diablo, a Mexican; and Babe Furhman, of German-Irish descent.

Billy Martin's conflicts in baseball were rarely over race. There were few signs of prejudice in his makeup and there was always a long line of Black and Hispanic players standing by his side.

What lingered in Billy Martin's character, what made his relationships with people such as Reggie Jackson and, of course, George Steinbrenner nearly impossible for Martin to manage, was their financial security.

Billy Martin was a classic Depression baby, someone who could never escape the bitter memories of those days, someone who saw financial turmoil just over the next horizon, someone who could never relax in the company of others he envisioned as more financially confident. It was probably the single most important aspect of Billy Martin's life, and it played desperately into the torturing hands of silver spooner George M. Steinbrenner.

Steinbrenner led Billy's list as his most hated adversary. Reggie Jackson was next, and Ken Holtzman, a pitcher Billy hated with uncontrollable venom, held the number three position. Steinbrenner was of German background. Jackson was Spanish and African American. Holtzman was Jewish. Were race and religion the key factors in Martin's sense of anger about these three? No way. It was all about money. Martin hated Steinbrenner for his wealth and financial control over him. He also saw Jackson and Holtzman as two of the wealthiest and most overpaid players in baseball history.

Martin's early character was set more on the ball fields around Berkeley than in the backyards.

"He was a good boy," recalled Mrs. Downey. "There was discipline in our house. When he was eight or ten or twelve he would play in the park all day and be home in time for bed at eight-thirty."

Billy Martin was an average student at Franklin Grade

School, Burbank Junior High, and Berkeley High School. He enjoyed history and geography, but had little time for studies. His main interest was baseball—playing it, talking about it with friends, listening to it on his floor-model radio. He rarely read about it.

"We couldn't afford newspapers in my house," he once told me.

When Billy was a high school junior, a teacher asked him to read a book for a report. He admitted he had never read a book and suggested he didn't intend to change.

"What will you do with your life?" the teacher asked.

"I'm going to be a baseball player," he said. "Baseball players don't have to read books."

The teacher reached into a shelf and pulled out a book. "Here," she said, "read this."

The book was *Lou Gehrig: A Quiet Hero,* by Frank Graham.

"I read it from cover to cover in one sitting," said Martin years later. "It had a strong influence on my life. I knew I wanted to be a baseball player. Then I wanted to be a Yankee. I admired Gehrig's courage, style, and class. That's who I wanted to model myself after."

No two Yankees would ever be more different in temperament than the quiet, dignified Gehrig and the bombastic young Martin.

That book was a connection Billy Martin and I would share. I had read that same book and fallen in love with the movie of Gehrig's life, *The Pride of the Yankees,* made shortly after the death of the Yankee first baseman in 1941. Billy and I often talked about what Gehrig had meant to the team and to baseball. The discussion would often bring him to tears, something not unusual for the emotional Yankees manager. Both would die tragically, well before their time, Gehrig from amyotrophic lateral sclerosis, Lou Gehrig's disease, in 1941, and Billy Martin, in a horrendous car accident in 1989.

Fifty years after she played the role of Gehrig's wife in the great film with Gary Cooper, Teresa Wright journeyed

down to Yankee Stadium from her Connecticut home. It was
her first visit ever. I chatted with her a bit. It wasn't the same
as chatting with Cooper or Gehrig, I imagined.

There was one other thing Gehrig and Martin had in common. They liked to hide from the snooping press in the off-
limits trainer's room.

"Babe (Ruth) was always out front with the sportswriters.
He couldn't wait to talk to them," clubhouse attendant Pete
Sheehy, who joined the Yankees in 1926 and lasted more
than fifty years, once told me. "Gehrig was the other way.
He liked to stay away from the press and I think he spent a
lot of time after games in the trainer's room if he saw a
writer enter the clubhouse."

Billy Martin could almost always be seen sitting on a
footlocker in the off-limits trainer's room, especially after a
tough loss. It was probably a useful defense mechanism for
the volatile Martin.

Martin had played baseball at Berkeley's James Kenney
Park with big leaguers when he was only twelve years old.
Several, including Cookie Lavagetto, Augie Galan, Nick Et-
ten, and Tommy Glaviano, lived in the area. They would fill
out the lineups for local pickup games with young kids like
Billy Martin.

"Sure, I remember Billy from those days," Lavagetto, a
former Brooklyn Dodgers star and later Martin's Oakland
Oaks roommate, once said. "He was the same, a cocky kid
who always wanted to play. You couldn't keep him out of a
game if you wanted to. He was always picking your brains,
how do you make this play, how do you make that play, a big
talker, full of fight."

Billy Martin signed with the Oakland Oaks after graduat-
ing high school in 1946 and was assigned to the Idaho Falls
club, moved up to Phoenix in 1947, and came home to Oakland in 1948. The Oakland manager was a failed big league
skipper named Charles Dillon (Casey) Stengel, then a year
away from moving back to the big leagues with the Yankees
and the unprecedented five straight World Series victories
with the New York Yankees.

Casey and Edna Stengel never had any children of their own. There were lifelong rumors suggesting ailments of every kind caused by Casey's rowdy, youthful baseball conduct. One story suggested that Stengel, in a fit of depression, jumped into the cold water of the Gulf of Mexico during a bitter spring training.

Martin lost his father before he ever knew him, and he had difficulty dealing with the absence of his hard-working stepfather. Father figures showed up for Martin throughout his tumultuous life. Stengel was the most significant surrogate. George Steinbrenner was probably not among them.

Stengel and Martin each loved the game of baseball with uncontrollable passion. Once a player proved to Stengel that he was passionate, the manager would dedicate endless hours to helping him improve. It was what Casey did remarkably well—with Martin and with so many others—throughout his brilliant career. While Casey had interests outside of the game, his true emotions only surfaced around the game. He saw a kindred spirit immediately in the aggressive, talkative, courageous Martin, a player of limited physical abilities who would need every edge to succeed.

Stengel related in the same way to sportswriters who showed a passion for his game. I first met him in 1959 as a young writer with *Sports Illustrated* magazine. I stood next to him as he ducked questions, for maybe the only time in his professional life, after the Yankees lost the 1960 World Series to the Pittsburgh Pirates at Forbes Field while stories filled the New York press that his Yankee days were over. He was soon fired and in an ebullient press conference explaining his withdrawal from the Yankees, he bellowed, "I'll never make the mistake of being seventy again." He was nearly seventy-five when he ran the Mets in 1962, and I sat with him one afternoon on the bench at the Polo Grounds before a night game scheduled some six hours later.

He started telling stories about his 1912 debut with the Brooklyn Dodgers and his 1913 days in Ebbets Field as my pencil moved rapidly through my notebook. He was on Jake Daubert or Wilbert Robinson when a television crew approached from across the field. Stengel had apparently agreed earlier to do a three o'clock interview, and now the cameraman, the sound man, and the talent, Gabe Pressman of New York's NBC station, approached the bench. Casey continued talking with me and showed Pressman—a somber, humorless newsman—no attention.

Pressman moved closer to Stengel and in a sonorous television voice said, "Casey . . ."

Stengel looked up at Pressman with a venomous glance.

"Can't you see I'm talking to my writers," he bellowed.

I had made the big time. I was one of Casey's writers and if I happened to be alone with him on that bench soaking up baseball trivia I was *all* of his writers. What a thrill. Pressman would get his interview a few minutes later, but on Casey's terms, in Casey's good time. I would forever after be one of "Casey's writers" and would see no wrong in his conduct.

On Casey, Billy Martin and I agreed.

Martin was angry with Casey when the manager was promoted to New York in 1949 and didn't bring Billy up to the big leagues with him. They connected again in New York in 1950 and Stengel promoted Martin's career every chance he had. In 1952 Martin made a wonderful World Series catch off the bat of Jackie Robinson, and Stengel retold the story endlessly until his final days. Martin, often leaning back in his office with a pipe stuck between his teeth, would quietly retell the pop-up story if anyone asked. Film of the play was consistently shown before almost every World Series.

Billy Martin blamed Stengel for his trade away from the Yankees after the 1957 Copacabana incident in which the birthday celebration of Martin and Yogi Berra, along with Whitey Ford, Mickey Mantle, Johnny Kucks, and Hank Bauer, turned into a brawl. General manager George Weiss labeled Martin the instigator, an embarrassment for the Yankees. He ordered Martin dispatched to Kansas City. Martin could not forgive Stengel for that for many years and avoided him as much as he could.

After Stengel left the Yankees and later returned to base-

ball with the Mets, Martin walked up to him before an exhi-
bition game. They began chatting as if nothing had ever happened between them.

"I kept thinking," Martin would tell me later, "that if
Casey died before we could talk again I would never get
over it."

They became close again for the next ten or twelve years
and Martin was truly distraught and emotional when Stengel
died of cancer in 1975. Billy Martin arrived at Stengel's ornate Glendale, California, home, sat in his favorite rocking
chair, drank his favorite bourbon, examined his favorite pictures, checked out his favorite pieces of furniture, and slept
in Casey's bed. He was tearful and taut throughout the long,
touching farewell to one of the game's most significant figures. Stengel was probably the closest male in Billy Martin's
life.

In a rare, quiet, touching moment Martin would entertain
me with stories of Casey in his Oakland days before I was a
sportswriter. He spoke of early Yankee success stories, of
some of the experiences he had had with Casey through a relationship that covered almost thirty years.

"I loved the man," he would say, with deep emotion.
Martin knew that he had a sympathetic ear in me with that
one.

Martin played for Stengel in Oakland in 1948, worshiped
him from afar in 1949 when Stengel won the first of his five
straight Yankee titles, and joined up again with the Old Professor in New York in 1950. He was a utility player that year
behind Jerry Coleman and Gil McDougald but showed off
all his cockiness by closing in on Joe DiMaggio. DiMaggio
was nearing the end of his brilliant career. While most players stayed away from him in the clubhouse and talked to
DiMaggio only when Joe spoke to them first, Martin became
an instant pal. They had in common the San Francisco area
background, the Italian background, and a sense of status.
DiMaggio always had to have a front man, a foil, a protector
at his side to keep unwanted press and public away. Martin
served that purpose well. He also was one of the few players

who could make the intense, ulcer-wracked, somber DiMaggio actually laugh.

DiMaggio would address most of the younger players as "Kid," as Babe Ruth did, because he never took the trouble of learning their names, not an uncommon big league experience between stars and rookies. Martin immediately won DiMaggio over with his brazen behavior. He called the great DiMaggio, the Yankee Clipper, Joltin' Joe, "Dago," in reference to his Italian background in a politically incorrect era when ethnic background and religion was the quickest and easiest identifiable aspect of a player's personality. DiMaggio laughed when Martin called him "Dago" and immediately responded by calling Martin, "Little Dago."

So Dago and Little Dago became pals, sharing meals together in Joe's hotel room on the road after a loss or dining together in a New York night spot after a glorious win.

"When Joe walked into the clubhouse," Billy once said, "It was like royalty coming in, a king or a United States Senator. He was always dressed so perfectly, so immaculately, his hair so perfect. The guys would say, 'Hi, Joe,' as they passed his locker and I would always burst out with, 'Dago.' And the other players, especially the younger ones would just stare at me."

DiMaggio told Martin in the middle of 1951 that this year would be his final season. Billy asked for a couple of DiMaggio bats as souvenirs and Joe presented him with several bats, a pair of spikes, and several Yankee jerseys on the final day of the 1951 season. The items remained in Billy's possession in his home until the time of his 1989 death.

Martin would shortly become closer to another young player named Mickey Mantle and would run with Mantle and Whitey Ford for all the years of his Yankee career from 1950 through 1957. Martin and Mantle treated each other as equals. Martin and DiMaggio would never have that kind of relationship. It would be more hero and hero worshiper, something that seemed satisfying to each of them in their own way.

Except for the catch off the bat of Jackie Robinson in the

World Series of 1952 and the .500 batting average against the Dodgers in the 1953 World Series, gaining the prestigious Babe Ruth award as outstanding Series star, Martin's Yankee career was unexceptional. He was a decent big league player, an average fielder, a .257 lifetime hitter, and rather successful in important games. Because of the great players around him he would clearly be described as an overachiever. He played in five Yankee World Series and batted .333. He always made a lot of noise and Stengel always advertised his presence.

Martin went to Kansas City in 1957 and played with a total of six teams in the years between 1957 and 1961. He finished his career with the Minnesota Twins and soon accepted a scouting job with Minnesota. Martin knew that someday he would be a manager in the big leagues, because Casey told him so and all the sportswriters told him so. Sportswriters create managerial candidates by writing about them as potential leaders in the dying days of their careers, allowing the players to explain their futures. Sportswriters insist certain players have managerial potential and a few have coaching potential. Owners and general managers as well as fans read these articles, so the potential soon becomes reality.

Martin went to Minnesota's farm club in Denver in 1968 and was named Minnesota manager for the 1969 season. He was fired in Minnesota, Detroit, and Texas before the Yankees became interested in him in 1975.

"The secret is to get on the managerial wheel," Yankees manager Joe Torre once told me. "It will spin and spin and spin until it drops you off in another town as field leader."

The Yankees were struggling again in 1975. George Steinbrenner was growing impatient. Bill Virdon was a solid baseball man but he didn't have fire, he didn't have chemistry, he didn't have star power, he didn't have any of the traits Steinbrenner envisioned for a baseball manager. Billy Martin had all of that. Steinbrenner had never met Martin but he knew all about him through his "baseball people," the baseball lifers Steinbrenner depended upon for information.

One of his best was Birdie Tebbetts, a former catcher and big league manager who smelled out a baseball player a country mile away and entertained for hours with stories of how he caught him.

Steinbrenner read of Billy's Texas firing and asked Tebbetts and Paul about him. "That man is a fiery manager," Steinbrenner said to Paul and Tebbetts one day. "Let's get him."

"I think you'd be making a big mistake, George," said Paul.

"I want him. Let's get him."

"George decided he wanted Billy and I started tracking him down," Paul told me years later. "He was nowhere to be found. We called down in Texas and people there said he was with Mantle and Ford. We called at their homes and they said they were off hunting and fishing some place in Colorado. We called Billy's father-in-law in Nebraska and he told us Billy could be reached at some lodge in Colorado. I finally reached him and asked him if he would meet with Birdie Tebbetts in Denver."

Billy Martin had held several baseball managerial jobs and blew all of them with his aggressive conduct. Now he was on the threshold of his life's dream, the managerial job of the New York Yankees, *his* New York Yankees, *his* team, as the true successor to his hero Casey Stengel.

Paul and Tebbetts soon arrived at the appointed motel.

"I checked in and didn't tell him I was there," recalled Paul. "I wanted Birdie to talk to him first. He knew Birdie from their playing days and from their managerial days together. Soon Birdie was in Billy's room and my room happened to be right next door. I could hear everything they said. I had to laugh when Birdie told Billy he had to excuse himself for a while to contact Gabe on this point or that. Then he would march up and down the hall for a while before going back into Billy's room for more conversation. The discussions lasted into the next day. Finally, a deal was struck and Birdie told Billy he would get Gabe Paul to initial the contract to make things official. I think Billy almost fainted when he only had to walk next door to see me."

"You're the new manager of the Yankees. Congratulations," Paul said to Martin.

Martin never answered. He was too choked up to talk.

On August 1, 1975, a Friday night, Gabe Paul met for a few minutes with Bill Virdon. The meeting followed a Yankees victory at Shea Stadium, the temporary home of the team while the Stadium was being remodeled for the first time since it had been opened in 1923 to a Babe Ruth home run.

"I'm sorry," Paul told Virdon. "We just decided to make a change."

The following afternoon, August 2, 1975, the press was called in early and waited in the lounge for Billy Martin to appear. He walked into the large room wearing a cowboy jacket, cowboy pants, and boots. He sat at a long table, looked out at the anxious members of the press, lit up a pipe, and answered all questions quietly for more than an hour.

George Steinbrenner was not in the room. Those of us who had been around Billy as a combative player; a feisty manager at Minnesota, Detroit, and Texas; and an opinionated scout knew this relationship was volatile. George and Billy had massive egos. George and Billy would never mix easily. What seemed different this time for Billy was the team he was managing. He was in Casey's chair now. He would have the opportunity of asserting himself in baseball legend as leader of the Bronx Bombers. He must have learned by now, after three big-league managerial failures, that only one man made the decisions for a team, the man who signed the checks. Around the Yankees that was George M. Steinbrenner III.

I was writing a story that day in the *New York Post* about the arrival of Billy Martin as the manager of the New York Yankees. I knew Billy's time in New York would be exciting. I also knew that eventually I would write of Billy's firing. That was always the way it played out.

George Steinbrenner and Billy Martin, a little Cain and Abel there, Frank and Jesse James, Butch Cassidy and the Sundance Kid, any love-hate relationship you could name. They really had only one thing in common that would bind them together for many years: Winning with the Yankees.

CHAPTER

FIVE

The scouting report on Billy Martin said he would have one personality for the first year of his managerial career and another—uglier, meaner, and more sarcastic—later on. He was 30–26 after taking over the Yankees in 1975, mostly calm after losses, always upbeat after victories, quick with wit about Stengel, Steinbrenner, any player, any sportswriter if the mood struck him.

When Steinbrenner issued a critical remark through a "source close to the owner," which was usually George returning a late-night phone call to me or another sportswriter and warning us never to say it came from him, Martin played the game with him.

"Let him come in here and manage these guys and I'll spend the day counting his money," Martin often said.

The tension that was always discernible between Steinbrenner and Martin would remain subdued throughout much of the last two months of Billy's first season as field boss of the Yankees.

In late February of 1976, I traveled to Fort Lauderdale, Florida, for my first full spring training with Billy Martin as Yankee manager. This was the time of year that sportswriters, baseball players, baseball executives, and fans all connected.

Spring training was the most joyous aspect of a sportswriter's life. The workday was short, the conditions were perfect, the atmosphere was pleasant, and the ego was stroked. Jealous desk men back home in New York might pass remarks about a story a sportswriter wrote but in their hearts they wanted to be him, or her, as the later years would suggest.

My first spring training in Florida with a newspaper was in 1962 for the *New York Post,* shortly after I had been hired. I had worked a couple of years at *Sports Illustrated* magazine, wanted daily journalism, and got a call from sports editor Ike Gellis that a job was available. I had applied several times before and been told no openings were available. On this one morning I was asked to come in early.

Gellis and managing editor Paul Sann sat at a long conference table. Gellis had only one question: "Do you smoke?" I told him I did not. He told me I was hired. Sann asked me to come to his office after Gellis finished our interview. Ike soon told me how I qualified for the job. It seemed that the previous baseball writer for the *Post,* Arch Murray, was a nonstop smoker. He also drank heavily. Murray had set his bed on fire several times while traveling with ball clubs on the road. A week earlier he had been in St. Louis on assignment, was drinking heavily, smoked in bed, and fell asleep. He died in the smoky fire. I had qualified as his successor since I didn't smoke.

Martin was smoking a pipe as I entered his office early one morning in 1976. I asked about the corncob pipe he seemed to enjoy so much and we started exchanging stories about smokers.

"I remember when I first came to the Yankees in 1950 and I used to walk over to say hello to DiMaggio. He would be sitting there in his underwear sipping half a cup of coffee and smoking a cigarette. Pete Sheehy, the clubhouse guy, always told me he had to have half a cup of coffee for the Dago and a pack of cigarettes ready when he came in. Joe used to smoke everywhere—the locker room, the trainer's room, on the bench. Half a cup of coffee and a Camel cigarette. That's what I always remember about Joe in the clubhouse."

Martin hardly ever told stories about his days with the Twins, the Tigers, or the Texas Rangers. He was a Yankee, always a Yankee, only a Yankee, no matter what the uniform of the time said or the paycheck recorded. One of Billy's first acts in coming to the Yankees was hiring Yogi Berra as a coach shortly after Berra had been fired by the Mets as their manager. It was Martin's way of linking the great Yankee past to its present. Of all the Yankee legends, from Ruth to Gehrig to DiMaggio to Mantle, none could possibly match the intensity Martin felt about the team. Maybe it was simply because none could match Martin's intensity.

George Steinbrenner was born on July 4, 1930, and enjoyed the centennial year of 1976 from beginning almost to end. The Yankees took off quickly under Martin, were in first place a week after the season started, broke through by July for a big lead over Baltimore, and clinched the Eastern Division title under Martin on September 25. They won by 10 games.

This was a team that Steinbrenner and Gabe Paul had put together in the previous couple of seasons and it was now nearing its peak. It included the best catcher in the American League, Thurman Munson, a combative kid from Akron, Ohio; a future Hall of Fame pitcher, Jim (Catfish) Hunter from Hertford, North Carolina; a solid first baseman named Chris Chambliss, son of a navy chaplain from Dayton, Ohio; a rugged, handsome outfielder named Lou Piniella from Tampa, Florida; a witty, mysterious guy called Puff by his teammates, Graig Nettles, because he often disappeared after a game like a puff of smoke; a flashy center fielder named Mickey Rivers from Miami, Florida; a maturing second baseman from Brooklyn named Willie Randolph; and a quiet, chess-playing left-handed pitcher, maybe the best in the game that year, from Lafayette, Louisiana, named Ron Guidry.

Martin had led and blended these players into a wonderful team—smart, talented, aggressive, outspoken, and confident.

"There was never a game we didn't think we could win, a pitcher we couldn't beat, or a team we couldn't outmanage that year," recalled Piniella. "The tougher the pitcher, the tougher the game, the more sure we were that we would win."

When the Yankees clinched the Division title in Detroit

with two weeks to go, the champagne flowed freely. Steinbrenner came down to join the celebration and was drenched in the bubbly. His perfectly coiffed hair, cut and styled weekly in his office, was mussed up just enough for a toweling.

"We did it," Steinbrenner announced before a television camera, "just the way I said we would."

Martin was happy but smirking as he caught Steinbrenner's public act. The Yankees hadn't won anything since 1964 and now twelve years later, with Billy Martin as manager, they were back on top. Martin knew where the credit should go. He wanted to hear it from Steinbrenner and Gabe Paul. He wanted to hear it from his players. He wanted to see it in large bold headlines in the press.

Martin's hero, Stengel, had won his first Yankee pennant in 1949 and announced after the triumph, "I never coulda done it without my players."

Martin led the Yankees to a title in his first full season after the team had been out of the money for a dozen years. He knew he couldn't have done it without his players. He also knew his players couldn't have done it without him. Why wasn't he getting more of the glory?

Martin knew he had to beat Kansas City in the playoff for the pennant and probably the Cincinnati Reds in the World Series for the total victory. Then he would truly get his acclaim. He knew that. He wished that. He aimed for that.

There would be a five-game series for the right to advance to the World Series. Martin, who had always been confident and had starred in so many Series games as a player, was ready for the emotion.

"The way you win a big game is by going into it knowing you will win," Martin said before the opener.

Catfish Hunter was the Yankee starter for the first game and Larry Gura, an ex-Yankee traded away by Martin earlier that year, was the Kansas City starter. Martin had used a little negative psychology on Gura to weaken him before the game. He referred to Gura's interest in tennis as a relaxing sport. "A goddamned tennis player," Martin would say in his most sarcastic tone, something he had worked into a verbal art form. He also threw around another word—*gutless*. That stings professional athletes very sharply. He suggested Gura wouldn't throw inside because he was afraid of the opposing player's reaction and that this made him useless as a Yankee pitcher.

Boston's Bill Lee, an outspoken iconoclast, had suggested earlier in the year that Martin often instructed his pitchers to headhunt opposing players, an evil but common baseball act. Beanball pitchers had earlier instigated a furious field fight in which Lee had suffered a broken collarbone in a scuffle with Graig Nettles and Mickey Rivers.

"Billy Martin has a bunch of storm troopers over there and he is the leader of the Brown Shirts," announced Lee, with his arm in a sling the next day in reference to the trained killers of Adolph Hitler and Benito Mussolini.

Martin laughed it off. He took it as a compliment. Besides, it came from Lee and no one took that flaky left-hander seriously.

With the pressure on Gura, with the tension enormous, and with Martin bellowing from the dugout, the Yankees got two quick runs in the first inning of their first postseason game in twelve years. Catfish Hunter was his usual brilliant self and the Yankees won the playoff opener 4-2. The Yankees were two wins away from their first World Series in a dozen years.

The Kansas City Royals won the second game. Dock Ellis, a militant black activist, was the winning Yankee pitcher in the third game and the Royals tied it 2-2 with a 7-4 win in the fourth game.

Now it was show time.

Professional athletes like nothing better than the heroism of a final big game. They start thinking about it as kids in Little League, do it a few times in high school and college, collect some press clippings from last-second minor-league heroics, and dream sweetly about hitting a Bobby Thomson home run in the final game of an important season.

Now fifty professional baseball players on the Yankees

and Royals would have that chance in this last game, that chance to separate themselves from the other fifteen thousand big league players with one swing of the bat or one magnificently pitched game. Who would enter that game as just another big leaguer and leave it as one of the game's historic figures?

Baseball players try to follow a normal routine every game of the season, whether it is a meaningless game in June or an October classic. Lou Piniella said that that day could not be normal, no matter how hard he tried.

"I didn't sleep for more than a couple of hours," he recalled. "I drank six or eight cups of coffee before I showered. I just thought over and over again about the game. I dreamed all day long of getting the big hit, a hard-line double to left. I didn't want to get too giddy and think about a home run."

On Thursday night, October 14, 1976, the Yankees and Royals played one of the sport's most memorable games, the pennant-deciding final encounter between two fairly evenly matched excellent baseball teams. It was the kind of game the 56,821 fans in the stands would long recall, reminisce about in middle and advanced years, lock deeply into their memory banks with the birth of children, the birth of grandchildren, a new job, a new house, the handful of life-changing events most people experience.

Even sportswriters get worked up at these games. It was the time to shine. This final playoff game, win or lose for the home team, would lead the paper. Occasional readers would join regular readers for that report. Editors, who didn't know first base from first fiddle, would expert the story. Egos and prizes were on the line.

While baseball players theoretically pull together for the good of the team and the winning game, sports reporters don't even make an act of it. They are out there to better the competition, to rise far above the crowd, to write something that will make the sports anthologies.

Dick Young, the columnist of the *Daily News* in New York, covered the Brooklyn Dodgers for many years. When they blew a pennant he would write, "The tree that grows in Brooklyn is an apple tree."

Young and I ended up with a bitter, hateful rivalry through the years but I am forced to admit (tears here) that I never wrote a line that would last as long.

The players were ready. The sports reporters were ready. The fans in the refurbished Yankee Stadium were ready. Millions of television viewers were ready.

In George Steinbrenner's loge-level private office, dozens of "A" list celebrities mingled. Gabe Paul looked down on New York's diminutive mayor, Abraham Beame; or Cary Grant, who had been drawn into Steinbrenner's circle by Bill Fugazy, the limousine company executive. Fugazy always offered a vehicle free of charge when the debonair Grant was in town. Grant sat in the softly cushioned chair in the shape of a fielder's glove in the middle of Steinbrenner's office with waiters at the ready.

"Another scotch and soda, Mr. Grant?" a waiter asked.

"Yes, please," said the actor in his most sonorous sound.

I was allowed in the suite for a few minutes with a *Post* photographer to record the event as Grant sat before me with the same perfect grace and style I had seen in so many films. I could think of only one thing as I watched our photographer take dozens of pictures of him in that chair, knowing the paper would use just one small shot the next day. Now I knew why people bought baseball teams. Would Cary Grant come for lunch at American Shipbuilding with an industrialist named George Steinbrenner?

For George Steinbrenner, winning was everything with the Yankees. Collecting "A" list celebs through the years wasn't bad, either.

The Yankees built a 6-3 lead into the eighth inning. I looked over from my press box seat and saw that Grant was still among the faithful in Steinbrenner's Stadium loge box seat. He would clearly enjoy another scotch and soda in the postgame party. Hey, these guys have egos, too.

Future Hall of Famer George Brett, one of the generation's best hitters, crashed a three-run homer to tie the game at 6-6 as the crowd sat stunned in the Stadium. This was not the way it was supposed to be. In the House of Heroes, it was supposed to be the guys in the pinstripes doing the damage—not the players in the powder blue.

The Yankees went out quickly in the eighth, Kansas City failed to score in the top of the ninth, and now the Yankees had that unanswerable chance of scoring a run in the bottom of the ninth and winning a pennant. As the Yankees trotted into their dugout and the Royals trotted to their positions on the field the Stadium crowd unleashed its frustration. They wanted that win and Brett had denied it to them. Now they could at least express their frustrations with a mini-attack on the field. Paper cups, paper airplanes, brown bags, soggy fruit, an occasional secreted liquor bottle, small batteries, hats, shirts, even an old shoe filled the field.

"Fans who insist on throwing things on the field will be removed from the Stadium and subject to arrest," proclaimed announcer Bob Sheppard, in a voice that clearly must have brought huge smiles to the face of Cary Grant down the runway from him. It did little to calm the crowd. Finally, their anger spent, the fans settled down. The groundskeepers had picked up most of the stray garbage except for an occasional piece of paper or a brown bag. Let the game resume.

The scheduled hitter was Chris Chambliss and the pitcher for Kansas City was Mark Littell. Chambliss had been obtained from the Cleveland Indians by the Yankees on August 26, 1974, with pitchers Dick Tidrow and Cecil Upshaw for pitchers Steve Kline, Fred Beene, Tom Buskey, and my old wife-swapping pal, Fritz Peterson. Mel Stottlemyre, a Peterson pal, former Yankee anchor pitcher, and now in decline with a bad shoulder, greeted the news with a rousing statement about Chambliss: "What the hell do we need him for?" Trade reactions of teammates usually have little to do with whether or not the stranger can play. The question more often is whether or not the stranger can party. Peterson was a tough loss for Stottlemyre but Chambliss would turn out to be a great gain for the Yankees.

Chambliss, twenty-seven years old, had batted .243 as a Yankee in his first frustrating season but came back to hit .304 the next year. He was a solid star with a .293 average, seventeen homers, and ninety-six RBIs in the 1976 season. Now he walked up to home plate as the noise level stayed intent but the brown-bag throwing decreased. The preacher man's son prayed a bit as he walked up to the plate. Later he recalled his master plan as he moved toward the plate.

"I decided to swing at the first pitch," Chambliss later told me. "I figured Lytell would lose his concentration and he might groove one."

Lytell pumped a high fastball sixty feet six inches away from Chambliss's moment with history. The left-handed hitter caught the baseball on the sweetest part of the baseball bat, that thick, round part above the trademark, making that sound that millions of kids and thousands of big leaguers can recall throughout their lives as a joyous, emotional moment. There was a strange silence in the Stadium as the ball rocketed toward the right field wall, clearly high enough, clearly far enough but not yet a fact of history until it damaged the hands of a fan or crashed into a seat. Whack. It was there, thirty or forty rows back, a hundred feet up, a home run, a winning home run, an historic Yankee home run, as memorable as any the Babe or Lou or Joe D hit in their years of glory. Catcher Thurman Munson, the next scheduled hitter, leaped in the air and waved farewell to the baseball as it made it into the seats.

Chambliss stood at the plate for a moment, the bat hanging by his side, his eyes fixed on the distant wall, his neck a little taut, his knees shaking a bit with the emotion of the instant. Now he was running, jogging, dancing toward first, around the base, moving past second, knocking a fan down at the base who had raced him there from the other side, sprinting as well as a man of his size, six feet one inch and 221 pounds could possibly move, and heading for home. There were fifty thousand people at home, or so it seemed to Chambliss as he approached the plate. He couldn't quite make it there and veered off in a tangle of teammates, fans, special cops, and even New York City policemen. He got near the dugout and Martin urged him back to the plate in a phalanx of supporters and law officers for the final, official magical touch of the plate. A home run. A *winning* home run. An historic Yankee Stadium home run. It would identify Chambliss forever as a Yankee figure of much note.

"I still think about it occasionally," he said recently. "Someone always brings it up, in the ballpark, around home, in church. Chris Chambliss? Oh, you're the guy ... Yeah, I'm the guy. I can still see it. High, up, just perfect, good swing, good follow-through. The rest of it, the crowds on the field, the fans, the cops, that's a little bit of a blur."

"Victory has a thousand fathers, defeat is an orphan," John F. Kennedy once said.

All those fathers seem to gather in the winning locker room of a winning team, especially a winning Yankee team, where politicians and show business people, where baseball players and baseball executives, where family and friends, where professional hangers-on with the magical skills of a Harry Houdini in getting in as he got out, challenge the supposed working press. They also come in hordes at these baseball events—editors, columnists, feature writers, news side experts—all participating in the reflected glory. Where were all these people on the brutally hot days in July as we climbed the stairs in the Texas ballpark?

Steinbrenner, Gabe Paul, Bill Fugazy, other pals of Steinbrenner were soon pushing through the hordes for congratulations and photographs, for a little reflected glory, for a share of the emotional triumph. Billy Martin, who had been there as a player so many times, sat on a trunk in the center of the clubhouse, his hat sweaty and matted, his eyes a little glassy, his uniform dark and dirty with perspiration.

"I got to thank George and Gabe," he told the press and repeated for a late television microphone. "I wish Casey was here to see it. This was his pennant."

Then Martin, always misunderstood, always underappreciated, always failing to gain the necessary glory, let his true personality show with a few words.

"Those guys who didn't think this team could do it," he said, with much emotion, "who picked against us, who said I'd never win one, where are they now? Now they can kiss my Dago ass. I won it. The Yankees are back where they belong, on top."

He took another swig of the New York State champagne, climbed down from the trunk, and marched off again into the forbidden trainer's room. He had said enough for one interview.

The Cincinnati Reds beat Boston in the seventh game of the 1975 World Series with Carlton Fisk's memorable twelfth-inning sixth-game homer getting the Sox into another sad Series loss. Babe Ruth had pitched the Red Sox to the 1918 Series title but after he was moved to New York in 1920, the "Curse of the Bambino" had kept Boston from a Series win.

Now the Reds, known as The Big Red Machine, with a powerful cast of characters from Pete Rose to Johnny Bench, Joe Morgan to Tony Perez, and led by colorful Sparky Anderson, were ready for the Yankees.

The Series was rather forgettable. Cincinnati simply was a much better team than the Yankees. They swept the Series four games to none and the joy of the 1976 pennant seemed to evaporate for Martin and many of the Yankees in the outclassed Series defeat.

One incident summed it all up for the Yankees. Johnny Bench, the future Hall of Fame catcher, was named the Series Most Valuable Player. He had batted .533 in the four games. Thurman Munson, the Yankee catcher, had been almost as good. He batted .529. Sparky Anderson was in the interview room under the stands of the Stadium as Munson waited his turn. Sparky puffed on a pipe and looked about twenty years older than his forty-two years of age. His hair was completely white and his face was craggy. He spoke in convoluted sentences, which, later on, would not keep him from a broadcasting job. He was asked about the relative merits of the two fine catchers after Bench had been interviewed and Munson, in an undershirt, sipped at a cold beer. Anderson did not know Munson was close by.

"I wouldn't embarrass anybody by comparing him with Bench," he said, without thought.

Most of us in the room just laughed. Sure, Bench was the best but Munson was the local favorite, the fine Yankee catcher, and he had just proved he was a class player in a Series overmatch. He also was an abrasive personality, quick to see slight when none was intended, and even quicker to blame the press for any lack of attention or recognition his personality seemed to prevent him from gaining. He was, most significantly, a duplicate Billy Martin personality— certain he was unappreciated, certain the world (especially those with typewriters) was against him, certain he had to excel each day to reach any measure of accepted glory.

He moved to the platform in front of a half-dozen microphones when Anderson left the room and attacked the Cincinnati manager, called the Reds lucky, and said that Bench was considered a great catcher because he got along with the press. Munson had proved to be a wonderful player but he would never prove to be someone who enjoyed the thrill and excitement of being a big league star. He carried too much Munson family baggage in his head.

Martin was still bad-mouthing the Reds when many of us returned from the interview room to the Yankee clubhouse. He was not, by any definition, a graceful loser. He always used a line, stolen from Vince Lombardi or someone else, in his more philosophical moments, "Show me a graceful loser and I'll show you a loser." Martin sat stony-faced on the same trunk he had enjoyed in the center of the clubhouse after the victory over Kansas City. This time he seemed spent, about a hundred years old, undernourished, someone who had lost his best friend and could use a big meal. He denigrated the Reds, attacking them for their style, their arrogance, their luck. "Bloopers, pop-ups that fell in, every umpire's decision, every break. That's why they won," he said. Steinbrenner stayed upstairs in his office as the press instigated and agitated Martin further. He had heard by now of the fuss over Bench and Munson in the large interview room and blamed it all on Sparky Anderson's romance with the sportswriters.

When times were good for Martin—a pennant win, a future Series win—he could charm the press with funny lines, amusing stories about the old days under Stengel or managers he had played for and maybe even learned from through the years. When he lost an important game (that meant *any* Yankee game), it was shoot the messenger time. The print press, especially those of us who attempted to record his ravings accurately, were abused verbally, criticized, and discounted. It was as if we were opposing players and really had something to do with the winning or losing of baseball games. Martin got messages to his players through his ranting with the press. He now understood that as good a team as the 1976 Yankees were, they still lacked a player or two who could give them the World Series over the Reds or anyone else.

Billy Martin and George Steinbrenner agreed on little. After the 1976 Series loss to the Cincinnati Reds they agreed on one thing at least. The Yankees had to improve the next year if they were to regain their manifest destiny, the World Series title that Billy Martin so desperately wanted to bring back to the Yankees.

There must be a player or two out there who could accomplish that for them. Steinbrenner, by signing Catfish Hunter and trading for other high-salaried players, had quickly proven that money would not be a factor in the Yankees move to the top.

Steinbrenner was about to show just how wide and high he would go for victory.

CHAPTER

SIX

Every summer for forty years I have traveled to the bucolic upstate New York village of Cooperstown for the Baseball Hall of Fame induction ceremonies.

I sat on the back porch of the Otesaga Hotel overlooking Lake Otsego where Indians once fished and baseball heroes of the past now think of their golf games.

There are a dozen or so rocking chairs on the balcony of the magnificent old structure where I chatted casually in the early afternoon sun with Ted Williams and Stan Musial, Warren Spahn and Bob Feller, Casey Stengel and Al Lopez. I talked gently with Rube Marquard, a pitching star with the New York Giants and the Brooklyn Dodgers before World War I, as he rested in a wheelchair. And I could see why Lefty Grove, now well into his seventies, was considered a great pitcher and as crusty as they come. I had a long talk one year with a man named Edd Roush, a Cincinnati and New York Giants outfielder who could not really explain why his mother spelled his first name as she did but could explain why he sat out the 1930 season. "John McGraw wouldn't pay me what I wanted," he said.

Roush became famous for skipping the 1930 season and forcing the Napoleonic McGraw to trade him back to Cincinnati. He won two batting titles, had a .323 lifetime average and was the game's finest defensive center-fielder of his time. No matter. He was known for staying home in 1930.

"I want what I deserved," he said.

Go back in baseball history 100 years or 130 years to the first organized professional leagues. There were always holdouts. There were always independent, heroic figures who were willing to stand up to ownership. In baseball's earliest days something called the reserve clause was written into a standard contract binding a player to his team for life unless sold, traded, or released. This was a clear violation of the democratic free enterprise system where a working person can take the best job at the best salary.

Holdouts were gloriously chronicled with Babe Ruth, Roush, and even Joe DiMaggio staying home until their prices were met. DiMaggio was soundly booed when he returned to the Yankees after a holdout during the depths of the Great Depression.

Forty years after Roush skipped the 1930 season, a St. Louis Cardinals outfielder named Curt Flood, traded to the Philadelphia Phillies, challenged the reserve clause. He sat out the 1970 season while the United States Supreme Court examined the reserve rule. It simply ordered baseball to come up with a better solution as it sent the case back to lower courts for examination.

Marvin Miller, a labor leader with the United Steelworkers in Pittsburgh, had by then become the leader of the Major League Baseball Players Association. Despite ugly and shabby treatment by selfish, wealthy baseball owners, Miller became the most important revolutionary person in modern baseball history.

A new agreement was reached in negotiation between the owners and players under the aegis of Miller, and late in 1976 it would be played out for the first time. The first free agent class in baseball would take the field in 1977. The most heralded of the free agent players was a charismatic outfielder named Reginald Martinez Jackson, Jr.

Late in November 1976, the owner of the Yankees and the American Shipbuilding Company of Cleveland would engage the son of a Philadelphia tailor in a romance worth of Tracy and Hepburn, DiMaggio and Monroe, David and Bathsheba. Jackson had starred at Oakland and, with free agency coming, had been traded to Baltimore for the 1976 season. Now he was free to sign with any club.

Steinbrenner understood star power. The Yankees had

won the pennant easily in 1976. They had lost the World Series. Steinbrenner saw that as a serious defeat. He wanted more; he wanted it all. He wanted the best. He wanted Jackson. He would not take no for an answer.

Steinbrenner brought Jackson to Manhattan. Reggie had already visited Montreal and San Diego, where the price had escalated to over four million dollars for five years, astronomical numbers in an era when two or three hundred thousand dollars a year was considered a huge baseball salary. It was only a dozen years since Sandy Koufax and Don Drysdale had held out together in a salary war against the Los Angeles Dodgers in breaking the artificial $100,000 salary limit. Koufax wound up with $125,000 a year and Drysdale got $115,000. Baseball salaries have not stopped breaking records since.

There was more than money involved in the pursuit of Jackson. Steinbrenner understood that better than most. Jackson was a man of fierce pride and enormous ego. Steinbrenner played on both of those characteristics as he wooed and won Jackson.

"I didn't talk money," Steinbrenner said of their first face-to-face meeting in November 1976. "I talked tradition. I talked the Yankees. I wanted to convince Reggie this was the only place for him to play. I wanted to convince him of the possibilities of business expansion here for him."

They enjoyed lunch at the fashionable Plaza Hotel where the elite meet to eat in Manhattan. They walked outside, down the steps, past the doormen, and close to a waiting horse and carriage, a Plaza hotel nicety for Central Park whirls.

"Hey, Reggie, hey, Reggie," yelled the driver of the carriage. "Wanna ride?"

Jackson only smiled and walked a few more paces away from the hotel entrance. A small, black boy, spotting Jackson from across the street, raced through the traffic and moved close to the baseball player. "Sign this, sign this," he shouted. Jackson did. Others turned toward him, smiled, and turned away. After all, this was New York, the Big Apple. Celebrities were a dime a dozen.

"See," Steinbrenner told Jackson. "Everybody knows and loves you already in this town."

He was playing the right tune at the right time for the right man.

Jackson and Steinbrenner talked some more as they walked along Fifth Avenue. Steinbrenner suggested it would be comfortable for Reggie to live in one of those magnificent apartments. He could easily commute to work at Yankee Stadium. He would be acknowledged as he dined in the finest restaurants in the world. He would be fawned over, appreciated, and honored as he played for the most famous team in baseball history. Still, Jackson gave Steinbrenner no hint of his feelings.

"After I left him at the Plaza," Steinbrenner later told me, "I decided Reggie had to sign with us. I knew he would be in Chicago the next day talking to other clubs. I called his agent, Gary Walker, and told him I wanted to see him one more time in Chicago. I wanted to be the first in and the last out."

"He's already got an appointment with another club for breakfast at eight o'clock," Walker told Steinbrenner.

"I'll be at the hotel at seven-thirty," Steinbrenner told Walker.

Steinbrenner flew to Chicago that night and sat in the lobby of the Hyatt Regency Hotel in Chicago at 7:00 A.M.

"I was alone in that lobby Thanksgiving morning," Steinbrenner remembered. "I felt like some little kid as I waited for my time to call. I kept thinking how I had promised my kids I would be home for Thanksgiving. This seemed more important."

Steinbrenner got half an hour with Jackson from 7:30 to 8:00 A.M. He repeated his offer of some three million dollars for five years and talked more of the gold and glory possible for Jackson outside of baseball in New York City, of the Yankee tradition, and of the fame imparted on a Yankee celebrity by Madison Avenue, the advertising-agency mecca.

Other baseball officials met with Jackson and Walker throughout the day. Late in the afternoon Steinbrenner went to the hotel coffee shop and had a cup of coffee. It was his only food all day. He read all the Chicago newspapers. He talked with fans in the lobby. He talked repeatedly to the members of his staff back at Yankee Stadium. He called his family often in Tampa and he wondered constantly what in hell he was doing sitting alone in a hotel lobby on Thanksgiving Day in 1976. He was the owner of the New York Yankees, American Ship-building, owned several homes, a horse breeding farm, and assorted other properties worth multiple millions.

He realized, Steinbrenner suggested later, that this was the fiercest competition he had ever experienced. That is what kept him there, kept him waiting for that call from Jackson, kept him on edge for a long, restless day. This was what he enjoyed about baseball, about life, about his daily adventures. It was not money or power or even victory. It was the competition—beating his opponents, rising above them, enjoying the smell of success. It was something that had been burned into him as a kid at the feet of his father, something he enjoyed in business, something he enjoyed through his players as he vicariously watched them win games with great pitches or big hits. There was no real way to describe it, to measure it or even to appreciate it. What is love? Who really knows? What is the joy of this kind of signing success? Who really knows?

"Paging Mr. Steinbrenner," he suddenly heard early that evening in the hotel lobby. "Paging Mr. Steinbrenner."

He walked to the house phone. Jackson was on the line. His voice was calm. "C'mon up, George," Jackson said, evenly. "We're finished."

Steinbrenner walked into Jackson's suite 1101 in the Chicago Hyatt Regency Hotel. Walker—tall, blond pal of Jackson's from college at Arizona State—sat in a large chair. Jackson stood in the center of the room. There was a smile on his face, Steinbrenner remembered.

"You're it, George," Reggie said.

Tears came to Steinbrenner's eyes. He shook hands with the large athlete standing before him and then impulsively hugged him.

Jackson moved to a small desk in the hotel room. There was a one-page note on hotel stationery. Jackson handed it to Steinbrenner. In longhand he had written out an agreement of acceptance of terms as generally outlined by Steinbrenner. "This will do until the lawyers get to writing it up," Jackson said.

George Steinbrenner has kept that note under glass on a dresser in his Tampa home. Every so often he looks at it, proud of his victory, proud of outhustling every other club that was after Jackson, glad he made the deal for the future Hall of Famer.

The four-paragraph note agreeing to terms ended with, "We are going on this venture together. I will not let you down." It was signed "Reginald M. Jackson."

A few years later Steinbrenner leaned back in his thick, deep, dark leather chair in the shape of the fielder's glove in his Yankee Stadium office. He stared at a large, personally autographed picture of his friend Cary Grant. He was, like his movie pal, impeccably groomed, his hair recently trimmed, his television blue shirt neatly starched, his trousers carefully pressed, his leather shoes shining.

"That was one of the hardest days of my life," he recalled of the pursuit of Jackson. "Also one of the most thrilling."

Jackson had homered the night before in another easy Yankee win.

"Reggie has finally become the leader of the club," Steinbrenner said. "Just as I always expected. He understands his role now. The magnitude of being a Yankee has superseded the magnitude of his being Reggie Jackson."

Uppity.

That was the word most heard about Reggie Jackson from most of his teammates after he joined the Yankees. He was a black baseball player who romanced only white women. He drank fine wine. He lived in a fashionable Manhattan apartment building. He drove to work in a $90,000 Rolls Royce.

Mickey Mantle, angered at something I had written about him in his declining years, once watched me as I approached him at the batting cage from the Yankee dugout. He turned slightly and said over his shoulder, "You piss me off just standing there."

Reggie Jackson also seemed to piss everybody off just standing there.

"To most of my teammates," he would often say in his sour moments, "I'm just an uppity nigger."

Baseball, like America, has struggled with race for most of its history. Jackie Robinson broke the color line in 1947 for financial and moral reasons advocated by Branch Rickey. He was an exceptional man, an outstanding talent, and soon to be an historic figure.

Reggie Jackson wore his race on his sleeve. How much the Yankee relationship with Jackson had to do with that and how much it had do with Jackson's arrogance, convoluted psyche, manner, and mien is difficult to measure. Ballplayers often disliked each other before 1947, before race was a factor in the game, before that obvious difference could be used as an excuse. The amount of tension in a baseball clubhouse in the twenty-first century will probably be no different than it was in the final days of the nineteenth century and throughout the twentieth century.

Ballplayers die twice—the day they are finally released and the day their physical life ends. For most, the first death is harder. It comes quickly, when they are still very young and far in advance of any planned farewell party. Sportswriters go on into their seventies, eighties, or nineties—John Drebinger of the *New York Times* was still writing well and eating enormously in his ninth decade. Athletes are finished early. It is clearly the most significant part of their relationships with each other, with friends and family, and with the media. There was never an easy day with Jackson for any teammate, manager, or friend.

"Reggie wasn't really a bad guy," Oakland and Yankee teammate Catfish Hunter once told me. "He would give you the shirt off his back. But then, of course, he would call a press conference to announce it."

Ron Swoboda was a popular outfielder with the World

Champion 1969 New York Mets. He was popular with the fans and unpopular with his teammates. He gained fame with a famous World Series catch against Baltimore's Brooks Robinson. Swoboda was almost always being interviewed by the New York media after games—win, lose, or rained out. The other players, especially those uncomfortable with the press, hated him for it. As a dozen or more reporters gathered around Swoboda's locker after unimportant games, several teammates would be snickering in the background. They didn't want any attention themselves. They just wanted to make sure Swoboda didn't get it.

Jackson had made an art form of relating to the press. He had spent a year in college, actually read books, listened to classical music, understood history and theater, and followed news outside of Yankee Stadium. It made him comfortable with sportswriters on planes, buses, and in hotel lobbies, and clearly uncomfortable with many of his teammates who could not see past the sports pages and wouldn't know an international crisis from a domestic crisis.

Ballplayers change their identities, their personalities, their character as soon as they walk inside a team clubhouse. Soft-spoken husbands and fathers become rowdy beer drinkers. College graduates forget the English language. Good-looking women become a major topic of conversation. On the road, teammates who enjoy family barbecues together at each other's homes, might share a girl for the night in sexual contests. It is this tight fraternity, this bonding, this linked mentality that combines twenty-five talented athletes from a variety of backgrounds into a single force, a team—led, motivated, and controlled by the manager.

When Mickey Mantle retired after the 1968 season, I asked him what he would miss the most about not playing anymore. I was certain he would talk emotionally about long home runs, marvelous catches, and winning games.

"Bullshitting with the other guys in the clubhouse," he said immediately.

It is a line we sportswriters never cross. We are outside that circle, uninvolved, separated from the men who stand up and face a fastball coming in at their heads at one hundred miles an hour. We cannot know what it is like to be a pitcher who faces down a hulking hitter with forty ounces of wood in his hand directed at the pitcher's face.

Reggie Jackson joined the Yankees in the spring of 1977. His teammates treated him like a sportswriter.

At Oakland he had been the central focus of the championship teams. He was tolerated for his ego and admired for his talent.

"He said the same things in Oakland he later said in New York," Catfish Hunter recalled. "The only difference was nobody paid any attention to him in Oakland."

He was called "Buck" by his Oakland teammates, as most black stars are. The term was first used in 1951 for a kid center-fielder on the New York Giants named Willie Mays. Jackson was also called "Nine" as in his uniform number nine, but most often he was addressed simply as Reggie, the name he liked, the press liked, and the fans liked.

When he came to the Yankees, Reggie had considered wearing uniform number 42 since 9 was in the possession of star third baseman Graig Nettles. He settled on 44 because, he said, "There was only one forty-two." That was the uniform number worn by Jackie Robinson of the Brooklyn Dodgers, a number now permanently retired by baseball as a late honor to the game's most revolutionary figure.

Jackson was called nothing when he joined the Yankees. He was simply ignored. As the members of the press gathered around his locker in Fort Lauderdale Stadium each and every day before and after workouts, most Yankee teammates walked by as if he was not there. An invisible black man. Billy Martin seethed when he was asked about Jackson. He was not interested in having him and had not been consulted about obtaining him. It wasn't Jackson's race. It was simply Jackson. His ego. His style. His flair. His flashiness. All the things Martin craved for himself, Jackson seemed to have. His very presence in that Yankee clubhouse, that House of Heroes, that room filled with the legends of

Ruth and Gehrig and Billy's pal, Mickey and all the rest of them, galled Martin.

Elston Howard broke the color line with the Yankees in 1955. The Yankees, with a long history of racism, were one of the last teams to put a Black on the field. Even Casey Stengel, my hero and Billy's hero, but still a man of his times, uttered a memorable racist line about Howard after he joined the Yankees. Howard was a strong hitter, good catcher, adequate outfielder, and fine fellow. In the late night at a hotel bar before a dozen sportswriters, including Harold Rosenthal of the *New York Herald Tribune,* Casey grumbled, "When I get a nigger, I get the only one who can't run." My pal Harold later repeated the line to me.

Howard had a wonderful career with the Yankees, starting as their token Black and working into coaching and front office positions. He had been accepted by the fans and was treated well by the club. This was true in part because he kept his mouth shut. His wife, Arlene Howard, was strong, tough, and militant, something Ellie could never quite deal with in his playing days

My wife, Janet, once drove to a Yankee wives' function with Arlene Howard. As they left Yankee Stadium, Arlene decided she wanted to make a left turn where a traffic sign clearly indicated no left turn was allowed. Arlene, after rigorous body language from the traffic cop on duty, made the turn anyway. As the poor unsuspecting cop stopped the car, Arlene Howard turned to my wife and said, "Watch this." Taking her driver's license, the cop repaired to a spot about twenty feet behind them and slowly slowly began to write out the ticket. Arlene became angrier and more exasperated as the minutes ticked by. She got out of the car, walked back to him, berated him with her sharp tongue, and snatched the ticket out of his hand. While my wife watched in astonishment, she raised the ticket up to his face. "Then she tore the ticket up," my wife recalled. "When she came back to the car she turned to me, saw the look on my face, and said, 'Don't worry, nothing will happen.' And nothing did."

Elston Howard would have accepted the ticket and congratulated the officer for doing his job. But of course, Elston would never have deliberately made that illegal turn in the first place.

Elston Howard suffered a serious viral infection around his heart in 1979. It would lead to his death in 1980 at the age of fifty-one. We talked about Reggie Jackson a few months before Ellie died. In the twenty years I had known him it was the first time I ever heard him speak harshly of the Yankees.

"Billy was jealous of him, hated the attention Reggie got, couldn't control him," said Howard, as he bit into a sandwich and sipped a cup of coffee in a Bronx diner near the Stadium. "That was part of it. The other part, the big part, was that Reggie's black. Billy hated him for that. I believe Billy is prejudiced against Blacks, Jews, American Indians, Hispanics, anyone who doesn't bow to him. He can get along with Blacks if they don't challenge him. But Reggie challenged him in every way. Billy was always hostile to him. Did everything to make him unhappy. Went out of his way to see him fail. I think Billy wanted Reggie to fail more than he wanted the Yankees to win."

Howard's voice suddenly grew quiet as he sipped his coffee and looked out the diner window at the mostly minority people walked down the River Avenue street near the Stadium. He looked back at me and just shook his head.

"George has been great to me," he said of the Boss. "He took care of me. He's been a good friend. But I would have liked a managerial offer. I might have turned it down but I would have liked an offer."

George Steinbrenner hired and fired Billy Martin five times. Why not try Elston Howard? Why not, indeed?

In the early 1960s I wrote a magazine article for *Coronet* ("Your best bet is *Coronet*") suggesting that soon there would be a black manager in baseball. I nominated Bill White, then a star with the St. Louis Cardinals. White had been a bright student at Hiram College in Ohio, a man who took a summer baseball job with the idea of paying for future medical schooling. The medical education never materialized. White went on to become the first black broadcaster in New York with the Yankees and spent several years as president of the National League. When I interviewed White for my article, he predicted that baseball would never see a black manager.

"The owners are all white. They want to take their manager to their private country clubs, show him off, play golf with him, drink with him at the club bar, dine with him at the annual dinners," said White. "Blacks make them uncomfortable in that setting. It's all right for them to be around us as athletes. We help make money for them. It's different when we have to cross over into that social setting."

It would be 1975 before the Cleveland Indians hired Frank Robinson as the game's first African American manager. General manager Phil Seghi, who knew Robinson from his Cincinnati days, pushed for it. Owner Nick J. Mileti accepted. Mileti did not play golf.

The pressure on Jackson—with the big contract, with the obvious antagonism from Martin, with the coldness from teammates, with intense media scrutiny—was enormous.

"It makes me cry the way they treat me on this team," Jackson told me one day in one of his philosophical ramblings. "The Yankee pinstripes are Ruth and Gehrig and DiMaggio and Mantle. And I'm a nigger to them. I don't know how to be subservient."

There was one exception to the coldness with which Jackson was treated. He had one friend on the Yankees—backup catcher Fran Healy. "When I was playing for Kansas City and he was with Oakland," Healy recalled, "I met him outside the players' gate. We talked a long while. I found him very intelligent, very interesting, a unique guy. We became friends, visiting and talking together each time we played each other. We just naturally became friends when he joined the Yankees."

Healy took a lot of heat from teammates for his relationship with Jackson. There were whispers of the hateful term "nigger lover" from passing teammates, scowls from many who saw Healy as flunky for the star, sarcastic remarks about how Jackson picked up all the checks in all the expensive restaurants on the road after Healy made all the reservations.

"There was nothing like that," said Healy recently, as he marked twenty years as a Yankee broadcaster. "I just found Reggie an interesting guy to talk to. That was all there was to it. If I worked in a factory and he was the guy loading the racks next to me the relationship would have been exactly the same."

George Steinbrenner had asked Thurman Munson to fly in from his home in Ohio to appear at Jackson's first Yankee press conference at the gilded princess suite of the American Hotel in New York City. Steinbrenner knew Munson would be the thorn in Reggie's side. Munson was not only jealous of Reggie's glory, he was bitter about his salary. Steinbrenner had promised Munson he would be the highest-paid Yankee. When Munson heard of the Jackson numbers he was livid. Steinbrenner explained to him that it was the signing bonus that made the difference. Munson would have none of it. Jackson was now the highest-paid Yankee and the squatty-bodied catcher hated Jackson for it.

Two things destroy baseball teams. One is salary jealousy. The other is sexual jealousy. When two players covet the same girl, things can erupt in a clubhouse. Babe Ruth was the highest paid Yankee in his time. Lou Gehrig accepted that. What Gehrig didn't accept was Babe's attempt at romancing Gehrig's wife, Eleanor Twitchell Gehrig. It caused a breakdown in the men's relationship for many years, only resolved on July 4, 1939. Gehrig was honored on that day after his consecutive game streak was ended and his fatal illness disclosed. Ruth put his burly arms around Gehrig, and before photographers, Gehrig accepted the Babe's gesture. He died June 2, 1941.

John Drebinger of the *New York Times,* who traveled with Ruth and Gehrig and the Yankees in the 1920s and 1930s, said that is the way it was between Ruth and Gehrig. So that is the way it was.

When I broke in as a regular beat reporter with the Yankees, I almost always sat next to Drebinger in the press box. I pumped him for stories about those two legends. "Get me a sandwich, kid, and I'll tell you," he would often say. Other sportswriters made fun of Drebinger's legendary appetite. They said he'd eat anything. Once he proved it. He ordered a grilled American cheese sandwich from the dining room at Tiger Stadium. While he wrote his wonderful story for the *Times* that day, he munched contentedly on the sandwich. He never noticed that Joe Trimble of the *Daily News* had put a yellow piece of Western Union typing paper inside, along with the cheese.

Trimble, a notorious drinker, was capable of some strange behavior. On an off day in Detroit, then Yankee publicity director Bob Fishel invited a dozen members of the press to dine with him in a flashy restaurant called the London Chop House. Trimble started preparing for the evening's entertainment by drinking at noon. When 6:00 P.M., the meeting time, came he was sloshed. We all walked out into the street toward the restaurant a couple of blocks away from the hotel. Trimble lagged behind, so blind with drink that he crashed into a large light pole. His face was bloodied. He rose slowly from the ground, looked at the pole, and meekly apologized, "Oh excuse me, sir, I didn't see you."

While players argue over women, sportswriters rarely do. They don't have the youth, sex appeal, and athletic charisma of the players. Sportswriters argue over stories. We all argued over the stories involving Jackson and Munson that spring, the younger sportswriters generally siding with Jackson, the older, established ones agreeing with Munson.

Jackson, for his part, made no effort to win over his teammates that spring. His actions did much to alienate them even further. He flashed money constantly in the clubhouse, around the hotel lobby, and on the team bus to out-of-town games. He talked loud and bragged about huge home runs he had hit. He often stood outside the ballpark or the team hotel with one or another of his beautiful blond girl friends. They were almost always beautiful, and they were always blond. "Living black, sleeping white," players called it. He dined alone or with Healy or occasionally with a sportswriter anxious for a detailed story of his life. I always skipped my chances for dinner with Reggie in Fort Lauderdale. He offered enough material during the workday. My wife and kids were more fun at night.

There is a hierarchy among the baseball press about a baseball team. Those of us who work with them every day, write about their good days and bad, travel with them to unpleasant places like Kansas City, Milwaukee, and Arlington, Texas, deserve the big stories. When they retire, when they are traded, when they have major things to say, we want them to say it to us. That is our payment for eating stale sandwiches in the old Kansas City ballpark.

One memorable magazine story angered *New York Daily News* columnist Dick Young for years. Jackie Robinson, who had a complicated relationship with Young throughout his career, announced his retirement from baseball in a *Look* magazine article written by sports editor Tim Cohane. Robinson got $50,000 for the story. Young got heartburn.

Magazine writers, often hit-and-run guys, will write controversial, exaggerated, newsy material and then disappear forever from the scene. These types are disliked by the regular beat writers. Sometimes players will say things to strangers they might never say to regular, familiar sportswriters. It was about to happen again in the spring of 1977.

A freelance writer named Robert Ward, never heard from before or since, was in camp chasing Jackson around for an article for *Sport* magazine. Jackson was followed daily by the regular writers, but he was repeating much of what he had said in late February. By the middle of March, it was all wearing a bit thin for the regular beat guys. But Ward had never heard any of it before. He somehow got Jackson wound up—easy to do—and let Reggie go.

The season began quietly as the defending American League champions under Martin set out for the goal of the World Series title. Martin batted Jackson fifth, sixth, or seventh in the Yankee lineup. He kept him far away from the prestigious fourth and third spots, using him occasionally in right field, and criticizing his play when he did. He talked derisively about him to the press, especially after a couple of drinks in the hotel bar on the road.

As the season moved on, Munson seemed to accept Reggie's presence. Munson had his favorite sportswriters. I was not among them. He also had a habit of walking up and down the clubhouse floor when he wanted to talk to members of the press. A reporter might be abused if he stopped Munson but he might also get something interesting to write.

Fred Stanley, a backup infielder on that team, recalled a day early in May when Munson homered to win the game. When the press entered the clubhouse they moved quickly to Jackson's locker for comment about Billy Martin's latest tirade about him. Munson was ignored. It fueled his anger.

"Thurman was waiting for the press that day," Stanley recalled. "They stopped at Reggie's locker. They never got to Thurman and that really pissed Thurman off."

Jackson's arrogance, his failure to explode as a Yankee star, and his unwillingness to cater to his mates made for a very uncomfortable scene in the bowels of Yankee Stadium each day. Now the shit was about to hit the fan—every Yankee fan who cared about cause célèbre Jackson/Munson/Yankees.

Sport magazine announced that its June cover story, "Reggie Jackson in No-Man's Land," would be out in advance copies in the middle of May. Jackson was hitting .250, had only five homers, had knocked in only eleven runs, had two errors, and had made absolutely no appreciable difference in the lineup of the defending league champions.

Ward's article was placed in the locker of every Yankee player by some unidentified flunky. I can only remember that happening once before, when an article by Stan Isaacs, a *Newsday* sportswriter quoting manager Alvin Dark on his racial attitudes, landed in the lockers of the San Francisco Giants. Dark said that Willie Mays could play but other Blacks couldn't quite cut it. This occurred in 1964 during the height of the American civil rights demonstrations and brought baseball kicking and screaming into the mainstream of political discussion. Every news columnist and television commentator was expressing opinions about Dark's positions. Dark may have been a hero back home in Lake Charles, Louisiana, but he was a villain in a good part of the rest of the country.

Ward's article didn't have national impact but it certainly mattered to those who cared about the Yankees or were steeped in baseball tradition. (Get off it, you Dallas Cowboys fans, the Yankees were, are, and always will be America's Team.)

"This team, it all flows from me," Ward quoted Jackson as saying. "I've got to keep it all going. I'm the straw that stirs the drink. It all comes back to me. Maybe I should say me and Munson. But really—he doesn't enter into it. He's being so damned insecure about the whole thing. I've overheard him talking about me." American sports fans would be discussing "The straw that stirs the drink" for a good, long while.

Ward had asked Billy Martin if he thought there would be any leadership problems on the club with Reggie Jackson now a member of the team.

"Not a chance," replied Martin. "We already have a team leader. Thurman Munson."

Jackson was almost universally criticized by teammates, as reported in the press, for demeaning Munson, who was, after all, the captain of the Yankees, the first since Lou Gehrig.

"See, the thing that people forget," explained infielder Fred Stanley, when questioned that day, "is that Thurman is our captain. He *is* Mr. Yankee. He wanted attention. He just didn't know how to get it. He wanted it as badly as Reggie wanted it."

Munson was playing well, Nettles was having a fine year, and relief pitcher Sparky Lyle was saving everything. Lyle was a wonderful character around the Yankees. He made a living with his nasty slider. He made a life with his crafty humor. One of his favorite clubhouse activities was sitting naked on the birthday cakes supplied regularly to players on their special day by clubhouse man Pete Sheehy. My personal tribute to Lyle came after the 1977 World Series team photo was taken. There was the picture of all the Yankees in their glory with Albert (Sparky) Lyle in the front row, his thick mustache drooping, his eyes intense, his long hair flowing in the breeze, his clefted chin glowing, and his hand on the open zipper of his fly. The picture died. Sparky Lyle lives forever in the memory banks of friends, fans, and press.

The intensity between Jackson and Martin colored everything around the team. Still, the Yankees played well, partied, laughed, and loved. No team with jokesters such as Lou Piniella, Sparky Lyle, Graig Nettles, Catfish Hunter, Mickey Rivers, and even "Squatty Body" Thurman Munson, when the mood hit him, could be serious all of the time.

On June 18, 1977, the Yankees were seen on national television in a game against the Red Sox. It was a mini-drama that would, in some ways, serve as the breaking point in the Jackson/Martin nonrelationship.

Boston's Fenway Park, one of the oldest and most historic stadiums in baseball, is a small field, almost always filled and ringing with passionate noise, especially if the hated Yankees are on the field. The Yankees stole Babe Ruth away and nothing has ever been the same since in Losertown, Massachusetts.

The Yankees had tortured the Red Sox for nearly six decades, maybe the worst of it the two final games of the 1949 season when an ailing Joe DiMaggio led the Yankees to victory.

Now, in 1977, the two best teams in the American league were at it again. Boston was having a big day on their way to a 10-4 win. Boston slugger Jim Rice hit a looping fly ball to right field. Jackson coasted after it, surrounded it, and picked it up finally as Rice cruised into second base. Martin, watching intently every move Jackson made on the field, was outraged. He called outfielder Paul Blair, a fine defensive player, and sent him to right field to replace Reggie.

Jackson jogged in slowly to the Yankee bench on the first
base side of the field. Jackson knew a confrontation was
coming. He put his glasses down with his glove and moved
to the screaming Martin.

"You show me up, I'll show you up," screamed Martin,
his neck muscles and veins popping from his skin.

"What did I do? What did I do?" bellowed Jackson.

Most of the players looked straight ahead at the field.
Two of the coaches, Elston Howard and Yogi Berra, experienced in this sort of thing from their Yankee days, got between the large outfielder and the sinewy manager. Mike
Torrez, a handsome Mexican American pitcher from Kansas
City, told Jackson in Spanish, "Go inside, cool off, go inside."

"I think Billy and Reggie were under enormous tensions," Torrez later told me. "It was only a matter of time before one or the other would explode. That was it."

Jackson did go inside the clubhouse. Martin finished out
the game with anger burning on his face. George Steinbrenner, in town for the series, spoke carefully to both the manager and the player. The press kept ringing the rooms of all
three individuals. Sometimes someone would answer and
develop their part of the story.

The break came late in the night when Jackson sat in
Steinbrenner's suite and told the Boss, "I don't want to be
the cause of a manager's firing. Don't fire him."

The story sold a lot of newspapers back in New York. The
New York Post loved it. We had always been the gossip central of baseball. I got a lot of calls from radio and television
stations to address the issue on the air. My pal, Marv Albert
of WNBC in New York, even sent a limousine to my house
after I returned home to do the television show *Live at Five*
with him.

Ron Swoboda, my old pal from the Mets, had a wonderful
line after a five-strikeout doubleheader the Mets had split.

"It's a good thing we split," he said, after the two bad
games, "or I'd be eating my heart out. As it is, I'm only eating out my right ventricle."

When I did something I knew would cause unrest among my sportswriting competitors, my wife and I would often laugh and one of us would say, "He's probably eating out his right ventricle." A lot of my competitors and even some of my neighbors were eating out their ventricles when Jackson's conduct earned me so much attention.

The Yankees were soon home from the trip. Jackson returned to the two-bedroom corner apartment he rented for $1,466 a month at 985 Fifth Avenue in Manhattan, just across the street from Central Park. Actress Cicely Tyson, wearing a jogging outfit, could often be seen coming out of the building, crossing the street, and jogging along the reservoir. Writer-producer-director-comedian Mel Brooks, father of the 2,000-year-old-man, and his actress wife, Anne Bancroft, often worked on new scripts in their fifteenth-floor apartment. The president of a jeans company lived on the twelfth floor. The chairman of the board of an airline company lived on the eighth floor. Psychiatrists, financiers, politicians, and industrialists maintained apartments in the building.

There were no signs of baseball in Jackson's apartment except for a huge painting of him in uniform, painted by famed sports artist LeRoy Neiman and presented to Reggie as a gift by his agent Matt Merola. There was a comfortable couch in the living room, several tasteful looking armchairs, a modest bedroom, and a small kitchen.

A small patio overlooked Fifth Avenue and Jackson often spent time out there working with and enjoying his flower garden.

Teammate Fran Healy often joined him there for a quiet dinner and after the Boston episode they spent an evening discussing all aspects of the event. They chose to dine in Reggie's apartment without furor instead of making a public appearance at one of several popular restaurants they often frequented—Oren & Aretsky's, Jim McMullen's, or baseball star Rusty Staub's Third Avenue spot.

The apartment was elegant, tasteful and strikingly decorated. I interviewed Jackson there once. Afterward, I thought of a line I had heard New York Jets owner and former show business agent, Sonny Werblin, utter often. Werblin admitted the line was not original. He had first heard comedian Joe E. Lewis use it in his act, but Werblin, a kid who grew up poor in Brooklyn, soon adopted it for himself.

"I've been rich and I've been poor," Werblin would say, with a wry smile. "Rich is better."

CHAPTER

SEVEN

There were days in the summer of 1977 when Billy Martin would show up at the ballpark with his face looking drained, his neck tight, his eyes a little watery, and his speech slurred. Often he would walk back and forth into the off-limits trainer's room until he felt strong enough, confident enough to face the press.

There were other days when he came to the park after an early visit to church. His face would be relaxed, his eyes would be clear, his hair would be combed, and his speech would be soft and distinct. On those wonderful days he leaned back in his managerial chair, discussed some of his Civil War heroes, examined the campaigns of Sherman or Grant in depth, puffed gently on his pipe and appeared, outwardly, a man at peace with himself and the world.

The bad days outweighed the good days by two to one in the final months of the 1977 season.

The Yankees stayed in a tired old hotel in Milwaukee called the Pfister. The rooms were small and room service was slow and ended early. Many times a player or a sportswriter would go hungry after a long night game because room service was closed and few restaurants were open after midnight.

A lot of us sportswriters took to wrapping a sandwich from the press room and bringing it home in our typewriter bags. Bars down the street from the hotel stayed open forever so it was easy to get a beer or a soda to wash it down with several hours after the game ended.

The Yankees had won a long game in Milwaukee and by the time I got back to the hotel, about three hours after the team did because of a long story and longer column I had to write about the drama, I was far too wound up for sleep. I turned on the television set, picked up a book, and relaxed in bed. Maybe an hour went by and the movie kept my interest. I remembered the sandwich I had brought home from the press room and the beer that made Milwaukee famous. It was all pretty comfortable when a sudden, forceful knock on my door startled me. No message after midnight in a hotel could ever be good news.

"Open the door," screamed a voice I knew only too well.

I opened it quickly; Billy Martin walked in and sat on my hotel bed as I moved to the one lounge chair in my room. I was tired now, not anxious to hear about Billy Martin's Civil War heroes. I was determined that this would be a short visit.

"Nobody is going to tell me how to make out a lineup," Martin screamed.

Reggie Jackson had been hitting well the last few weeks but Jackson, mostly as the designated hitter, had been batting in the fifth or sixth spot in the Yankee lineup. Billy began a laborious monologue about how George Steinbrenner was always looking for stardom out of his stars, how George wanted Reggie Jackson in his cherished fourth spot in the order. Billy insisted he would not do it. Nobody tells Billy Martin how to make out a lineup. Nobody tells Billy Martin who to play. If Steinbrenner didn't like it he could take his goddamn job and stuff it.

It is hard now to reconstruct accurately what Billy Martin said in my hotel room that night. He did a good imitation of his hero Casey Stengel. He rambled from one subject to another, moving in and out of the Yankee lineup to his own Yankee heroics. Quickly he moved on to how much he didn't need the job (which he did—desperately). Always he kept coming back to the pride of the Yankees thing. He spit out the names of Jackson and Steinbrenner with great venom and boasted loudly of how he had made a star out of Thurman Munson.

"Don't you write a goddamn thing about Reggie batting fourth, because he ain't," Billy screamed.

It was about all any of us *had* been writing on this trip.

Jackson had a big RBI game a few days earlier and when he bragged about his abilities in tough games he held several New York newspapers in his hand. He was on the back page of the *Post* and the *News*, led the sports section of the *Times*, and was spread across several pages in Long Island's *Newsday*.

"Sometimes," Reggie said, oh-so-philosophically, "*I* can't even appreciate the magnitude of me."

Those few of us standing there tried not to smile. As we walked away we burst out laughing. "The magnitude of me." Wow. Reggie had out-Reggied himself with that one and for the remainder of his Yankee career it became a gag line in the press box as he got a big hit or even failed to get one. "The magnitude of me." I could never understand why it was not placed on his Baseball Hall of Fame plaque. Then again, the word "Black," or "Negro," does not appear on Jackie Robinson's Hall of Fame plaque.

Billy never discussed "the magnitude of him" that night in Milwaukee but it was clear that Reggie Jackson's presence on the Yankees had become a burr under Billy's skin that would never be softened.

He rambled on for an hour and a half, asked if I had any beer, and when told I did not, called room service. Room service did not answer at that late hour. Then he warned me not to write that Jackson would bat fourth on the Yankees. My eyes began closing and even Billy could see that my interest had waned. Suddenly he got up and walked to the door. He was out and down the hall to his own room as I locked myself securely in mine. If he came back, I decided, I would hide under the covers, not listen, not answer, and not explain to him why I was writing another story about whether Reggie Jackson was batting fourth in the Yankee lineup.

A few days later Jackson's name *was* fourth in the Yankee lineup. Everybody knew George Steinbrenner had ordered it. Billy delayed it but he couldn't prevent it. Jackson was there in that famed spot of Ruth, DiMaggio, and Mantle. The torch had truly been passed.

The Yankees had won the division title again and now would play the Kansas City Royals for the American league pennant. These were clearly the two best teams in the league and the rivalry was intense. The Royals believed they were the better team in 1976 even if Chris Chambliss's home run proved otherwise. Now they were certain they were better than the Yankees and would prove it in the play-off. The two teams split the first four games of the five-game series. The pennant would be settled on Sunday afternoon, October 9, 1977, at the Harry S. Truman complex in Kansas City.

George Steinbrenner, team president Gabe Paul, and Billy Martin sat in Steinbrenner's suite at the Crown Center Hotel in Kansas City half an hour before the team bus was scheduled to leave for Royals Stadium at the complex.

Martin was tight lipped, his eyes hollow, his skin taut on his bony body as he addressed his two baseball superiors.

"I'm not starting Reggie," he told them.

"You're the manager," said Steinbrenner.

"I don't think he can hit this guy," Martin said.

"You're the manager," Steinbrenner repeated.

A left-hander named Paul Splittorff was starting this final game of the playoffs for Kansas City. He had compiled a 16-6 record that season and had been a difficult pitcher for the left-handed hitting Jackson to hit.

Steinbrenner, Paul, and Martin finished their conversation and left Steinbrenner's suite. There was little conversation on the team bus as it moved along the interstate to the attractive complex. Steinbrenner and Paul got off the team bus and disappeared into the bowels of the stadium. Martin led his team into the visitors' clubhouse. He wore a gray suit, a white shirt, no tie, and dark sunglasses. He hung his clothes up quickly in the large closet in the manager's office, changed into his baseball underwear and pants, and sat at his desk. He wrote out the lineup card and coach Elston Howard placed it on a nearby wall. All the players scanned the lineup casually.

As we reporters crowded into Billy's office he explained the reasons for the dramatic lineup change.

"The records show Reggie doesn't hit him," explained Martin, without a record in sight.

Reporters raced over to Jackson's locker. He had already seen the lineup card without his name on it. He sat in his undershorts. His huge chest seemed to burst from his skin. He was clearly bruised, emotionally wounded, and deeply shocked by this development.

"I know what I can do," he said. "If he did, we might be a lot better off."

Reporters now charged back to Billy's office. We, tattletales all, told the manager Jackson was distraught and we wanted a few more words on the subject before we would let Billy manage the game and the Yankees play it for the pennant.

"I'm the manager of this club," Martin snarled. "I make out the lineup card. If he doesn't like it he can kiss my dago ass."

Splittorff remembered his elation at finding out Jackson would not start the game.

"I had good luck against him but my God, he *was* Reggie Jackson. He could hit it out on anybody," Splittorff said. "That was an edge for me. You know what else was important? Billy Martin had told the world Reggie Jackson was afraid of me. Can you imagine what that did for my ego?"

Steinbrenner and Paul sat behind the screen in the stands, behind home plate. When I snuck over to them and asked what they thought of Billy's incredible move Steinbrenner answered quickly. "Billy's the manager," he said. "See me after the game."

Steinbrenner was giving out a clear message. He knew how much of a gamble this was for Billy, for the Yankees, and for all the fans of the team in the final game of the year. If it worked Billy would be seen as a courageous hero, ready to make one of the most dramatic moves in a big game any manager could claim. If it didn't work and the Yankees were shut down, it could not only defeat the Yankees—it might even end the mysterious aura around Billy's managerial skills. Anyway you sliced it, the decision was the biggest Billy had ever made as leader of any team.

Paul Blair went to right field for the Yankees in the bottom of the first inning, Jackson went to the right corner of the bench, and Martin stood, one bent knee on the top step, in the left corner of the dugout. The game was as good as it gets. Kansas City led in this deciding game of the year 3-1 into the eighth inning. Splittorff, a tall, bespectacled hard thrower, had worn down. Kansas City manager Whitey Herzog, a baseball lifer, had once been a top executive with the Mets. He had energized this Kansas City franchise and now he made a dramatic move of his own. Knowing Jackson was sitting in the corner of the Yankee bench he brought in his best relief pitcher, Doug Bird, to face the next hitter.

"Get a bat," Martin yelled to Reggie, and Jackson walked forward to pull his darkened forty-ounce bat from the rack. The crowd reacted emotionally. There was some booing from Kansas City fans, some cheering from Yankee fans who had made the dramatic trip out west, and much gabbing from neutral fans. The star was on the stage. Could he fill the role?

Bird was a high fastball pitcher. Jackson was a high fastball batter. This was strength against strength. There would be nothing fancy here, just what the ballplayers call good old-fashioned hardball—a fastball pitcher against a fastball hitter—and let's see who is best.

The Yankees had two on and two out when Jackson lined Bird's fastball into center field for a hit. This was probably the biggest pinch hit of Reggie's career, maybe, emotionally, the biggest hit of any kind in his career. He stood at first now, with a small smile on his face and, thanks to the baseball gods, in his heart. The Royals now led 3-2.

The Yankees rallied for three runs in the ninth and closed out the game and the second Yankee pennant in two years under Martin with a 5-3 victory.

While television cameras covered the champagne celebration in the Yankee clubhouse and most of the players acted with youthful enthusiasm, Jackson and pal Fran Healy sat alone, deep in a corner of the clubhouse. Billy denied Reggie's hit had anything much to do with the game and applauded the team effort, the clutch hits of others, and his own careful maneuverings of his players for the victory. There was satisfaction enough to go around. Billy celebrated in his own way and Reggie celebrated in his.

Steinbrenner had accepted the triumph carefully and now knew that what mattered, what *really* mattered, was winning the World Series. If he was to be on top of the other owners, his team had to beat the Dodgers for the title.

These two cherished franchises in baseball, the Yankees in New York and the Dodgers, once in Brooklyn and since 1958 in Los Angeles, would be settling the baseball crown. Few things in sports can get people as excited as a Dodger-Yankee World Series, a tradition that goes back so many years and has so many memories.

The Dodgers were managed by TommyLasorda—a colorful character. Lasorda, who counted Frank Sinatra among his closest friends, was eager to show him off to Martin during the Series.

The Yankees won the first Series game, the Dodgers took the second, and the teams flew to Los Angeles for the next three games. Martin was invited to dinner at La Scala, one of Hollywood's most fashionable sites, with Lasorda, Sinatra, and a band of hangers-on. When asked the next day who picked up the check, Martin replied, "When you go out with Frank, Frank pays." There was a precedent for Billy's remark.

A year or two earlier, before a flight west, the Yankees had been dining together in a popular Manhattan restaurant. Sinatra was in the same room. When the team was ready to leave, traveling secretary Bill Kane asked for the check. It had already been taken care of by Sinatra. "When you dine with Frank, [even when he is not part of your party], Frank pays."

On the off day the focus was on Jackson, of course, because he had criticized Billy's use of a tiring Catfish Hunter. "If he doesn't like it," Billy said, "he knows what he can do."

More important for the other Yankees were the bad locations of their Series seats. Everybody—players, executives, and press—must pay for Series tickets. None are free. The players expect perfect seats for the only time during the year when they have to buy tickets.

"Look at these seats they gave us," shouted Thurman Munson, as he displayed tickets for wives, family, and friends way up in the upper deck of Dodger Stadium. "If these seats aren't exchanged for better locations, I'm going home."

Munson stayed. The tickets could not be exchanged. Most of them had been sold in advance. It just gave Munson and some of his Yankee mates a little more to grumble about. They acted unconcerned about the Dodgers.

The Yankees won the third game of the Series and with Jackson hitting a home run they won the fourth game. Jackson homered again in the fifth game on his last time up, as the Yankees lost 10-4.

Now the 1977 Series moved back to New York for the sixth game, one of the most historic in baseball.

Reginald Martinez Jackson made it so.

Jackson walked his first time up. Then he hit a home run off Dodger right-hander Burt Hooton. Then he homered off curveballing right-hander Elias Sosa. Finally he homered off knuckleball pitcher Charlie Hough. Three straight home runs. Only Babe Ruth, who had done it twice, had ever accomplished that World Series feat. "The magnitude of me," indeed.

As he watched the last one climb into the upper deck at the Stadium, he began jogging around the bases slowly. Jackson stopped running about fifteen feet before he reached home plate, and walked the rest of the way home. He savored every second of the event, walked on into the dugout, and held up three fingers. He later said it was to signal his mother, watching the game from her home in Baltimore, that he had hit three home runs and was now in the same class as Babe Ruth.

The noise from the fans did not cease for well over a minute and Jackson finally stepped back out onto the field for a curtain call as teammates looked on admiringly from the dugout. They might not like the guy, as clearly they did not, but they all seemed forced to recognize and appreciate his abilities. He may have been for those Yankees a bore, a phony, a braggart, an unappreciated teammate, but he was certainly an incredible home run hitter and scene stealer. This they all had to recognize, even Nettles, even Lyle, even Thurman Munson. Like it or not, there was a lot to the "magnitude of me."

It had been fifteen years since the New York Yankees had last won the World Series, in 1962. Steinbrenner, Gabe Paul, New York City mayor Abraham Beame, singer Robert Merrill, and Steinbrenner's new best pal, Cary Grant, were pulled into the raucous clubhouse celebration, and Jackson let his guard down. Some players came over to shake his hand and some sportswriters, writing critically of him for most of the season, listened patiently for his winning speech.

"After everything we have gone through here . . ." His voice broke and his words ended. He grabbed a bottle of champagne and walked into the manager's office. Billy Martin, holding court with his press favorites, stood up to greet him. Martin leaned over to shake Jackson's hand, and soon the two men were bear hugging. "You did a hell of a job, big guy," Martin said, with true affection.

Maybe a Yankee Series win was more important than personal differences. Maybe they could get along, appreciate each other, bring endless triumphs to the Bronx scene. And maybe the moon is made of green cheese.

They slugged from the same bottle of New York State champagne. They patted each other on the back. They posed for pictures together. Their smiles were deep and seemed sincere, like those of two lifelong friends. What miracles World Series triumphs wrought.

The kids in the city ran into the streets, and parties started everywhere. There was no noise and no joy louder than that coming from Seventh Avenue and 125th Street in Manhattan, the main intersection of the black ghetto in Harlem. Small children held up baseball cards and newspaper pictures and glossy photos of Reggie Jackson.

"Why not?" asked black congressman Charles Rangel of Harlem. "Who else do these kids have for heroes—Sammy Davis, Jr.? Of course they love Reggie. He is the black Babe Ruth."

It all seemed worthwhile now, the pressures and the pain, the conflict and controversy with Billy Martin, all the anguish and the anger created by coming to a team where he was really not wanted by anyone other than the owner. Billy Martin had treated Jackson shabbily but Jackson had survived. He had ended his first Yankee season in the most dramatic way possible, three homers in a row in one game, four in a row in two, and five in the Series. What more could anybody want?

Steinbrenner, Martin, and Jackson, linked forever after in baseball history as a result of the 1977 season—each had their private memories of that year. What mattered most were the accomplishments on the field in one of the great Yankee seasons of them all.

A baseball glow lasts a few months. Then there is a title to defend in a new season.

For Reggie Jackson it would even include the sticky, gooey Reggie Bars raining on the famed Stadium grass on the next opening day.

CHAPTER

EIGHT

Reggie Jackson and Billy Martin stayed away from each other throughout the winter of 1977–78 and it appeared for a while that the World Series win would make things a bit more peaceful around the Yankees.

How foolish we sportswriters be.

This threesome—Boss Steinbrenner, manager Martin, and Reggie ("Magnitude of me,") Jackson—had colliding egos, and anytime they were in the same room, same ball park, or same universe an explosion was sure to follow.

Jackson had several business interests in his hometown area of Oakland and had phoned Steinbrenner in late February for permission to take care of some business matters, especially his antique automobile dealership. Wealthy men lined up to buy flashy cars at a showroom owned by Jackson. Reggie never phoned Billy about traveling back home, and Steinbrenner never bothered to inform Billy—until a couple of days before spring training—that Reggie would be late.

"Some guys don't need spring training," snarled Martin.

"I had business," Reggie said. "George understands that. He is a businessman."

The meaning was clear as Jackson explained it to the press. Martin was *only* a baseball man, an uncouth jock, who could not possibly possess the intellect, the skills, and the subtlety needed for business matters.

When he finally did arrive in Fort Lauderdale about a week after the other regulars, he was greeted by waiting sportswriters. Jackson knew how to play out his scenes. He knew when to arrive and he always knew what to say. Martin sat in his small side office with one or two of his favorite sportswriters. About a dozen or so of us gathered around Jackson's locker. We listened to him discuss the antique auto business, watched him strip slowly and get into his uniform, and waited for his next sarcastic crack about Billy.

Reggie was a little too smart for that. He never really discussed his manager that day. Why should he? He had electrified baseball with the World Series finish, five homers and three in the last game, and the feisty little manager could hardly match that.

The most significant change in the 1978 Yankees picture over the previous year was the arrival of Al Rosen, the former fine third baseman of the Cleveland Indians. Gabe Paul had finally had enough of Steinbrenner's taunts and treatment. He had gone back to Cleveland as part owner of the new, rebuilding Cleveland franchise.

Steinbrenner called Rosen, whom he had known well in Cleveland, and asked to meet with him. Rosen was working as a public relations man for Billy Weinberger's Caesar's Palace in Las Vegas. It was one of those jobs often given to former star athletes just so the wealthy owner could have him around and brag about his relationship with a famous athlete.

Rosen was different than most former athletes. He was Jewish and had grown up reasonably wealthy in Spartanburg, South Carolina. His father ran a dry goods business and young Al was ticketed for that profession until he began showing early signs of being an exceptional athlete. He handled anti-Semitism in a combative way, punching out most of the kids who passed remarks at him, threatening any others with the same if they dared try it. Because of his exceptional abilities, his toughness, and his determination, he soon escaped anti-Semitism and was honored as a local sports hero.

Rosen won two RBI titles with Cleveland and was a star on the 1954 Indians, one of the great American League teams of the century. He stayed in Cleveland after his career ended, became involved in several private businesses, and drifted into the casino business with Weinberger.

Rosen was handsome, personable, a fine speaker, and slow to anger. He seemed perfect as the barrier between the volatile owner and the volatile manager. Martin quickly determined that Rosen would be on his side in any disputes with Steinbrenner because he had big game experience as a former player.

"Al played the game. He understands what it is like," Martin said. "Gabe got in the way. He didn't know the game."

Rosen traveled with the team in the early days of the 1978 spring training season. A quiet peace descended on the Yankees.

It all ended opening day when Reggie Jackson homered. Reggie bars, created by Standard Brands Company, fell from the Stadium—maybe ten or fifteen thousand candy bars in all—flying from the upper deck, the mezzanine, and the field seats. When the game was over Jackson was asked if he knew how the barrage started. Could Standard Brands have planted a candy-bar thrower in the upper deck to remind the fans of the yellow-wrapped gooey candy with the Jackson picture on the wrapper?

"Oh my, no," said Jackson, gooey sincerity pouring from his lips. "I just think it was an honest expression of appreciation for what I've done to help the ball club."

The Red Sox showed early speed with Jim Rice, who was having an MVP year, and Fred Lynn, who was proving to be one of the best all around players in the game. Carl Yastrzemski was solidifying his future Hall of Fame credentials and Mike Torrez, the former Yankee pitcher and Reggie pal, was now adding to Boston's pitching depth.

In a June game at Fenway, with Steinbrenner at the park, a tall, college-educated pitcher named Jim Beattie was slapped around, then fired immediately for his efforts.

"He was scared stiff," said Steinbrenner, as he left the Stadium. A few of the sportswriters followed him. "What the hell was he doing out there? He spit the bit."

Steinbrenner owned a breeding farm in Ocala, Florida, and when one of his horses seemed not to like racing, he would fire the jockey, the trainer, and maybe the horse. He would suggest the horse "spit the bit," meaning he just couldn't handle the pressure of a competitive race. The term was a serious and ferocious criticism of a big league ballplayer. Beattie later became vice president and general manager of the Montreal Expos, so Steinbrenner's criticism didn't seem to have a major impact on his career.

As the race wore on and the Red Sox pulled further away, finally getting a fourteen-game lead on July 17, Billy Martin was again drinking heavily. On the road, he would leave the ballpark and head to the hotel bar. In New York, he'd spend most of his evening at a friendly bar with coach Art Fowler.

Fowler was a good old boy from Converse, South Carolina, who had attached himself to Billy in his playing days. Fowler went everywhere Billy went. Almost. Baseball coaches are Boy Scouts, loyal to the manager, never a threat, and willing to share most off time together. Fowler was perfect for the job. He had no personal ambitions as a coach. He simply wanted to help Billy with the pitchers, and he could keep up with Billy drink for drink throughout their time together.

Martin assumed he would bring Fowler along when he took over the Yankees late in 1976. Gabe Paul would have none of it. "He's a drunk," Paul shouted at Martin. Martin, also a recognized baseball drinker, certainly was not turned off by that qualification.

Martin couldn't get Fowler to run with him as the Yankees insisted Bob Lemon become his pitching coach. Lemon, a Hall of Fame pitcher with Cleveland, was also a heavy drinker. Billy suggested Lemon was even a heavier drinker than Fowler. Lemon made fun of his own drinking habits. Often he could be found asleep in the clubhouse after a long night.

Lemon had a favorite line he liked to use when he had too many drinks for a good conduct medal. "I never take the game home with me," he would say. "I always leave it in some bar."

As the Yankees began to fall back in the race, Steinbrenner was determined to shake things up. Lemon had left the

Yankees by now and Fowler had become pitching coach. He was doing his usual job of helping Billy stay up late at night. Steinbrenner decided to get rid of him. He called Billy to his office one day and announced that Fowler was gone. Clyde King, a minor league pitching coach, a fine fellow and a tee-totaler, would be brought in for the pitching. Martin begged Steinbrenner to keep Fowler. Loyalty, Billy understood, worked both ways.

Steinbrenner, that old softy, relented. Fowler could stay. But King would also arrive. A few days later King was handling the Yankee pitching, Fowler was handling Billy and his drinking, and the Red Sox were handling the Yankees.

Don Zimmer had moved his Boston team to a commanding lead, was playing very aggressive baseball, and saw no danger of letting this one slip away.

Zimmer had not counted on Reggie Jackson to save the Yankee season, this time with a failed bunt.

On Monday night, July 17, in a tie game against Kansas City in the tenth inning, Martin flashed the bunt sign to third base coach Dick Howser with Jackson at bat. Thurman Munson had begun the inning with a line single to right off relief pitcher Al Hrabowsky.

There are hardly any more embarrassing acts for a slugger such as Reggie Jackson than being forced to bunt in such a spot by his manager. It is about manhood, ego, the macho sense of an athlete that the pitcher is better than he is. Hrabowsky was a tricky pitcher with a strange set of motions on the mound, a little voodoo before he let go of the ball and a lot of hokum. He was no Goose Gossage with a fastball that could come at a hitter's head at one hundred miles an hour.

Martin wanted that run. Maybe he would have asked Babe Ruth or his pal Mickey Mantle or even Joe DiMaggio to bunt in that spot. Nah. This was Reggie. Billy decided he couldn't hit Hrabowsky and Reggie would have to swallow a little humility for the team. The next thing you knew Billy would be asking Jackson to get hit by a pitch in a big spot, what the players call "taking one for the team."

Jackson made a halfhearted bunt attempt on the first pitch and drew back. Third base coach Dick Howser looked over into the dugout. Billy was sending out lots of signs, the last one a touch of his cap with the small cross in front. That meant he wanted Jackson to swing away now.

Howser moved down the line toward home plate. "Billy took the bunt sign off," Howser said.

"I'm going to bunt," Jackson said.

What we had here was the baseball version of the World War II case of Private Eddie Slovak, the only man executed at General Dwight D. Eisenhower's orders after refusing to return to his combat outfit. Disobeying a manager's order is a baseball crime, a very high crime and misdemeanor, worthy of severe punishment.

Jackson bunted at the next pitch and missed. Billy screamed at him from the bench. He flashed the hit sign again to Howser, giving Jackson the benefit of the doubt. Maybe, just maybe, he really missed the sign. Then he bunted at the next pitch and fouled it back. He bunted again at Hrabowsky's fastball, fouled that one back, and was struck out. He walked past Billy in the dugout and the two men ignored each other.

The Royals scored two runs in the top of the eleventh inning to win the game 9-7. When the press was allowed into the clubhouse, Martin was marching back and forth like a caged tiger. Jackson stood calmly in front of his locker. Billy smashed a clock radio to the floor. He flung a drinking glass against a door. He ducked and dodged reporters, those of us he knew would protect Jackson in this episode and those he knew would defend him. The media world around the Yankees had clearly been divided into pro-Billy, anti-Jackson cliques and anti-Billy, pro-Jackson cliques. Never the twain would meet.

"No interviews, no interviews," screamed Billy as his press pals marched behind him.

Jackson stood quietly in front of his locker, waited for his press favorites, including me, and laid out his case. He was asked why he bunted.

"I was trying to advance the runner," Jackson replied carefully.

He was asked if he had missed the sign to hit away.

"I don't miss signs. My job was to advance the runner. I tried to do that. How can they say I'm a threat if I swing the bat? I'm not even an everyday player. I'm a part-time player."

Private Slovak might have said the same thing if he had worn a baseball uniform instead of an army uniform.

Executive Vice President Cedric Tallis, a lifelong baseball official, always remained calm in the wildest storms. With Al Rosen upstairs in his Stadium office and George Steinbrenner back in Tampa, Tallis was in charge. He was not about to take on this decision alone. That's how he had survived in the game for forty years. Stay away from decisions that might explode in your face. Tallis called Steinbrenner in Tampa with Billy standing at his side listening to everything that was said. Tallis called Rosen in the upstairs office and Rosen chose to stay away from the clubhouse, not wishing to interfere in any decision Martin, with the support of Tallis and with Steinbrenner's blessing, decided to make.

Tallis faced the vultures of the press, hungry for more back-page newspaper controversy, and simply announced, "Reggie Jackson is suspended immediately without pay."

Jackson flew home to Oakland that night as the Yankees flew on to Minnesota for the start of a road trip to the Twin Cities, Chicago, and Kansas City. The Yankees swept Minnesota and won two straight in Chicago for a five-game streak without Jackson. The suspension was rescinded after five games and Jackson was ordered to rejoin the club for Sunday's game in Chicago. The team bus left at 10:00 A.M. Jackson was not on it. He came down to the lobby a few minutes later with his pal Fran Healy, signed a couple of autographs, and got into a cab for Comiskey Park.

"Reggie was tense, as tense as I had ever seen him," recalled Healy. "This was a hot situation. Even Reggie had never gone through anything like this before."

Baseball clubhouses, especially in the older parks of

decades ago, had room for a team and a few sportswriters. There were over thirty reporters waiting at Jackson's locker when he showed up with Healy. A dozen long-stemmed red roses, with a card reading "Love from Andrea and Diane," sat on his locker stool. Telegrams were piled in his locker. Packages of mail with postmarks from every part of the country were neatly tied in a bundle and set on the floor. Jackson took off his sports jacket and faced the waiting press.

Dick Schaap of NBC had flown in on Saturday night just for the first viewing of Jackson in the flesh after the suspension. He asked Jackson how he felt at the furor.

"Nervous," Jackson said. "This is a bitch. It's hell to have to go through this."

Jackson's name was not on the lineup card Billy handed to Elston Howard for posting on the clubhouse wall. He sat in the far corner of the dugout, alone, watching the game, saying nothing to teammates and never being addressed by them. The Yankees won again and Billy Martin soon settled in the press room of Comiskey Park, a lounge called the Bard's Room. He drank four scotches and ate nothing. Some sportswriters ate four sandwiches and drank nothing. I had one sandwich and a soda pop. I was working and knew something would happen in this tension-filled atmosphere.

Steinbrenner had given a recent interview to the *New York Times* suggesting that Billy's drinking was getting out of control. Steinbrenner said Billy had been examined by doctors recently, told he had a spot on his liver, and ordered to cease drinking. He did not.

Bill Veeck, owner of the Chicago White Sox and one of the most brilliant, witty, and creative baseball executives in history, came into the Bard's room. Veeck had a wooden leg from a World War II injury in Bougainville and clomped on it noisily throughout the press box and on the wooden floor of the Bard's room. Veeck was a master of public relations and won over almost every sportswriter with personal intimacy and great stories. He once invited me to his Chicago apartment for an interview and I almost collapsed when he

put out a cigarette—he was a chain smoker—against his leg.
I had forgotten it was a wooden leg and I didn't notice the
little metal ashtray he had sticking out from the wooden leg.
Another time I arrived for an interview in a New York hotel,
and Veeck, in that gravely voice of his, called for me to come
in. I didn't see him but he said I should keep walking to the
back of his room and into the bathroom. I obeyed. There he
sat in a warm bathtub, ready to talk of the White Sox, the
war, and the ways of the world.

On this summer day he told Billy Martin that he and
Steinbrenner had talked about switching managers—with
Bob Lemon coming to New York and Martin going to the
White Sox. It never happened. It agitated an agitated Martin
even more. The White Sox? He was the manager of the New
York Yankees, *his* Yankees, and great successor to Casey
Stengel. He wanted to go nowhere else.

The team boarded the bus for the ride to O'Hare Airport
in Chicago and the flight to Kansas City. Martin, looking ill,
tense, angry, and alcoholic, asked sportswriter Murray
Chass of the *New York Times* for a few minutes of his time
when they got to the airport. Chass, dedicated and determined to become a sportswriting star, was never without his
notebook. No story was too small or too big for him. He believed, as most *Times* sportswriters from John Drebinger in
the 1920s on down, that no story was official until it makes
the *Times*, the paper of record.

Now Billy was ranting and raving to Chass about Jackson. He said it was on the record. It was as much a hot newspaper story as it was therapy. Martin was clearing his psyche
via Chass. "If he doesn't shut up," Billy said of Jackson, "he
won't play. I don't care what George says. He can replace
me right now."

Chass stopped at a pay phone, called in Martin's ramblings for an update story, and returned to Billy's side before
they boarded the plane. Martin's anger only grew. He was
spilling out all his frustrations, the way George Steinbrenner
treated Reggie as an equal, with dinners at "21" or at Jimmy
Weston's or P. J. Clarke or at a meeting in Steinbrenner's

Stadium office. Billy was never privileged to experience any of this. It was a flood of venom now, about Jackson, about Steinbrenner, about their relationship outside of his hearing. He knew they talked about him, lied about him, criticized him. He couldn't stand it.

"The two of them deserve each other," Martin blurted out. "One's a born liar, the other's convicted."

Martin had heard Graig Nettles, the team's wonderful third baseman and resident wit, utter the statement to several teammates in the clubhouse. Martin thought it was a perfect description of the hated player and the obnoxious Boss.

Chass's story was big, big, big. It was gossip central around the Yankees, once labeled The Bronx Zoo by Sparky Lyle, and no one could ignore it. Steinbrenner was outraged. He ordered Al Rosen to Kansas City. He wanted Billy Martin out of his sight. Jackson, the focus of all this rage, actually seemed calm when he simply responded by saying of Billy, "The man is sick."

It was no exaggeration. Martin's nerves, taut at any time, seemed gone. He looked pale, thin, and washed out. There was a line about Babe Ruth, spoken by owner Jacob Ruppert that kept Ruth from a managerial chance at the Yankees. "He can't manage himself," Ruppert said of the hard-drinking, high-living Bambino. "How can he manage the Yankees?"

Billy Martin had finally come to the point when he no longer could manage himself. He seemed so tangled, so angry, so depressed that most of us around him every day considered a suicide watch. Whether it might be a war hero or a baseball hero, every human being, especially those wound as tightly as Martin always seemed to be, cannot cross a certain line and survive. Martin was at that line.

He knew enough to save his life by getting out of the line of fire.

Billy Martin had decided to leap before he was pushed. Al Rosen was on his way to Kansas City after Martin's remarks about George and Reggie made the newspapers. Martin would certainly be fired if he didn't leave voluntarily. Rosen called his old teammate and pal Bob Lemon in Long

Beach, California, at 4:15 in the morning New York time, 1:15 California time.

"Keep yourself in cold storage, Meat," Rosen told his old pal, using his Cleveland nickname. "I just wanted to know if you were home. We might be making a change."

Billy Martin called his young agent and friend, Doug Newton, back in New York and told him he was thinking of resigning the Yankee job, the only job that ever really mattered to him. Martin stayed secluded in room 1138 of the Crown Center Hotel in Kansas City. A real estate businessman named Bob Brown, who had helped Billy make some money in shopping centers, was with him. Billy told him he was gone. Brown, anxious to keep his connection with the manager of the Yankees, always a good business instrument, urged caution. It was a little late for that.

Mickey Morabito, the twenty-seven-year-old publicity director of the Yankees, flew in from New York Monday morning. He had left his assistant, Larry Wahl, twenty-three, in charge of the Yankee press. Rosen had called him late Sunday night after several conversations with Steinbrenner. Morabito, always kind, understanding, and sympathetic to Martin, went directly to the manager's room.

"He looked like hell," Morabito recalled. "He was sitting there wearing those dark sunglasses, his face was drawn like he hadn't slept, and his clothes seemed to hang on him. I saw the notes in his hand."

George Steinbrenner had just completed a tour of his Kinsman Stud Farm in Ocala. All was in order. His Kentucky Derby hopefuls were ready. So was his manager across the country in Kansas City.

Morabito saw Billy's handwritten resignation statement on a small piece of hotel notepaper. Morabito told Martin he would type it up for him so it would be easier to read when he faced the press. Morabito raced to his room and in some few minutes was back with the one-page, typed statement. It probably would have been faxed or e-mailed in these days but typewriters were still an important piece of publicity equipment in 1978. Morabito told Billy that all was ready for his adventure with the press. Newspaper reporters salivate over this kind of story. It is part of their "ghoul pool" mentality.

The "ghoul pool" was a favorite *New York Post* game in which a reporter would select a prominent public figure to die within the next year. There might be three or four hundred dollars in it from the pool if your guy died as you had predicted. The best "ghoul pool" legend concerned Spain's leader Francisco Franco. He became deathly ill early one year, lingered for months, and was still breathing although incredibly weak as October turned into November. Soon the year would end, and still Franco lingered on. "Die, you bastard," shouted a *Post* reporter, whose name is lost in the legend, as the clock moved relentlessly on. Somebody else's entry died ahead of Franco, and the pool was ended. The Franco man, angered at his loss, wrote a fake headline on a *Post* page announcing, "Franco Still Dead."

Now the reporters gathered in a hotel ballroom—pushing, shoving, cursing, screaming at each other—as Billy Martin appeared from behind a fig tree in the lobby.

Martin held his statement in his right hand and an unlit cigar in his left. He announced he was resigning from the Yankees but would answer no questions about it. "That means now and forever," he said. "I am a Yankee and Yankees do not talk or throw rocks. I owe it to my health and my mental well-being to resign. I am sorry about those things that were written about George Steinbrenner. He does not deserve them, nor did I say them."

This was "shoot the messenger time." Billy would not accept the blame for his outrageous statements. He preferred blaming the sportswriters for his anguish. It was an old story with Billy. Tears came to his eyes and he continued. "I'd like to thank the Yankee management, the press [ha], my coaches, my players, and most of all, the fans."

He broke down, weeping, and walked off with Yankee pal and broadcaster Phil Rizzuto, his old shortstop teammate from the 1950s. Rizzuto, himself, had never seemed so distraught. Few had ever seen Rizzuto at any Yankee press briefing. He was usually too busy on the golf course or home with wonderful wife Cora. He made his own honorable lifestyle public and even refused an invitation one time to join other sportswriters and broadcasters for a viewing in Minneapolis of the heralded sex film, *Deep Throat*.

"I can't go," he told the group of sportswriters preparing to leave by cab for the distant movie house. "Cora would kill me."

An hour later the sportswriters sat in the dingy theater and as the film started, the raunchy scenes began. As actress Linda Lovelace performed oral sex on screen, a voice was heard from the last row of the theater, shouting "Holy cow."

Rizzuto's presence at Billy's resignation was even more startling. He walked away from the mad scene in the hotel with Martin, sat with him in his room until it was time for Billy to leave for the airport, and wished him well as Martin got into a cab. Rizzuto was certain Billy would be back. Baseball was always that way.

It was over now. Billy was on his way home to Oakland. Steinbrenner was walking quietly around his farm. Morabito was preparing a news release. Lemon had been told to fly to Kansas City to take over the Yankees.

Martin never mentioned Reggie Jackson by name as he made his farewell address. Jackson stood at the other end of the large room, hidden mostly by the crowd of media, watching the scene at the Crown Center Hotel.

It was July 24, 1978. Billy was gone, Lemon was coming, and Jackson was ready. The rest of the Yankees were moving forward, and the Boston Red Sox were way ahead of the Yankees. Were those Yankee footsteps they were hearing?

The 1978 baseball season, one of those classic Yankee years, was just beginning.

CHAPTER

NINE

Robert Granville Lemon, born September 22, 1920, came out of service in World War II to join the Cleveland Indians in 1946. He had been signed originally out of high school in 1939, had made it to the Indians as a third baseman for a few games in 1941 and 1942, then was drafted. He served his country for the next three seasons and resumed his career on a fine Cleveland team after his tour of duty with the navy.

Lemon opened the 1946 season as Cleveland's center fielder but was on the mound by the end of that year because manager Lou Boudreau saw that he could throw very hard and hit rather soft.

He had seven twenty-game seasons on a brilliant Cleveland staff through the years. He played with fellow Hall of Famers Bob Feller, Hal Newhouser, and Early Wynn, burly Mike Garcia and hard-luck Herb Score, whose potentially magnificent career was cut short by a line drive off his eye hit by Yankees shortstop Gil McDougald.

Lemon started his managerial career at Hawaii in 1964 after scouting and coaching, got to the big leagues with Kansas City in 1970, was named the White Sox manager by old boss Bill Veeck, and was fired by Veeck in June of 1978. Veeck replaced him with his former teammate Larry Doby. Doby was the second African American in big league baseball behind Jackie Robinson and the first in the American League. Now he became the second black manager behind another Robinson—Frank Robinson, named Cleveland manager in 1975.

The same names are continually recycled in baseball's managerial chairs. Yankees manager Joe Torre, who managed the Mets, the Braves, and the Cardinals before coming to the Yankees in 1996, said it best.

"Once you are on the managerial wheel," said Torre, "you hang on while it is spinning until you are dropped off at another job."

Lemon was as easy to take as Martin was difficult. He was so low-key he seemed asleep half the time we reporters talked to him. While most managers led with their egos, he seemed to have none. He had quiet pride in his performance as a player and felt confident in his abilities as a manager. He just didn't seem comfortable bragging about his accomplishments, Hall of Fame or not. He was unusual in that respect, and no sportswriter who cared about the game of baseball could help but care about an individual like Lemon. He never talked over or under a sportswriter's head. He made it clear that baseball was a rather simple game and that if a guy like Bob Lemon, with little education and no obvious unique talents, could make a living at it for over thirty-five years, anybody could. This was no Billy Martin, no Alvin Dark, no Tony LaRussa, no Buck Showalter, who clearly indicated in their communications with the press that the game was just beyond those pencil pushers.

Lemon came to Kansas City as Yankees field boss on July 25, 1978. Neville Chamberlain would have loved Lemon. He provided a new atmosphere around the Yankees—"Peace in our time."

The Yankees were fourteen games behind the Red Sox on July 19 after game 90 of their 1978 season. Billy Martin's team had cut the lead to only nine-and-a-half games by the time Lemon took over the managerial post. Boston, hearing footsteps again as the Red Sox had for more than half a century, was already sniping at manager Don Zimmer. Pitcher Bill Lee, king of the baseball flakes, had labeled Zimmer a gerbil for not pitching him at certain times. Carl Yastrzemski was growling, Jim Rice was having pugnacious sessions with the press, and Mike Torrez, the former Yankee obtained as a free agent by Boston, was already thinking it might have all been a great mistake. It was just much more fun being part of the Yankees, even if a good part of the time was spent involved in "The Bronx Zoo."

Lemon made the lineup out each day, sat back quietly on the bench, and reacted almost the same after a win or a loss. Steadily the Yankees moved forward, aiming for a series in Boston in early September, four games that would probably settle the entire thing.

In the meantime, after Billy resigned, George Steinbrenner sat at home in Tampa watching the Monday night game on television. Coach Dick Howser handled the game that night before Lemon could arrive for the Tuesday game. Steinbrenner stared at Howard Cosell's yellow ABC jacket on television, thought about Billy Martin, and considered his options.

"What kind of a man would I be," George said later, "if I let a guy go for saying something about me that was true?"

Steinbrenner *was* a convicted felon from his legal plea in the Nixon reelection scandal, and Red Smith of the *New York Times* hardly ever referred to the Yankees Boss without describing him as "Convicted Felon George Steinbrenner."

Billy Martin hardly did worse.

"I'm the leader of the team. I had to be able to take the heat. I knew he said it. I also knew it was true. He had made a mistake. I had made a mistake. The only guy who had never made a mistake was the guy with the long hair, the guy who walked on water. I kept thinking about that all night long," Steinbrenner recalled.

Steinbrenner watched the game that night with an old newspaper friend, Tom McEwan, sports editor of the *Tampa Tribune*. He discussed with McEwan a strange idea he had. What if he brought Billy back?

Martin had flown to Miami where his old pal, Mickey Mantle, was playing in a celebrity golf tournament. They could spend a couple of days together, have a few thousand drinks, laugh a lot, make fun of Steinbrenner, and get over some of the pain.

Steinbrenner picked up the phone and called Doug Newton, Billy's agent, in New York. "Tell Billy I'll talk to him at the Carlyle tomorrow night. Tell him to call me when he gets in. I'll send a car to the airport for him. I want to see him tomorrow night."

Martin arrived in Miami, called Mantle, spent the night at the hotel bar with him, played golf the next day, and finally answered Newton's phone message. Steinbrenner wanted to see him in New York on Wednesday. It all seemed to happen so fast. Steinbrenner and Martin met for breakfast at the fashionable Carlyle, where Steinbrenner always stayed while in New York. They moved upstairs to Steinbrenner's hotel apartment. Steinbrenner told Billy he would honor his managerial contract for 1979 and would give him a new contract for 1980 at $100,000—a princely baseball managerial salary at the time. What's more, all of the clauses put into the old contract by a devious and suspicious Gabe Paul, especially the one about grounds for firing for "conduct detrimental to the Yankees," would be expunged in the new deal.

Now everything was put into place for a Steinbrenner show. Billy Martin's return would be announced on Sunday, Old Timer's Day, before a sellout crowd. Clubhouse man Pete Sheehy, who had administered to Babe Ruth and Lou Gehrig, Joe DiMaggio and Charlie Keller, Mickey Mantle and Yogi Berra, put out the old Yankee uniforms. Publicity director Mickey Morabito got to the clubhouse early, made sure Billy's number 1 uniform was ready, hung it up in a locker next to Mickey Mantle's, and left the room.

Mantle arrived before noon, thrilled as always to be back, and headed for his old locker. Mantle often told the story that after his retirement he had a recurring dream.

"I would come to the Stadium in a cab and when I got out I couldn't get into the Stadium," he would say. "I could hear Casey yelling my name and I could hear the public address announcer calling out my spot in the lineup but I couldn't get in. I would get on the ground and see if there was a hole somewhere that I could sneak through. I could never get in. That dream was damn upsetting."

But this was no nightmare. Mantle, always a great friend of Martin's, was inside the Stadium without any problems. Morabito took him to a private room where Martin was being hidden away. "Ain't this somethin'? Wait till the people hear this one," Mantle said to Martin.

Yankee announcer Frank Messer was introducing the old-time players. The cheers were huge, especially for Whitey Ford, Yogi Berra, Mickey Mantle, and Joe DiMaggio—the legendary favorites of the fans. "I'll now turn the program over to public address announcer Bob Sheppard." Sheppard sat high above the Stadium in his loge booth and began by saying, "Bob Lemon will assume the duties of general manager. . . ." The words were also being printed on the message-board lights and a murmur filled the Stadium. "Managing the Yankees in the 1980 season," intoned Sheppard in his melodic voice, used as a Stadium instrument and to teach speech at St. John's University in Queens, "and hopefully for many years after that will be . . ."

The pregnant pause was so dramatic. Sheppard continued as Martin showed himself for the first time, coming out of the Yankee dugout, holding his cap in his hand, a smile fixed on his face, ". . . Billy Martin." The crowd erupted. The noise rolled through the Stadium in huge waves. Martin kept waving his hat. Some of the Yankee players in the dugout—Munson, Piniella, and Nettles—applauded. Three others—pitcher Ed Figueroa, outfielder Roy White, and number 44, Reggie Jackson—had fixed, bewildered stares on their faces.

Mickey Morabito handed out press releases in the working press room under the Stadium. It stated the facts. It gave none of the reasons for this highly emotional, incredibly dramatic turn of events in Yankee history. Martin was soon standing before the reporters, still in his Yankee uniform, content to say very little. The press knew Billy wanted to rejoin his pals in the clubhouse so they accepted the quick statements. Steinbrenner refused to answer any questions, unusual for him, and quickly walked away. He turned to Morabito as he left the press room and said, "Stay with Billy and make sure he doesn't say anything."

Steinbrenner had been the Boss of the Yankees for almost six years by now. It was the first time any of us could remember George refusing to comment on something. He seemed more willing to talk about his "convicted felon" status that day than to talk about Billy.

Steinbrenner later said he was simply determined to give Billy another chance. Steinbrenner also recognized that Billy was as popular a Yankee figure as there was—a streetwise guy, pugnacious, tough, a Yankee through and through who had an emotional hold on the fans. Steinbrenner knew he would take a pounding from the press and public if the Yankees slipped out of the race under Lemon. They would stay away from the Stadium, berate Steinbrenner for his attitude toward Billy, and make a rebuilding task in 1979 and 1980 even more difficult.

Bob Lemon said little about his new job in the front office for 1980. He was busy trying to get this team into the 1978 race. The Red Sox gave every sign that they would choke, their legendary summer condition. Their fourteen-game lead had slipped to four games by the time the Yankees moved into Boston for a four-game series on September 7.

Lemon's managerial style remained intact. Most of the baseball stories in the New York press were simply about the games—runs, hits, and errors. Very little was written now about Martin, and he stayed away from the team, busy regaining his health and his self-confidence.

By early September the Yankees were getting healthy after a long tough season. Thurman Munson, his knees improving, was hitting again. Piniella got clutch hits almost every day. Nettles played a brilliant third base and smacked winning hits. Ron Guidry, a quiet, chess-playing kid from Louisiana, was simply the best pitcher in baseball. He was too skinny at 160 pounds to throw hard but somehow he did. Ed Figueroa was a solid starter. Goose Gossage, Fu Manchu mustache drooping lower, was the most intimidating relief pitcher in the game. Sparky Lyle, no longer the ace out of the bullpen, was effective in a new role. Roy White, Chris Chambliss, Paul Blair, Mickey Rivers, Bucky Dent, and Willie Randolph were solid performers each day.

While the Yankees improved in September the Red Sox disintegrated. Catcher Carlton Fisk couldn't throw. Outfielder Fred Lynn had a severe stomach injury. Third baseman Butch Hobson had a bad elbow. First baseman George

Scott was growing fatter by the day. Carl Yastrzemski suddenly felt his age, thirty-nine years old, the real thirty-nine, unlike Jack Benny's fake thirty-nine, a tough age for an everyday big-league baseball player.

The Boston press, always aware of the team history and cynical about the summer lead, began piling on. The Red Sox players grew more tense as the race tightened. While Billy had been gone, Lemon's laid-back style had taken hold. The Yankees needled each other freely, especially on team buses, the focal point of team togetherness.

Reggie Jackson once accused Mickey Rivers of not only having a low IQ but of not even being able to spell it.

"Yeah," responded Rivers, "and you don't know who you are. You got a black momma, a Spanish father, and a white man's first name."

The story the Yankees loved to tell the press about Rivers was how he bragged one time about having a winning horse in a big race at Belmont in New York. Rivers was a compulsive gambler at the track.

"He wanted to brag about his knowledge of horses and how he had the winner," said teammate Piniella. "The way he did it was by betting every horse in the race to win. It only cost him about a hundred bucks to win two dollars."

The loose Yankees and the tight Red Sox met in Boston's Fenway Park from September 7–10. The Yankees won 15-3, 13-2, 7-0, and 7-4 to tie for the division lead. The Boston press buried the Red Sox, and the Yankee press began counting magic numbers, the amount of Yankee wins and Boston losses the Yankees needed to seal the season with a triumph.

The Yankees got up by two games in the race and it appeared to be over. The Red Sox, with the pressure off, suddenly started winning. The two teams were tied for the lead after Boston won on the final game of the year and Cleveland defeated Catfish Hunter at the Stadium.

The Yankees boarded the team bus after that final Sunday game for the trip to the airport and the short flight to Boston. The needling on the bus was as outrageous as usual—racial, religious, and sexual innuendo flying back and forth from almost every player. They acted as if they were about to play a meaningless game in June instead of only the second playoff game in American League history. Boston had played one in 1948 against the Cleveland Indians. Of course, they lost.

George Steinbrenner, emerging at the airport from his limousine with team president Al Rosen for the charter flight of some fifty-five minutes, was still seething about the Stadium loss. He had paid Catfish Hunter all that money and Hunter had let him down in the final game of the season. It was a bitter pill for the Boss to swallow. Would he have to admit a mistake? How could Steinbrenner possibly know that the loss on Sunday would set up one of the most memorable games in Yankee history.

Ron Guidry, 24-3 on the season, was the Monday scheduled starter for Bob Lemon, and former Yankee Mike Torrez, wooed and won away by free-agent dollars, was the Red Sox starter in this one game, winner-take-all contest in Boston.

"We're in good shape, we're going with our best," Rosen told Steinbrenner on the plane to Boston, in reference to Guidry, the game's best that season.

It was only late the next day, after the game, that Rosen admitted how concerned he was at the one-game playoff format.

It might have been just one of the great baseball acts of all time. I didn't cover the game when Lou Boudreau led the Cleveland Indians over the Boston Red Sox in the 1948 playoff at Fenway Park. All I could do was listen and watch on a pal's small television set when Bobby Thomson hit his home run off Ralph Branca ("The Shot Heard Round the World") in 1951. I still love you, Ralph, and my kids have never forgotten your kindness when we sat together at Grossinger's Hotel in the Catskills in New York at a sports banquet and you helped us cut the meat at dinner for two small, restless children.

But 1978 was different. I was there, I was involved, I was working, and I was watching everything. Didn't these Yankees know it was for the division title and the right to play Kansas City and move on to the World Series?

Publicity director Mickey Morabito and traveling secre-

tary Bill Kane approached the game with calm. They handed
out the usual pregame press releases and traveling schedule
for the trip to Kansas City. All seemed normal. The players
kidded each other on the team bus, played cards, enjoyed a
snack, drank a couple of beers, and settled into their rooms
at the Sheraton Boston in Prudential Center.

The fifteen-minute bus ride to Fenway the next morning
at ten o'clock was again routine. Maybe the Yankees knew
something. They certainly knew the Yankee team history of
almost always winning when it mattered. They knew the
Boston team history of almost always losing when it mattered. They also knew something else. Their pitcher that day
was the best in the game, Ronald Ames Guidry, a skinny
twenty-eight-year-old left-hander from Lafayette, Louisiana.
Baseball historians have argued the value of a good pitcher
in a game, 75 percent, 80 percent, 85 percent. Let's say
Guidry was 100 percent of the Yankee confidence that day
and let it go at that.

Guidry came from Cajun country in Louisiana and had
just enough French Cajun accent in his talk to make conversations with him difficult. He earned the nickname of the
"Ragin' Cajun," even though he almost never raised his
voice and was a focus of furor around the Yankees before he
made it big. He was so thin at five feet eleven inches and
maybe 158 pounds that the Yankee brass thought he could
not possibly be a winner. He never won more than six games
in any of his six minor league seasons and was being considered as a left-handed relief specialist when he joined the
Yankees late in 1976. A skinny guy named Billy Martin saw
something in Guidry in 1977 and gave him twenty-five
starts. He was 16-7. The next year he was the best in the
game with a 25-3 mark and an amazing 1.74 ERA.

Guidry enjoyed playing chess with sportswriters on long
flights, tried to convince New York suburban types that hunting was a thrill, and stayed away from all of the politics of
Billy, Reggie, George, and the rest. Now he was about to
pitch the biggest game of his life and the lives of most of his
Yankee teammates.

There was the usual banter around the Yankee clubhouse before the game. The press hung around as we always did. Bob Lemon sat back in his small Fenway office chair and told a couple of tales about being in the same room in 1948 as a pitcher for the Indians. He recalled when Gene Beardon beat the Red Sox with Lou Boudreau managing the team and leading them with two home runs as the heart of the Cleveland offense.

George Steinbrenner was in his seat next to the Yankees dugout on a crisp fall afternoon. Al Rosen was next to him. Billy Martin was out west hunting in Boulder, Colorado. The Red Sox jogged onto the field and the game began.

Boston took a quick 2-0 lead and held it into the top of the seventh. Mike Torrez, a handsome Mexican American right-hander who had moved on to Boston from the Yankees, seemed strong. The Yankees got a couple of runners on, and shortstop Bucky Dent was at the plate.

Dent was a popular Yankee with a boyish smile, a beautiful wife named Karen Lynn Dent, nicknamed Stormy (Bucky and Stormy, ahh, you had to be there), two adorable kids, and a choked-up stance. With two on in the top of the seventh, Dent fouled a pitch off his right foot, maybe baseball's most famous foul ball. He hobbled around at the plate and trainer Gene Monahan sprayed some painkiller on the foot. Before Dent could step back into the box, Mickey Rivers, the next hitter, gave the batboy his own bat to give to Dent. Dent accepted it quizzically and stepped back into the batter's box. Torrez stood at the mound waiting.

"I lost my concentration," Torrez would say later. "I lost my good groove."

He threw a fastball on the inside of the plate, just a little high, just a little too sweet a spot. Dent, bent in his crouched stance, his hands about six inches from the bottom of the bat, exploded on the pitch, and drove a hard, high fly ball to the famed Fenway wall, the Green Monster, as legend had described it. The ball sailed gently to the screen above the wall, plunked itself right in the middle and fell softly at the feet of left fielder Carl Yastrzemski for three Yankee runs.

Another run scored, then Reggie Jackson homered in the eighth and that was the run that would win the game. The Red Sox scored two in the eighth. Goose Gossage was on the mound in the ninth to protect the victory and the playoff win.

Rick Burleson, the Boston shortstop, walked; and Jerry Remy, the second baseman, singled with one out. Jim Rice hit a huge fly to right field and Burleson moved to third base after the catch, with the tying run. Ninety feet from a tie. Hey, this is Boston. Ninety feet, ninety miles, it's all the same.

"Pop him up, pop him up," shouted third baseman Graig Nettles, the Yankees resident wit as he guarded third base.

Gossage, the husky, hard-throwing, right-handed relief pitcher with the straggly hair and the Fu Manchu mustache, turned his back on the action. He faced the wall in center field.

"I thought if I got him out we would go on to the playoffs against Kansas City," Gossage would say later. "If I didn't get him out I would be hunting back home in Colorado. Either way it wasn't so bad."

Gossage turned toward the plate again, stretched on the rubber, took a deep breath, and fired a fastball at future Hall of Famer Carl Yastrzemski. Gossage remembered the last thing he heard before he let go of the ball.

"Pop him up, pop him up," Nettles was still yelling.

The ball was a little high and a little inside and Yastrzemski could only get the thinnest part of his bat on the pitch. "I just wanted a single, a plain old-fashioned single," Yastrzemski would say later.

"Pop him up," Gossage recalled Nettles yelling as the ball hit the bat. Then, typical of Nettles, as the ball slid toward third he heard Nettles yell, "But not to me."

Nettles crossed into foul territory and the ball came down slowly, spinning and turning as foul balls almost always do. Nettles held his glove six inches above his face as he looked up into Boston's crisp October sky. The ball fell gently into the well-used leather glove, and the Boston season, a year in which they led in the pennant race by fourteen games, was over in defeat. The curse of the Bambino.

Writer Roger Angell described the game later in a *New Yorker* article, as he captured the emotion of a Boston drunk in a local bar. Just before the depressed fan's head hit the bar counter he was heard to say, "Bucky Fucking Dent."

No true Boston Red Sox fan would ever again be able to recite the name of the Yankee shortstop that day without its full measure of three-word ignominy.

The Yankees went on to Kansas City the next night, beat the Royals three games to one, moved on to the World Series against the Dodgers again, and won that Series four games to two.

The season was over. The comeback from fourteen games down would be considered historic. Bob Lemon had soothed the tensions created by Billy Martin, Reggie Jackson, and George Steinbrenner. All seemed light and pleasant around the Yankees. Yeah, of course, this was all in November when no baseball games were being played. When the year ended, baseball fans would only remember one thing, one event—that home run into the screen at Fenway Park.

Move over Bobby Thomson. Make room for Bucky Bleeping Dent.

CHAPTER

TEN

Bob Lemon had ridden in an open flatbed truck down Lower Broadway, the street of heroes, in Manhattan after the World Series triumph. The Yankees had been honored by the city, had withstood the confetti cover and dined at City Hall. Now it was time to return home, and Lemon was anxious to spend time again with his wife, Jane, and his three fine sons, Jeff, thirty-one, Jim, twenty-nine and his young favorite, Jerry, twenty-six. He flew home to Long Beach, California, a few days later and relaxed in the quiet California climate. I called him the first few days he was home for a gentle story in the *New York Post* about his triumph. Lemon was always friendly, considerate but careful about what he said. He would not rock a boat with his words or deeds. Pitching was about getting batters out. Managing was about winning games. There wasn't much else to say.

Wives deserve most of the credit when the children of ball players are decent, responsible, respectful young men and women. The wives do the raising. The husbands are away most of the spring, summer, and early fall. In the winter many of them golf, fish, hunt, and travel rather than help raise children. They turn around and those babies they once held in their arms are thirty-year-old men and women. Where did the years go?

Lemon was close to his sons. That fall of 1978, October 27, after his dad was home a couple of weeks and the off-season schedule was fixed, Jerry Lemon took off from his Long Beach home in a new jeep to spend some time with his brother Jim in Phoenix, Arizona. Thirty miles outside Phoenix, on a clear night, Jerry Lemon somehow lost control of the jeep, flipped over twice across two lanes of traffic on Interstate 10, and was thrown onto the highway. He was unconscious when Arizona State police oversaw his evacuation to a West Phoenix hospital. He died four days later.

Bob Lemon had always been an easy guy to be around, quick with a quip, refreshingly modest, and truly honest with the press. He answered what he could and explained why he could not answer other things. I sent him a condolence card, could think of nothing to say on it, and simply signed the names of my wife, Janet, and myself. His formal response card came a few days later.

I stared at it for a while and just thought how unimportant winning and losing baseball games seemed. Or even writing stories about them.

The Yankees were the defending champions. The Yankees went through a casual spring in 1979. A pitching staff anchored by Catfish Hunter, Ron Guidry, and relief terror Goose Gossage had now added Luis Tiant, a fine pitcher from Boston, and Tommy John, the spirited left-hander from the Dodgers. Strengthened with the addition of Tiant and John, another pennant seemed a lock. A World Championship team adding two quality pitchers would hardly have to worry about defending its title.

The rest of the team was solid and presented the same lineup, with Chris Chambliss, Willie Randolph, Bucky Dent, and Graig Nettles in the infield, and Reggie Jackson, Mickey Rivers, and Roy White in the outfield. Thurman Munson, showing some wear and tear, was still a splendid catcher. Who could possibly beat this team?

George Steinbrenner didn't like what he saw in spring training. George Steinbrenner *never* liked what he saw in spring training. Any loss anytime, during spring training or the regular season, during the playoffs or the World Series, was simply unacceptable.

As the Yankees marched casually through spring training, Manager Bob Lemon hardly noticed. Lemon, who had always been easy to talk to, friendly, unpretentious, and comfortable, without an ounce of phoniness in his big body, had become a different guy. Al Rosen had always called his for-

mer teammate and Yankee manager, "Meat," a nickname
dating back to their Cleveland days together. Now Rosen began calling him "Lem," as most baseball people and many
sportswriters did. Lemon's eyes seemed not to focus properly and he seemed more ragged after each game and less interested in the previous day's game when confronted by the
press each morning in his Fort Lauderdale Stadium office.
His youngest son was gone. A part of Bob Lemon died with
him.

Rosen, a warm, intelligent, and compassionate man, tried
his best to involve Lemon in as much of the business of the
Yankees as he could. They dined together often. Rosen
stayed up late with his old pal, watching him drink heavily.
He never showed any reaction from it and he was always in
the park on time the next day with a hollow glare. It pained
Rosen severely and he began thinking, ever so carefully, that
maybe his pal needed a little time away from the team. But
what would he do? He was a baseball guy, and baseball guys
need the action, the games, the drama, the competition.
Rosen remained puzzled as to a proper approach. Maybe it
would all resolve itself with the start of the season, he thought.

After a shaky couple of weeks at the start of the 1979 season, Steinbrenner seemed anxious for action. Losing a game
or two or three was simply not to be tolerated. "Good clubs
always play this way early," Rosen fibbed to the Boss. "We
have to sit back and wait for them to get started."

Rich (Goose) Gossage, the most intimidating relief
pitcher in the game, with a huge body, a scary countenance,
that Fu Manchu mustache hanging loose from his face, and a
one-hundred-mile-an-hour fastball, sat in front of his locker
after a losing game. Reggie Jackson, home run hitter extra-
ordinaire and needler supreme, saw the hulking utility
catcher and pinch hitter, Cliff Johnson, crossing in front of
Gossage's locker.

"How did you hit Goose when you were in the National
League?" Jackson asked, with obvious sarcasm. Nobody hit
Gossage very much when he was in the National League. Or
in the American League for that matter.

"He couldn't hit what he couldn't see," added Gossage with a sharp needle.

Johnson threw a rolled-up piece of tape at Gossage. Jackson laughed and walked away.

Several minutes later Johnson was coming out of the shower as Gossage emerged from the sauna. "Did you really mean that?" Johnson asked. "Do you think I couldn't hit you?"

Gossage just laughed. Suddenly, Johnson, a big black man, and Gossage, a big white man, were throwing punches and rolling on the clubhouse floor. Ball players are not skilled pugilists. Mostly they hurt themselves by falling on weaker parts of their body.

In the first year of the New York Mets, in 1962, a field fight between the Mets and the San Francisco Giants occurred. It excited the fans. It did nothing for the losing image of the Mets. The headline over my story the next day in the *New York Post* read, "They Can't Fight, Either."

Gossage broke his thumb in this scuffle. He would not return until July. Johnson was soon traded to Cleveland. Dick Tidrow became the Yankees relief pitcher. He failed quickly and was traded to the Chicago Cubs.

Steinbrenner grew more impatient with his team, as the Yankees showed little fire. Rosen was the man in the middle. He was Bob Lemon's pal but he was George Steinbrenner's employee. He had to right the Yankee ship before it became the Titanic of the summer. He seemed unable to shake the depression from Lemon's psyche. A losing Yankee start did not help.

Billy Martin was still on the Yankees payroll and despite another public scuffle with a sportswriter in Reno named Ray Hager the previous fall (oh these troublesome sportswriters) he seemed to be behaving himself. There were no tales of drinking bouts, no outrageous statements when he ran into a media man or woman, and no public criticism of Steinbrenner or the Yankees under Bob Lemon.

Bob Lemon was a fine fellow but dull as a manager. As long as the Yankees were winning, as they did so dramati-

cally in 1978, he was unimportant. When they were losing in
a lackluster way in 1979, he became very important. If the
Yankees were to salvage the season, they had to make a big
trade, obtain another star pitcher, or shake up the troops with
a new manager. The reporters needed something dramatic to
write.

Steinbrenner summoned Billy Martin to a Yankee Stadium meeting. The word quickly leaked and a lot of us gathered in Steinbrenner's outer office for a statement.

The meeting lasted two hours. Billy Martin, looking
healthy and relaxed, left the Stadium, said nothing to the
press, and jumped into a waiting limousine. In the meantime
Steinbrenner invited a few of us into his inner office. Cary
Grant's picture was still there. Steinbrenner hadn't blamed
him for the slow Yankee start. The Boss sat on a side couch,
sipped a soft drink on this hot June afternoon, and talked
with a few reporters.

"It was a very good meeting with Billy," he said. "It was
maybe the best I ever had with him. Billy will be doing some
scouting for us soon."

Scouting ballplayers, young ones and established ones,
happens to be the most important, least appreciated job in
baseball. When Lee MacPhail was the general manager of
the Yankees he said it best: "It takes a hundred signings to
get one big leaguer."

MacPhail thought the toughest part of the art was looking
at a seventeen- or eighteen-year-old kid and projecting what
he might do at the age of twenty-three or twenty-four.

"I lost more great prospects to their girlfriends than I lost
to other teams," he once said.

A Mets scout named Red Murff once looked at a skinny
high school pitcher in the tiny town of Alvin, Texas, was duly
impressed, and considered telling his bosses to sign him. He
worried about one thing. The kid was over six feet tall but
only weighed about a hundred and forty pounds. Murff went
to the family home. The boy's father, a burly man who had
worked a farm all his life, answered the door. Murff identified himself as a Mets scout. He had only one question.

"How big were you when you were your boy's age?" he asked.

"Oh," said the boy's father, "I was about the same size."

That was enough for Red Murff. He told the Mets they should draft the skinny kid and sign him. That's how the Mets finally obtained the kid from Alvin, Texas, Nolan Ryan, a future Hall of Fame pitcher and maybe the hardest thrower in baseball history.

Billy Martin could work as a Yankees scout, but it was not what he wanted to do. He wanted back at the managerial job. Steinbrenner told him that day that he was thinking of making a change even more quickly than originally planned. Lemon was supposed to manage through the 1979 season, move over in 1980 to the front office, and become Billy Martin's boss. Wow. Hardly a promising prospect for a depressed man struggling to get over the loss of a loving son.

Steinbrenner talked to Rosen almost every day about the lowly plight of the ball club. He was paying big salaries and he expected a winner. Three pennants in a row and two World Series wins in a row were not enough. Hell, the Yankees under Casey Stengel had won five World Series in a row from 1949–53. That was Steinbrenner's goal. Not five. Six World Series. The best record ever.

On June 15, 1979, Steinbrenner walked out of his room at the Inn of the Six Flags in Arlington, Texas, for a breakfast meeting in the hotel coffee shop with Brad Corbett. He and the owner of the Texas Rangers talked about their respective teams, discussed possible deals and considered ways of generating more income for their franchises.

Steinbrenner went back to his room and called his manager, Bob Lemon. The old Cleveland pitcher, a baseball man for nearly forty years, got the message when Steinbrenner gently asked, "Can I talk to you?"

Steinbrenner and Lemon talked about the team for a couple of hours. Steinbrenner could not understand why a club that had won the World Series only nine months earlier couldn't even get into the pennant race against Earl Weaver's Baltimore Orioles. The same star players from the previous year couldn't hit in the clutch, get big hitters out, or make the catches against the wall they had made so easily a year before. What kind of a crazy game was this, anyway?

Steinbrenner decided he had no choice. He had to fire somebody. Lemon was the logical guy. Steinbrenner had fired secretaries for missing phone calls, office clerks for dropping a letter on the wrong desk, high-salaried executives in his shipbuilding business for being beaten out of an order, and barbers for cutting a hair on his head in the wrong direction.

"I think we'll have to make a change," Steinbrenner told Lemon. Why not? That's the way baseball has always worked. Nobody had a better grip on the baseball firing pin than George M. Steinbrenner III.

When Steinbrenner and Corbett met again later in the afternoon to move some deals closer for both of their struggling clubs, Steinbrenner suddenly blurted out, "I'm making a change. I'm bringing Billy back."

Corbett had employed Billy Martin as manager of his Texas team. He respected his skills on the field. He wasn't sure he would want to go through the irritation that came with employing Billy Martin once again. That was for George to accept now. Corbett only smiled when Steinbrenner told him about the move.

Corbett later sat in the press level of his cute little ballpark in Arlington. He saw one of his favorite writers from the *Dallas Morning News*.

"George is bringing Billy back," Corbett told him.

"When?" asked the reporter.

Corbett told him it could happen as early as tomorrow. The story was soon on its way as an exclusive to the sports pages of the Dallas paper, angering the New York sportswriters who thought they knew everything about the team all the time. The competition among the New York sportswriters was pretty fierce. The competition between writers from different cities was gentle. Once in a while New York sportswriters will share information with their friends. Most of the time they will guard information the way atomic secrets were guarded at Los Alamos. When a New York sportswriter offered important information to a colleague it was only because he thought of himself as superior, unable to be damaged by the same story appearing in a competitive paper. I never got involved in that stuff. I always thought my stories were mine. That's what the *Post* wanted. That's why owner Dorothy Schiff paid all that expense money to send me to such exotic places as Kansas City, Pittsburgh, and Arlington.

Harold Rosenthal of the *New York Herald Tribune* used to tell a story of a sportswriter named Mike Gavin, who became seriously ill during spring training one year. All of the other sportswriters covering the old Brooklyn Dodgers wrote stories under Gavin's byline, protecting Gavin and keeping his readers oblivious to the fact that their man was not on the job. When Gavin was finally stronger, Til Ferdenzi of the *New York Journal American* showed him the Gavin story for that day. Gavin took a quick look at Ferdenzi's pinch-hit story and said, "Yeah, that's the kind of shit they want."

Gratitude, huh? Ferdenzi could handle that kind of insult. He could always pull an old clipping from his wallet about his days as a football star for Boston College. The clipping headlined Ferdenzi's heroics that Saturday. Another smaller story ran under the report of Ferdenzi's doings. The headline simply read, "Yankees Buy DiMaggio from San Francisco."

The beaten New York press jammed Lemon's office after the game and told him a Texas paper reported he had been fired.

"I don't know anything about it," said Lemon.

It all became official on June 18, 1979. Old pal Al Rosen told Bob Lemon that he was being relieved of his duties as field boss and that Billy Martin was now manager of the New York Yankees for the second time.

George Steinbrenner told the press that he had noticed significant changes in Billy's manner. George thought that Billy was drinking less (of course Steinbrenner hadn't seen him for months), that Billy seemed more cooperative, that he paid attention, and was less argumentative in recent meetings.

When the new Billy heard about this transformation of his, he smiled and said, "The only difference is that now I have a mustache."

Billy Martin visited New York often, dined in the city's popular restaurants, attended several baseball events, and spent some time with his agent, Doug Newton, in the new western wear store they had opened together on Manhattan's Madison Avenue. Newton was the money man, and Billy was the front man.

Newton and Martin, who had been introduced by Mickey Mantle, an old pal of Newton's, stocked the store with the finest of western wear. There were beautifully tooled cowboy hats, belts, hats, and shirts. They catered to both men and women, with classy and expensive outfits.

Newton wrote in their 2000 catalogue about their grand opening. "It felt like Billy and I were going down Red Canyon (Newton hailed from Colorado) when we started selling western goods on Madison Avenue, back in the 1970's. Somehow, Billy managed to order all our boots for the 'grand opening'—75 pairs—in only one size: his."

The Yankees were nine-and-a-half games out of first place when Martin called his first team meeting at Yankee Stadium after he was rehired. Twenty-four players attended. Reggie Jackson was nursing a sore leg and stayed away from the clubhouse. Jackson had been agitated when reports filtered from the press to the players (sometimes from the players to the press if the contacts are reliable) that Lemon was gone and Martin was coming back. Jackson, thinking of himself as a Steinbrenner intimate had phoned the Boss in his Arlington hotel room a couple of days before Billy was rehired. Steinbrenner said, "I don't have to tell you anything." Then he hung up on Jackson.

Jackson made it clear that he was bitter about Billy's return. He talked about wanting to be traded, about being unable to play for a manager who hated him. He felt certain another major confrontation could not be avoided.

Jackson was injured and was not in Martin's first 1979

lineup that night. Billy talked after the game about the huge crowd reaction when he brought out the lineup card and about the excitement of the fans when he jogged out to coach third base. This was an old trick used by Casey Stengel when Casey wanted to liven up his team—sort of baseball's answer to a country showing its flag. Nothing happens. The manager and the country just want everybody to know they are there.

The Yankees had come back from fourteen games down to win in 1978. They were not nearly as far back now but few believed it could happen again. This team was suffering from serious injuries to Jackson, to Ron Guidry, to Goose Gossage, to Mickey Rivers, and to team captain Thurman Munson.

Steinbrenner had a press briefing a couple of weeks after he fired Lemon as manager and rehired Martin. He sat at his desk chair in front of eight or ten of us. He was flawlessly groomed, as usual. His hair was neatly cut. His shoes glistened. He wore a blue tie, a pink shirt, and dark pleated slacks. He was angry because most of us had criticized the Lemon firing and Billy rehiring, a scenario we knew would be agonizing over the next months. Billy Martin as manager made sportswriters work too hard. That's not why we are there.

Steinbrenner said Lemon would be taken care of financially. He would remain with the Yankees in the front office and regain his confidence after the tragic loss of his young son. He had made the change to Billy, he said, because he thought it was the right move at the right time.

"That's how I operate," he said. "I go by my instincts. I do that in business. I do that in baseball. I just felt it was right."

Then Steinbrenner, who loved to drop a name, dropped Frank Sinatra's. Billy had told him that Sinatra had sent Billy a telegram after Steinbrenner rehired him as manager of the Yankees. Sinatra's telegram read, "The next time you get in a fight make sure it is defending an eighty-year-old woman." This was a reference to Billy's battle with a young sportswriter in Las Vegas the previous fall, which caused headlines around the country.

"I think Old Blue Eyes has it just about right," Steinbrenner said. "Billy has to pick his spots, pick his causes. He can't be careless anymore."

Al Rosen remained depressed over the Lemon firing even though his old Cleveland pal was learning the front office tricks in the office upstairs at the Stadium next to Rosen's. Rosen understood that Lemon was really a field guy and Steinbrenner's face-saving plan simply wouldn't work. After several contentious conversations with Martin, Rosen knew that he, Rosen, was the odd man out in the latest Billy Martin drama. It always worked that way. Either Billy ran a team his way or he ran away. Steinbrenner wanted Martin's managerial skills more than he wanted anyone else's front office acumen. More and more Steinbrenner understood that these upstairs pencil pushers, all high salaried, important public executives, were only in the way. Two guys were going to make the Yankees win again, Billy Martin on the field and the Boss, George Steinbrenner, off the field. That's the way it would be. That's the way it really was from the beginning. That's the way it would always be.

Rosen turned in his resignation.

Cedric Tallis would handle the paperwork upstairs without conflict. Steinbrenner would make major decisions. Martin would make all the other decisions. Now, less than a year after his embarrassing, tear-filled resignation in Kansas City, Billy Martin was in his strongest position ever as Yankees manager.

CHAPTER

ELEVEN

Oscar the Grouch of *Sesame Street* was not modeled after Thurman Munson of the Yankees. He easily could have been.

"He's not moody," relief pitcher Sparky Lyle, a good pal of Munson's, once said of him. "Moody means you're nice some of the time."

"When he gets on a waitress in a restaurant," his biographer Marty Appel (Bob Fishel's successor under George Steinbrenner as Yankees PR director) once said, "Diane spends the rest of the night making up for him."

Diane Munson was an attractive woman, a grade-school sweetheart, a devoted wife, and the mother of their two daughters and a hyperactive four-year-old son.

Munson had joined the Yankees out of Kent State University, scene of a bloody anti–Vietnam War demonstration between students and the Ohio National Guard. He had played outstanding baseball in the Cape Cod League for college students in 1968, been drafted by the Yankees, assigned to Binghamton where he hit .301 in seventy-one games, moved up to the Syracuse club in 1969, and brought up to the Yankees after only ninety-nine professional games.

Bill Clinton was not the only youngster in the late 1960s to dance around his military obligations. Major League baseball teams constantly changed the military status of their players and moved them from one reserve unit out of the area to one in the area with a few quick phone calls and enough tickets left for the officers at the big league will-call windows.

Shortly after he came to the Yankees, Munson's reserve unit was moved to Fort Dix, New Jersey. That meant he could fulfill his military obligations in the reserve and stay out of the Vietnam draft. It also meant he would be available for the Yankees for most of their home games.

Munson was unique when he first walked into the Yankee clubhouse. He had none of the awe most players carried when they first appeared at the Stadium—the House That Ruth Built, and DiMaggio, Berra, Ford, and Mantle had brought so much glory to. He seemed incredibly self-confident, as if great success in the Cape Cod League made for an easy transition to big league baseball. There was an intensity about his manner and a total lack of humor. It was as if the mission he was on, success in baseball, was not for a career but for survival. What manner of goblins were marching through the head of this guy?

Yogi Berra had been an odd-shaped Yankee catcher, destined for the baseball Hall of Fame. Munson immediately attracted that same kind of special notice. He was a husky right-handed hitting catcher with a very strong arm. He was a line drive hitter who could smack baseballs to the deepest part of the field. Unlike most catchers, he ran well and would often surprise the opposition by taking an extra base or stealing a base. Manager Ralph Houk, a backup catcher behind Berra in his playing time, drooled over Munson. He saw him as his monument to Yankee lore, as Casey Stengel had always envisioned Mantle. Houk, careful with praise, puffed hard on his cigars, blew smoke through his managerial office, and bragged about Munson. It was as if Houk had admired him the way he admired the guys he fought with in World War II. Instinctively, Houk knew that Munson, if the cause was just, would take a bullet for him or climb a rocky hill as Army Rangers did.

Munson's physique was odd for a professional athlete. He was not tall, trim, and graceful on the field. He appeared shorter than his full height of five feet eleven inches, heavier than his 195 pounds, and wider than a bread basket. Players are notorious for immediately capturing any physical irregularity and using it against a player for comic relief.

A World War II player named Pete Gray batted .218 for

the 1945 St. Louis Browns a year after the team had actually won the 1944 American League pennant. Gray had lost his right arm in a childhood accident. Instead of admiring the grit it took to play ball and actually make the big leagues with one arm, his teammates rode Gray mercilessly about his handicap. They called him every rotten name one could imagine for a man with one arm, sort of the white Jackie Robinson, abused for a condition he could not control. Gray had one characteristic in common with Munson. They were both angry, crusty men.

What allowed Munson to deal with the riding was simply the fact that he soon proved to be an exceptional player, and his teammates publicly admired him for that. "I'd play Adolf Hitler," Billy Martin once said, "if he would help us win." Reggie Jackson was about the only player I could recall who, although an exceptional performer, was still detested by most of his teammates.

Fritz Peterson, my pal, was the quickest with the quips about Munson. He tagged him Tugboat, Squatty Body, and Burly Boy after his large girth. Peterson would scout the stores around the Stadium and on the road for postcards of fat men and women. He would send these cards to Munson at the Stadium where Pete Sheehy, subtle and quiet, would manage to put them on top of Munson's fan mail. Peterson once saw a comic book filled with drawings of a fat character named Humphrey Pennyworth. He cut out several of the pictures, pasted them in Munson's locker, and waited for his reaction. Munson, grown used to this ribbing by now, ignored the pictures. If Peterson couldn't get a rise out of Munson for these fat pictures, why bother?

Munson batted .302 in his first full year of 1970 and was named the American League Rookie of the Year. He hit .301 in 1973, .318 in 1975, and .302 in 1976, when the Yankees won their first pennant in twelve years. He was named the American League's Most Valuable Player that year and had already been named captain of the Yankees by Steinbrenner, the first captain the team had had since the death of Lou Gehrig in 1941. Not DiMaggio, not Mantle, not Berra, not any of the heroes of previous teams had earned that honor. He took the honor with a growl. All he seemed to care about was the extra $500 he got for the title from the club.

As grouchy by nature as Munson was through 1976, it only grew worse starting in the spring of 1977. Reggie Jackson showed up, announced that he was "the straw that stirred the drink," and became the self-appointed center of the Yankee universe. It didn't matter that Munson had another terrific season with his third straight year over .300 at .308 and his third straight year with one hundred RBIs. Jackson was the story. Jackson was *always* the story. Munson would march around the clubhouse with a scowl on his face after a Yankee win, maybe a game in which he had delivered the winning hit, and stare over at the crowd of sportswriters around Jackson.

Munson was born in Akron, Ohio, on June 7, 1947. His father was a German immigrant who had come to the United States as a small child, retaining all the traditional Teutonic stiffness of the German nature. He was incapable of any softness, gentility, or ablility to communicate with his son. He worked as a cross-country truck driver and was away a good part of the time. His mother was gentle and kind but seemed to retreat into a shell when her husband came home. Munson turned early to sports, was outstanding in every game he played, and soon recognized that baseball was his best game.

The Munson household was always tight with money and that became a motivation for athletic success. Munson later became difficult in salary negotiations with the Yankees, pushing hard for every penny he could get and investing carefully in shopping centers, land deals, and local real estate. Munson and teammate Lou Piniella, a business whiz, often exchanged ideas about how to make their baseball salaries grow dramatically.

Late in 1977 Munson took up flying private planes. He took lessons from friends in Akron and soon purchased his own small private plane. While most ballplayers rent homes in the cities they play in, Munson preferred to keep his family back home in Ohio. He flew home to Akron from New Jersey's small Teterboro Airport, a center for private planes, as often as he could manage. He spent those off days with family, friends, and Ohio business associates.

The flying added to the tension in Munson's life. He was always checking schedules, the weather, and the lateness of games. Extra inning games, unfortunately too common, annoyed him beyond belief. While he continued to play remarkably well for the 1977 and 1978 Yankees, his anger became more obvious.

I had given up trying to talk to him after games by then and had just decided, as was always possible, to write around him. If he won a game with a big hit I might write about the batter before him. If he threw out a key runner attempting to steal a base against him I would write about the great tag at second base. If he had little to do with the winning or losing of the game it was always easy to march to Reggie's locker and listen to his lecture for a while.

He had a run-in with a fan in Minnesota who aggressively pursued him for an autograph. He stomped around the clubhouse shouting curses when sportswriters whom he had ignored now ignored him after he won a game. He even had hot words with Billy Martin, a devotee and supporter, just before Martin resigned in 1978. Munson had been playing his stereo cassette at an ear-splitting level on a Yankee charter flight. The card players couldn't get him to stop. Someone went up to the first class section, told Martin about it, and asked for his help. Martin asked Munson to lower the volume. Munson refused. Martin and Munson lunged at each other in the aisle of the plane but peacemakers Yogi Berra and Elston Howard calmed things down.

On August 1, 1979, the Yankees ended a series in Chicago. Munson had played first base that day because his aching knees were hurting badly. Catchers need more rest than shortstops and centerfielders. Munson knew he could no longer catch every day. His Yankee future had to be at first base or as the team's designated hitter with an occasional catching game.

Fritz Peterson, out of baseball by now, was working as a spokesman for the Baseball Chapel, an organization of the game's religious players. Peterson had found a new wife and religion at about the same time. Peterson called Munson in the clubhouse. He wanted a social visit with his old catcher.

"Can't do it," Munson told him. "I'm flying my plane home right after the game."

Munson had purchased a Cessna Citation twin-engine jet about six weeks earlier for $1.5 million. The stubborn catcher had been warned that the plane was too fast and too sophisticated for a pilot of his skills. Munson, inflexible about this as he was about most things, insisted he could handle it.

He had asked Lou Piniella and Bobby Murcer, recently returned to the team, if they wanted to fly home to Akron with him on the Monday off day. Each refused because of family obligations.

Piniella recalled, "Thurman was concerned about the how the plane was acting. He also heard about showers in the area and wanted to get home before the showers."

He flew home without incident, arriving at his Akron home at 3:00 A.M He got four hours sleep, spent some time with his wife and children, visited with his in-laws who lived nearby and were always kindly to him, and went downtown to Lucia's, a popular hangout.

Two friends, trained pilots David Hall, thirty-two, and Jerry Anderson, thirty-one, agreed to go up with him while Munson practiced touch-and-go landings with the Cessna at the Canton-Akron airport. Munson sat in the pilot's seat of his plane, Hall sat in the copilot's seat, and Anderson sat in the single passenger seat.

They took off at 2:45 P.M. on a clear afternoon. The men in the control tower watched the sleek silver plane with the NY 15, Munson's Yankee number, disappear to the left on a clear, cloudless sky. Munson flew the plane over the Ohio countryside for about fifteen minutes, circled back toward the airport, and called the tower for landing clearance. The plane came in slowly to the airport. Investigators later suggested "pilot error," because the plane was moving too slowly as it neared touchdown.

At 3:02 P.M., a thousand feet shy of runway nineteen of the Canton-Akron airport, the plane sliced into some trees, flew past Greensburg Road, crashed into the ground below a rise that led to the runway, and quickly caught fire. Hall efficiently kicked out the right side door and fell to the ground. Anderson, singed on his hands and neck, stumbled out after him. They turned to look for Munson. He was still in the plane. They ran around the burning plane and looked into the cockpit. Munson's head was tilted sideways. He was motionless. From outside of the damaged plane the two friends tugged and pulled at the catcher. He was harnessed into his seat. They tried desperately to release him. They could not. Suddenly, the fuel was ignited and the plane was covered in flames and smoke.

Detective Williams Evans, called to the scene by a witness from a nearby farm house, logged his arrival at 3:07 P.M. He found Anderson thirty yards from the plane, on his back, gasping for breath. Hall was leaning on a tree some forty yards in the other direction, his clothes charred from the flames, his eyes glassy, his mouth open as he sucked in air. Evans raced to the plane, still smoldering in flames, but couldn't get closer than ten feet.

Firemen arrived at the same time as an ambulance. Both survivors were rushed to nearby Timken Mercy Hospital.

Thurman Lee Munson, thirty-two years old, Yankee catcher and captain, was dead.

Investigators later reported that Munson had died of smoke inhalation. According to the medical examiner's report, released by Anthony Cardarelli, sheriff of Summit County, Munson was dead when the second fire burned up the plane.

Neal Callahan of the Chicago district office of the FAA, notified by the control tower of the crash, was responsible for notifying the Yankees after the Munson family was called.

He put in a call from his Chicago office to the Yankees offices in the Bronx and reached the head telephone operator,

Doris Walden, who cheerily answered, "World Champion Yankees."

"I have to speak to Mr. Steinbrenner. It's a matter of life and death," Callahan blurted out.

Walden had heard this kind of excuse before from outraged fans hoping to get through to Steinbrenner. But Callahan insisted it was that serious and she decided to put the call through to Steinbrenner's office. A young man named Gerry Murphy, who had served as traveling secretary and was now Steinbrenner's personal assistant, answered the phone. He heard Callahan again insist he had to speak to Steinbrenner on this matter. He did not wish to reveal these tragic facts to anyone other than the Boss. Murphy hesitated. He knew by now most of the people who could get through to Steinbrenner directly—limousine pal Bill Fugazy; Jimmy Nederlander, the show business producer and longtime pal; a few team owners and acceptable newspaper men.

Steinbrenner might explode at him if this guy was a phony. He gambled and put the call through. Steinbrenner picked up the phone and heard Callahan identify himself as a representative of the FAA in Chicago. He had bad news.

He said there had been a crash outside the Canton-Akron airport. "Your player, Thurman Munson, he's been killed."

"Are you sure?" Steinbrenner asked. He was shocked, tense, and starting to sweat.

Callahan explained the situation. He told Steinbrenner that friends of Munson were on the plane with him but had escaped death. They identified the Yankee catcher. Steinbrenner, careful now, quiet, in complete control, asked if the family knew about the crash.

"By now they do," Callahan said. "We just dispatched the police to their home."

Steinbrenner's first call went to Billy Martin's apartment in New Jersey. He was out fishing that afternoon with his young son, Billy Joe, enjoying the light breezes on a friend's boat. The ship-to-shore phone rang with an urgent message, "Call George Steinbrenner immediately."

Martin responded quickly. He got his friend to take him

in to the nearest dock, bought his son an ice cream, and moved to a pay phone in a luncheonette.

"George, this is Billy. I got your message to call."

"We have just gotten some terrible news," Steinbrenner said. "Thurman has been killed in a plane crash."

Both men broke down. Steinbrenner later recalled that Billy could not control himself as he sobbed on the phone. Steinbrenner collected himself enough to issue another order. "Call me later," he said.

Now Steinbrenner began calling his players. He reached Bobby Murcer, Munson's closest friend, told him the news, and quickly accepted Murcer's decision to fly to Canton with his wife, Kay, to help Diane Munson and the children as best they could. He contacted Lou Piniella. "I couldn't believe it, I didn't want to believe it," Piniella later said. "The whole thing seemed like a nightmare to me. I expected to go into the clubhouse the next day and see Thurman and realize the whole thing had just been a terrible dream."

By now the Associated Press had the story and was moving it across the country. Someone from my desk at the *New York Post* called with the news. My reaction was bland. Munson was only thirty-two but he had caused a lot of unrest in the homes of a lot of sports reporters. We try to judge players as men, not as athletes. Munson was a great athlete. He was a sour man.

I suddenly thought of a line we sometimes used in the privacy of the press box when a well-known personality died. Jack Mann, a Long Island, New York, *Newsday* sports columnist, was the originator of the line. Mann had been called at home when Ty Cobb—a mean, crusty, bigoted, angry man, and the most successful batter in baseball history—died in 1961 at the age of seventy-four. He was asked to write Cobb's obituary for his paper. Mann acknowledged the writing assignment, but explained to the desk the kind of man Cobb had been and that he would not soften the obit now that Cobb was gone.

"The only difference now," said Mann, "is that he's a dead prick."

The line popped into my head when I heard about the death of Munson but I set about my chore of getting reaction from Yankee teammates. Reaching a big league baseball player on an off day is no easy task. Few stay home for a barbecue with the family. Most go fishing, sailing, or hunting with teammates, shopping for new cars or appearing at shopping centers signing autographs for big bucks. Lou Piniella was home with his family.

"George was all choked up when he told me," Piniella said. "He could barely talk. He was very emotional."

Marty Appel, Munson's biographer and the former Yankees public relations man, recalled that day that he had told Steinbrenner of manager Joe McCarthy's 1941 pledge at Lou Gehrig's gravesite that no other Yankee would ever be named captain of the team. Steinbrenner had defied that tradition in naming Munson the captain in 1976. Now the irony of the early death of the Yankee captain had struck again.

The Yankees were scheduled against the Baltimore Orioles the Friday night after Munson's death. At game time the Yankees ran out to their positions. Like the riderless horse with inverse boots at a presidential funeral, there was no catcher at home plate. Each player stood still at his position as Munson's face was flashed huge on the electronic scoreboard. The fans began applauding and would not cease their farewell to their hero until more than eight minutes had passed. Not a player moved. The entire Stadium paid unique tribute to Munson and testimony to his tragic death. Backup catcher Jerry Narron walked quietly to his position behind the plate seconds before the game began.

The players would not talk to the press before the game but a few were willing to express their emotions when it was over. Lou Piniella leaned back in his locker, his handsome face etched with pain, his eyes red, his skin ashen. "We had this fishing trip planned, me and Thurman and Donnie Gullett and Charlie Lau and we were all going down to the Florida Keys and catch us some fish as soon as the season was over. Thurman was the closest friend I ever had in baseball. If there are eighty-one days on the road that we are together there must have been eighty-one nights we ate dinner together. We just loved being together, having dinner, talking baseball, drinking a beer, sharing good times. And the fishing trip . . . now there won't be any fishing trip . . ."

Both Piniella and Bobby Murcer later told me that Munson had asked them to join him for the trip to Canton from Chicago. Each admitted privately that the real reason they begged off with manufactured excuses about family obligations was their concern about Munson's ability to handle the complicated and expensive new Cessna he had recently purchased. This would all come back hauntingly to me on July 17, 1999, when John F. Kennedy, Jr., crashed off Martha's Vineyard while flying a Piper Saratoga after only one hundred hours of flying time. Kennedy could fly visually but not by instruments. It was Munson's arrogance and Kennedy's insouciance regarding flying that cost both young men their lives.

On Monday the Yankees were flown by chartered jet to the Canton-Akron airport, in sight of the crash, for a short bus ride to the Canton Memorial Civic Center. Diane Munson sat in a side waiting room and was greeted and hugged by the wives of most of her husband's Yankee teammates. They pledged their love and support through tear-filled eyes. The two small Munson daughters sat quietly with their grandparents while young Michael, dressed in a cut-down Yankee uniform number fifteen, scampered in and out of the room looking at his father's friends.

Lou Piniella read from the Scriptures and then said, "We don't know why God took Thurman, but as long as we wear a Yankee uniform Thurman won't be far from us. As a baseball player he was one of the best competitors. He played rough but fair. He was also a kind, affectionate, friendly man." His voice choked and he walked off the platform.

Bobby Murcer delivered the main eulogy and said, "He lived, he led, he loved. Whatever he was to each of us, catcher, captain, competitor, husband, father, friend, he should be remembered as man who valued and followed the basic principles of life. . . .

"As Lou Gehrig led the Yankees as the captain of the thirties, our Thurman Munson captained the Yankees of the seventies. Someone, someday, shall earn that right to lead this team again, for that is how Thurm—Tugboat, as I called him—would want it. No greater honor could be bestowed on one man than to be the successor to this man, Thurman Munson, who wore the pinstripes with number fifteen. Number fifteen on the field, number fifteen for the records, number fifteen for the halls of Cooperstown.

"But in living, loving, and legend, history will record Thurman as number one."

Clubhouse man Pete Sheehy locked the clubhouse tight that night, worried more than ever about theft.

Sheehy, on orders from Steinbrenner, had cleaned out Munson's locker. He left only a pinstriped shirt slung over a hanger, the NY facing out, a pair of pinstriped baseball pants hanging loosely on a hook, a Yankee cap on the top shelf, and across from the shirt, his catcher's mask on another hook. Atop the locker was a metal plate bearing simply the number 15.

There it remains, twenty years later, as a new generation of Yankee heroes, Derek Jeter, Bernie Williams, Paul O'Neill, Tino Martinez, David Cone, and Scott Brosius walk past the locker through the clubhouse to the trainer's room for treatment and privacy from the press.

Munson's figure still draws huge applause when it appears on the Yankee Stadium electronic scoreboard, and his name is always mentioned on Old Timer's Day. Steinbrenner gave Thurman's son, Michael, a chance at a baseball career by signing the youngster, never considered a pro prospect, and he donates heavily to a dinner in Manhattan in Thurman's honor each winter to benefit ailing children.

The Baseball Hall of Fame ballots for Munson decreased each year after his death, and his chances for enshrinement in the game's Valhalla seem remote.

He hit .292 in eleven big-league seasons, was a fine catcher, had a strong arm, could run exceptionally well, and was a very aggressive player. His legs were tiring in 1979 and his production was in serious decline. No matter how insulted he was by Sparky Anderson's remarks after the 1976 World Series, Anderson was right. Thurman Munson was no Johnny Bench.

I am among the more than 570 members of the Baseball Writers Association of America who cast ballots in the annual Hall of Fame vote. I have never voted for Thurman Munson. Gotcha.

CHAPTER

TWELVE

Billy Martin and barroom brawls went together.

On October 23, 1979, Martin was in the Minneapolis area, where he had managed the Minnesota Twins, for a hunting trip with an old pal, Howard Wong, owner of an expensive Chinese eatery. Wong tried to get Martin a room in a Bloomington hotel near the airport before Martin's projected flight to Dallas, where he would spend a week hunting and drinking with Mickey Mantle. There wouldn't be much hunting.

A national convention of beauticians had taken up most of the hotel rooms in the area and Wong had to settle for a one-night stay in Bloomington's finest establishment, the Hotel de France, with its elegant rooms and swank bar.

Wong and Martin had a couple of drinks at the bar, talked about their hunting trip, had a couple more scotches, talked about the next trip, and passed the evening without Billy showing any signs of wanting it to end.

Hotel barrooms are public places and there is no admission fee. Billy Martin had a membership card for any hotel bar he visited. In the elegant surroundings of the Hotel de France, a man named Joseph Cooper, a fifty-two-year-old marshmallow salesman in town for a tour of client stores, was near him. Cooper recognized Martin. This is part of the price of fame, a burden famous sports figures carry throughout their travels. Cooper struck up an unwelcome conversation. It all went well for a while. Cooper, a large man from Lincolnshire, Illinois, decided he would lecture Martin on the recently announced manager-of-the-year awards. The American League honor went to pennant-winning skipper Earl Weaver of the Orioles and the National League honor to

Dick Williams for building the new Montreal Expos into a competitive team.

Martin would hear none of it. When Cooper suggested that Williams was a brilliant manager, Martin responded, "Dick Williams is an asshole. They're both assholes and so are you for saying it."

Cooper bristled but said nothing. Martin suddenly reached into his pocket, pulled out a roll of bills, and said, "Here's five hundred to your penny I can knock you on your ass."

Cooper reached into his pocket, pulled out a penny, placed it on top of the five one-hundred-dollar bills Martin had placed on the bar, and said, "Let's go."

In the confusion that followed, Cooper somehow wound up with a cut lip and blood dripping on his clothes. Waitress Peggy McKenny rushed over with a wet towel. Then she called the Bloomington police, and Cooper was soon on his way for treatment at the Fairview Southdale Hospital.

Billy Martin later issued a statement through the Yankees publicity department, saying, "A guy was talking baseball with us and I decided I didn't want to talk baseball anymore and left. As I walked through the lobby I heard a noise. I turned around and saw the guy laying on the floor. A security guard told my friend Howard Wong the guy fell and cut his lip. I left and went to my room. I'm sorry the guy got hurt."

Fans somehow have a way of falling down and getting seriously hurt when they are around the Yankees. The most celebrated incident in Martin's brawl career, of course, was his 1957 birthday celebration at New York's Copacabana Club when another fan allegedly fell down in the restaurant kitchen after teammate Hank Bauer tried to quiet his offensive manner. Sammy Davis, Jr., was entertaining that night and the fan had apparently made some remarks about Davis and about the Yankee group, which included Bauer, Martin, Mickey Mantle, Yogi Berra, and rookie pitcher Johnny Kucks.

After the brawl was over, Martin was traded to Kansas

City, ending his Yankee days as a player but advertising him as a notorious night crawler.

The *St. Paul Pioneer Dispatch* put the story on page one the next morning and the wire services moved it around the country. Night sports editor Steve Bromberg of the *New York Post* got the story and alerted night managing editor Alan Whitney. "Kalech!" yelled Whitney across the *Post* city room. One of the secrets of journalism is knowing a story when it falls in your lap. This one was tumbling rapidly into the *Post* city room.

A *New York Post* reporter named Marc Kalech, later to become the paper's managing editor, called the Yankees PR man Mickey Morabito as soon as the wires moved the story of the incident.

"Billy Martin's been in a fight," Kalech told Morabito at about 4:15 in the morning.

"Are you shitting me?" Morabito asked.

"Nope," said Kalech. "We have a wire story from St. Paul. Have you talked with him?"

Working for George Steinbrenner was never easy. Working for George Steinbrenner when Billy Martin was the manager was even worse. Sleep was not an option. Morabito was starting to look worn and ragged around this time. What remained remarkable was his loyalty to Martin. He did all he could to help and defend Billy in each of his strange episodes.

Martin called Morabito, discussed the incident, and prepared a statement. The first edition of the *Post* was already out on the street with the huge front-page headline, "Billy Martin in New Brawl."

Steinbrenner was informed of the incident by a television reporter when he got off a plane in Tampa. Neither Martin nor Morabito had called Steinbrenner yet. Steinbrenner was shocked. "When he told me I just felt sick to my stomach," Steinbrenner later said.

In a few days the decision was made. Martin would go. On Sunday night, October 28, 1979, Morabito read Steinbrenner's statement to the press. "Billy Martin has been relieved of his duties as manager of the New York Yankees and Dick Howser has been named to succeed him effective immediately."

Martin's escapades had become tiresome. The soap opera running daily, involving Steinbrenner and Martin had by now been played out. The Yankees had finished in fourth place, thirteen and a half games out. There had been the death of Bob Lemon's son, the injury to Goose Gossage, the firing of Lemon, the return of Martin, and the final, fatal blow to that star-crossed season, the death of Thurman Munson in the August 2 air crash.

This time there was no public outcry after the firing of Martin. Very few fans reacted with a letter or a phone call to the Yankee offices as had happened repeatedly after the 1978 firing.

Billy Martin was simply following the script as he always had ever since he was a Yankee player. A few quiet seasons, a fight or two along the way, and then the final act of self-destruction in some barroom, some hotel lobby, some airport gateway.

One nasty letter arrived at the Yankee offices addressed to "Mr. Steinberger." A few phone calls asked George to resign but none of this made the press at the time. There were no calls for Billy's return by his old Yankee pals Joe DiMaggio, Mickey Mantle, Whitey Ford, or Yogi Berra. Berra, especially, had survived in baseball by getting along well with everybody—boss, teammates, and sportswriters.

He had been a Yankee hero ever since he first walked onto the field late in 1946, an awkward-looking kid from St. Louis with a quick bat and an abundance of malaprops. Old friend Joe Garagiola, as an NBC baseball broadcaster and later as a coanchor on the NBC Today show, raised Berra to the position of folk hero with his childhood stories of Dago Hill in St. Louis. Most of the Berra stories were true and simply exaggerated. Most were created by Berra's inability to offer cogent expression of his ideas. He knew the game cold. He just couldn't express it clearly. Garagiola and others helped make this quality famous and funny. A group of sportswriters stood in a hotel lobby in Minnesota one evening during a Yankees off day. The major topic of conversation was the selection of the restaurant where we would all dine together that evening at the expense of the Yankees, a noble adjunct to traveling with a baseball team.

Several places were named until someone suggested a Minneapolis steak house named Charlie's.

"Ahh," said Yogi, upon hearing the suggestion, "nobody goes there any more. It's too crowded."

There was much laughter at the time at Yogi's verbal flop. Then there was much thought. Nobody, meaning the Yankee coaches and press, goes there any more, because it is too crowded—with the general public. What could be clearer?

Yogi—his given name was Lawrence Peter and he was called Lawdie as a kid, an Italian usage of Larry—became an instant star when he joined the Yankees. The name Yogi would come from friends who had seen a movie with an Indian yogi and had noticed Berra sitting as still as a yogi as he waited his batting turn in American Legion baseball games.

Even Ted Williams, seeing him on the field for the first time, changed his opinion. Williams first asked, "Who's that guy?" as he stared at Berra's awkward shape. He changed his tune after Berra swung the bat a few times against the Red Sox. "Wow, what a hitter," said the best hitter of them all.

His verbal gymnastics became legendary. "It ain't over till it's over," he said of a tight pennant race. "Thank you for making this day necessary," he said when he was honored by the Yankees. One of my favorite Berraisms after four decades of listening to them is, "When you come to a fork in the road, take it."

My wife and I have taken that fork in the road many times after a few verbal squabbles about directions, a genetic imbalance between husbands and wives.

Billy Martin brought Berra to the Yankees after he was fired by the Mets in 1975. Yogi contributed in many ways to the team's success over the next years. While Yogi's awkward English made him a folk hero, his innate intelligence, common sense, and fierce pride made him a significant base-ball figure. Yogi isn't a joke teller or a raconteur. He is sim-ply a kind, decent, honorable man with a beautiful wife, the former Carmen Short, three fine sons, a holiday house filled with grandchildren, and the deepest level of affection from fans and friends.

He is a Hall of Fame catcher and one of America's most beloved public figures.

So Yogi and the rest of the team remained quiet as Billy Martin disappeared from the Yankee scene—again.

Reggie Jackson was on a business trip in Los Angeles when he heard the news on television in his hotel room. "Too bad," he said later. "I was getting along fine with Billy at the end. I can't say I'm real surprised. Billy seemed in better control of himself. Maybe not."

Al Rosen, who had resigned after being forced to fire his pal, Bob Lemon, and bring Billy back under George's or-ders, was working in Atlantic City, New Jersey, for the Bally Manufacturing Company, a firm that built casino equipment. He was asked by a friend what he thought of the firing of Billy Martin. He simply smiled and responded, "I'm like Will Rogers. I never met a man I didn't like."

Rosen is in retirement now in California, enjoys his golf games with pals, hardly ever thinks about his Yankee days, and smiles easily when asked about the Yankees. "That was then," he says. "This is now."

On Thursday afternoon, November 1, 1979, the Yankees ushered in an era of good feeling with the naming of Dick Howser as the new manager and Gene Michael as the new general manager.

These were two exceptionally bright, honest, creative baseball men. The Yankees would be in good hands as the team moved into the decade of the 1980s.

The press conference announcing the new management team was held under a domed glass roof in the main dining room of the famed Tavern on the Green restaurant in Man-hattan's Central Park. The sun poured through the room, and the free drinks and free gourmet meals after the press conference made for another memorable afternoon at the expense of the Yankees. Sportswriters aren't rich. They only live as if they are. They stay in the best hotels on the road with the team, eat in the finest restaurants—often as guests of the club or else on their newspaper's expense account. They fly in chartered planes, moving from airport to hotel or stadium in chartered buses. They have all their needs taken care of by the team's traveling secretaries. "I've been rich and I've been poor," Sonny Werblin, owner of the New York Jets, always said to me. "Rich is better." You bet. If you can't be rich, be a sportswriter. It will give you a good imitation of rich.

Gene Michael became one of my best pals in baseball. He had come out of Kent, Ohio, starred as a basketball player at Kent State University, been pursued by the New York Knickerbockers, and drafted as a baseball player by the Pittsburgh Pirates. He stayed in the Pittsburgh organization for seven years until he got a chance with the Pirates in 1966. He batted only .152 in thirty games and instantly recognized that he would not be a superstar. He went to the Dodgers for a year and came to the Yankees in 1968. He was one of the most astute baseball players I had ever met. He had a great understanding of the subtlety of the game. He even pitched occasionally when the team was in trouble.

Michael, at six feet three inches and weighing 185 pounds when he was a player, was far heavier than one would expect from a shortstop called "Stick," by his teammates. He could never explain why he wasn't better with the stick, the baseball bat, throughout his career. He ended up with a .229 lifetime average in ten seasons. A bad average. A nice career.

He was always thinking on the field and even saved the Yankees a few games with the hidden ball trick. He would secret a ball in his glove after a play, move toward the pitcher, deceive the runner into thinking he no longer had the ball, and tag out the unsuspecting base runner.

Michael could take good care of himself in a scuffle and once knocked out a Boston first baseman named Tony Hor-

George Steinbrenner in his private Yankee Stadium box with friends (*from left*) Joe DiMaggio and New York City mayor Rudy Giuliani
Jackson Pokress

Mike Kekich
New York Yankees

Fritz Peterson
New York Yankees

Yankee catcher Fran Healy (left) with author Maury Allen in 1977
Lou Requena

Thurman Munson, Squatty Body of the Yankees
New York Yankees

Ron Guidry
New York Yankees

Reggie Jackson
New York Yankees

Yankee greats at a 1979 Old-timers game (*left to right*), Joe DiMaggio,
Mickey Mantle, Roger Maris, Billy Martin, Yogi Berra, and Whitey Ford
Lou Requena

Yankee star Dave Winfield (*left*) and author Maury Allen at a 1991 Baseball Writers Dinner *Jackson Pokress*

Manager Joe Torre
New York Yankees

Darryl Strawberry *New York Yankees*

Joan Downey, Billy Martin's mother in 1985
Fred Larson

Billy Martin (*left*) and author Maury Allen in 1978   *Jim Cheal*

Outfielder Bernie Williams hits 1999
homer   *Jackson Pokress*

Jim "Catfish" Hunter
New York Yankees

Derek Jeter
New York Yankees

David Cone
*New York
Yankees*

El Duque, Orlando Hernandez
New York Yankees

Willie Randolph
New York Yankees

Mariano
Rivera
*New York
Yankees*

Don Mattingly being interviewed by Mickey Mantle *Lou Requena*

Famous Chris Chambliss 1976 home run *New York Yankees*

ton with one punch when Horton attempted to push him off the bag on a pickoff play. Michael would not be pushed. He simply punched his way free.

Horton later underwent psychiatric treatment for serious emotional problems. He was also the victim in Boston of Steve Hamilton's Folly Floater. Hamilton had invented a pitch that drove batters nuts. He would stop in his motion, hook his baseball shoe into the ground in front of the mound, and float a pitch to home plate fifteen or twenty feet in the air, the way a father would first play catch with a young son. Big league hitters cannot deal with that kind of silliness. They are bracing for the one-hundred-mile-an-hour fastball. When Hamilton threw it to Horton, he popped it up for an out behind home plate.

As the ball came down he took a few steps back toward the Boston dugout as the Fenway Park crowd howled. He was soon on his hands and knees crawling into the Boston dugout with his own teammates in hysterics. It was not long after that that he sought professional help for his emotional problems.

As smart a baseball player as Michael was, he was even smarter as a card player. We had regular, friendly (nobody was allowed to lose his salary) card games on the road. Michael could remember every card in every different game we played and almost always emerged as the winner. He instigated a poker game called "Crisscross" in which bets are made on open cards and then those cards are changed by purchase of other cards. He almost always won. When a sportswriter won at Crisscross it was equal, for us, to the ninth-inning, game-winning home run with two out.

Michael joined the Yankees in 1968, and except for one season at the end of his career in Detroit, he has been on the Yankees payroll ever since as a coach, scout, manager, general manager, and close confidant and aide to the Boss.

"I get along well with George," he said. "I say 'yes sir' at all the meetings and then I go out and do what I think is best for the team."

I always admired Stick Michael, learned a lot about the

game of baseball from him, and respected his personal integrity. I also admired his card playing. I brought Crisscross to a neighborhood poker game. When I win it is always with the dedication, "Thanks, Stick."

Dick Howser was from Tallahassee, Florida, and went to high school and college with a bruiser of a guy and a fine football player named Burt Reynolds. They remained fast friends long after their school days when Howser was playing professional baseball and Reynolds was the handsome, sarcastic, popular leading man in many movies.

"I never believed that could possibly happen," Howser once said. "Burt was just too shy in school."

Howser played eight years in the big leagues, including the 1967 and 1968 season with the Yankees, the last year as a teammate of Stick Michael's. He was named a Yankees coach in 1969 and succeeded coach Frank Crosetti who had been a Yankee shortstop from 1932 through 1948. Crosetti then became a Yankees coach and was legendary for collecting many World Series checks and spending none of them. As he neared his ninetieth birthday in 2000, Crosetti was as crusty as he had ever been as a player and coach.

Crosetti was the player who drove across America from San Francisco to St. Petersburg with Yankee rookie Joe DiMaggio and a third Italian teammate, Tony Lazzeri, in the spring of 1936 for the opening of the Yankees training camp.

"We got to about the middle of Arizona," Crosetti once recalled, "and Lazzeri turned to the kid, DiMaggio, and asked, 'You wanna drive?' DiMaggio said he didn't know how. That was the last words we heard DiMaggio say until we got to Florida."

Crosetti was also the Yankee coach who screamed at infielder Phil Linz on a Yankee bus in 1964 when Linz played *Mary Had a Little Lamb* on his harmonica instead of brooding about a Yankee loss. Yogi Berra was the manager, and after Linz refused Crosetti's suggestion that he stop playing, Yogi ordered Linz to quit. Linz threw the harmonica at Berra, who threw it back in one of the more celebrated Yankee internal feuds. It hit first baseman Joe Pepitone on the knee.

It caused a big newspaper fuss. Linz made $10,000 from a harmonica endorsement, paid a $200 fine to the Yankees, and helped them win the pennant. Crosetti collected and never spent another Yankee Series check.

At sixty-eight, Crosetti was forcedly retired and Howser took over his job. Crosetti hasn't got over that yet.

Howser stood only five feet eight inches tall, weighed less than 155 pounds, was a decent line-drive hitter, and a solid infielder. He typified the kind of person who inspires youngsters to the game of baseball. More than 140 years after the professional game began, there are still big league ballplayers built like Dick Howser. Basketball and football players are usually huge, totally identifiable men in a hotel crowd. Basketball teams, especially, cannot travel anonymously. There are few occasions when ten or twelve black men, all close to seven feet or over, walk through an airport without being identified as a professional basketball team.

Howser studied the game carefully, increased his skills with his knowledge, and related well to all the players with his helpful hints and winning smile. He was a manager in waiting when he left the Yankees early in 1979 to become the head baseball coach at his alma mater, Florida State University.

The Yankees would be rebuilt for the 1980 season, with the addition of Rick Cerone as the new catcher obtained from Toronto to succeed Thurman Munson, and the trade of 1976 home run hero Chris Chambliss. Catfish Hunter was retiring after some good years as a Yankee and then some painful shoulder problems.

George Steinbrenner, as always, was loyal to his former Yankee star and had invited Catfish back for a few happy weeks in spring training. Spring training that most joyous time of the year for baseball players and sportswriters, especially established players and proven sportswriters.

Hunter had left the Yankees with that big baseball bonus contract guaranteeing financial security for his family. He went home to his tobacco farm in Hertford, North Carolina, switched much of the crop to more profitable soybeans, and arrived at spring training for his three weeks of guest privileges. Hunter was close to his family and he spoke about managing his son's Little League team in an early spring-training interview.

Lou Piniella, sharp and witty, saw the article, and when Hunter arrived at the ballpark the following morning, Piniella rushed over to him. "You're managing a Little League team? You can't manage a grocery." Hunter took it with a laugh, called Piniella a funny name, and slapped him on the backside with a towel as he moved toward the shower. This, as Mickey Mantle said after he retired, is what they miss the most.

Dick Howser's first spring training in 1980 was organized and orderly. Most of the regulars found out early they were not going to coast through the spring as they had the previous March under Bob Lemon. Bus trips across Florida were the bane of every established player's existence. Some took as long as four or five hours.

One infamous Mets trip in 1962 just about ended Gil Hodges's playing career. He sat on the team bus from St. Petersburg, Florida, across the state to Vero Beach, Florida, where he had trained with the Dodgers for so many years. Mets manager Casey Stengel wanted him there as an attraction against his old team. When the bus arrived in Vero Beach after three hours on a bumpy road with Hodges asleep in the same position most of the way, he could not straighten his leg when he got up to walk. Soon after, knee surgery ended his playing days.

Sportswriters rent comfortable cars in spring training and travel from game to game with one or two pals to share the expenses and help pass the time. Bus rides to and from airports are enough inconvenience for members of the fourth estate.

Veteran players hope to avoid long trips by complaining about minor injuries. Many of the Yankees that spring would arrive at Lauderdale Stadium, take off their street clothes, march into trainer Gene Monahan's quarters, pick up an ice pack, and deposit themselves on a long table as teammates came into the room to gossip. Howser saw to it that players who needed ice pack treatment continued it on the bus on the way to the next game. The ice pack socials, among players staying back in camp and avoiding the trips, were over. Hey, was this guy Howser going to be a tough guy?

"There really was a different attitude around the club that spring," recalled outfielder Lou Piniella, friend and frequent dinner companion of Howser when he was a Yankee coach. "Dick was serious about the job. After all, we had finished fourth the year before and George wasn't about to take much more of that. I could understand that. I saw the changes immediately and I appreciated it the day we beat the Mets in a spring game. George always thought those games were more important than any other spring game.

"The ticket windows in New York will have lines out there before they open," Steinbrenner told his players after the game. Piniella said Steinbrenner always told him of his fondest Stadium dream, lines and lines of people standing all night long, waiting for the windows to open so they could buy the hottest ticket in town, a Yankee Stadium game ticket.

A win over the Mets wouldn't quite seal that dream for Steinbrenner but it did give him the sense that the tragic events of the 1979 season were behind him, behind the Yankees, and behind all their dedicated fans. This was a new team with a new general manager, a new manager, several new players, and a completely new attitude. There were no longer to be fights between the owner and the manager. All Yankees, front office and players, were on the same page. The idea was simply to win.

The team that Howser put on the field in 1980 was far different from Billy Martin's teams in the 1970s. Hunter was retired, Chris Chambliss was traded, Ed Figueroa was gone from the pitching staff, and outfielder Roy White, probably the most underrated and least appreciated Yankee of his time, was off for Japan.

White had hit only .215 as a part-timer in 1979. Steinbrenner thought he was finished, so wouldn't sign him again when his contract was up. White tried other clubs but nobody would pay him the rising salary level because he was an outfielder who simply didn't hit big home runs. He had hit twenty-two homers in 1970 but could manage only three in 1979. Baseball clubs are reluctant to pay big bucks to outfielders who don't hit home runs.

White had spent fifteen years with the Yankees, starting as a spindly infielder, moving to the outfield, developing rapidly as a fine fielding outfielder, solid hitter, excellent base runner, and smart, hustling player. He had a weak arm and rarely threw anyone out. An old baseball expression, often repeated by sportswriters, was that hitters like White could "take two and hit to right." Because of his weak arm, the nasty expression soon became, "Take two and hit to White." Nobody ever said sportswriters were kind.

A lot of dull hours pass in press boxes, and sportswriters fill the time with tall tales and endless games. White's name always came up on the all-colorful teams with others such as Pete Gray, Dallas Green, Bill White, Joe Black, Vida Blue, Red Schoendienst, and Whitey Herzog.

Roy White was always a gentleman around the clubhouse, never seemed to cause anyone any trouble, was honest, hard working, sincere, dedicated, and a solid major league ball player. Steinbrenner rewarded him with a front-office job after his retirement. Nice guys *can* finish first.

The team that Howser took north in 1980 was a solid contender. Tommy John, called baseball's "bionic man," for his complicated elbow replacement surgery, had won twenty-one games in 1979. He would anchor the staff. Ron Guidry had won eighteen games. Goose Gossage, healthy again, had saved thirty-three games. Rick Cerone, playing under enormous pressure as Thurman Munson's replacement, would be the catcher. Jim Spencer, Oscar Gamble, Lou Piniella, Bobby Murcer, and Reggie Jackson would provide most of the offense.

The Yankees, under Howser, lost the first two games of the season in Texas. Panic time. George was restless. Howser knew better, but he was feeling the heat. The players were all waiting to see how the new managerial setup with

Gene Michael on top and Howser below him would work.

Then it rained in Texas. It would stop, as it always had, as Gabe Paul repeated, but not until that game was called. The Yankees took it as a positive sign of the season.

"So far," laughed Lou Piniella, "it is our best day of the year."

Piniella, always insecure about his hitting despite a .291 lifetime average over eighteen seasons, was up during the nights in Texas swinging his bat in his hotel room in front of a huge mirror. This was a routine he followed carefully when he wasn't hitting. He had to get that stroke down right, get that timing, get that stance correct, get those pitches in the perfect zone where he could smash a line drive.

When he was hitting, it might even be worse. Keep that stroke, keep that timing, keep that stance, get those pitches in the perfect zone. Ted Williams always contended hitting a baseball was the hardest act in sports. He could do it. Michael Jordan couldn't.

CHAPTER

THIRTEEN

The Yankees opened the 1980 season at home against the Milwaukee Brewers on April 18. By now, Opening Day in Yankee Stadium had become one of the premier New York social events of the season. George Steinbrenner invited forty or fifty of his closest friends to dine with him, to share a few drinks in his loge-level office, and to sit with him in the boxes overlooking the field.

There were a few family members, a few baseball executives, a few local politicians. Always there was one supercelebrity dominating the crowd. Sportswriters were not invited.

There is a long ramp between the Stadium press box and Steinbrenner's private area. Many of us would walk that ramp before the game to get a glimpse of the attendees and make a note of it for the next day's paper. I took my ramp walk just before the game began. Most of Steinbrenner's guests were still in his large office suite finishing off the last canapé, the last sandwich, the last drink. One man sat alone on the right side of the box in a back row.

As I moved closer to identify him I suddenly realized I had seen that face before, many times, mostly on television, but on one memorable afternoon, up close.

Former president Richard Nixon, a devoted baseball fan and longtime pal of Steinbrenner's (convicted felon George Steinbrenner) was watching the exchange of lineups at home plate. He wore a dark suit and was, as always, impeccably groomed. He held a Yankee yearbook in his hand, waiting for the game to begin.

In the summer of 1969, baseball celebrated its one hundredth birthday as a professional sport. The All-Star game was being played in Washington, D.C., and all of the players on the American and National league teams were invited to a reception in the White House. Chalk up another sportswriting fringe benefit.

In the famous East Room, Nixon came out to address the large group. He spoke casually, reminiscing over how much he cared about baseball, what a fan he had been growing up in Whittier, California—long before the Brooklyn Dodgers and New York Giants moved west to California—and how he had always rooted for the Chicago White Sox. He did not explain why he selected that team. Then he began reciting the starting lineup for the White Sox in the late 1930s, an impressive baseball feat.

I was in the front section of the crowd, my press pass hanging from my neck, and my pencil recording in my notebook much of this for the next day's *New York Post*. This was the summer of 1969. I could not separate this baseball fan in front of me from the man who pursued the endless Vietnam War, ignored the protesters daily in the streets of America, and showed no signs of concern for the raging racial politics of the time.

Nixon looked out at the group, smiled shyly, and confessed, "If I had my life to live over I think I would be a sportswriter."

In a few minutes we were all in a line to shake hands with the President. I was standing near Baseball Commissioner Bowie Kuhn, baseball broadcaster Joe Garagiola, and Joe Reichler, a former aide to previous Baseball Commissioner William Eckert. Eckert had been nicknamed "The Unknown Soldier," by sportswriter Larry Fox of the *New York Daily News* upon his election, because no one knew who he was—other than a retired air force general. A secret service man was standing in the line next to President Nixon. Kuhn knew most of us and recited our names to the secret service man, who whispered it to the President. When my turn came the President shook my hand and said, "Glad to meet you, Maury."

"Thank you, Mr. President," I said. "I wish you *had* become a sportswriter."

The president had a quizzical look on his face. I wasn't

sure he heard me since there was so much conversation and so many people in the room. The United States Marine band might still have been playing, "Hail to the Chief." Garagiola, who clearly heard the remark, had a big grin on his face. Reichler, a longtime columnist with the Associated Press and now back with them after his turn with Eckert, had an impassive, glazed stare.

It is thirty years later and I can't recall now whether I planned to say something like that or not. I did have strong feelings against the war and strong feelings against Nixon for pursuing it. Maybe those emotions just slipped out.

Reichler put my remark to the President out over the Associated Press wires and I gave several interviews the next day about my "conversation" with the President. It got a little exaggerated. Some stories tend to grow in the retelling. I know the President either didn't hear it or clearly ignored it. I never forgot it, and those sportswriters who were there that day often remind me of it.

This particular evening, as Steinbrenner's special guest, there was a guard at the entrance to Steinbrenner's private suite. There was no way for me to greet Nixon, newly resurrected after Watergate, before the game.

The Yankees lost that first day but soon assumed their rightful position at the top of their division in early May. Howser had a talent for getting all of his players involved and keeping them interested over the long season.

Steinbrenner made a few cracks about Howser and a few about Michael during the season but mostly he stayed calm as the Yankees pushed ahead and stayed in first place.

Graig Nettles was out a good part of the season with hepatitis but still managed to agitate other players when he was around the clubhouse.

Piniella had not been playing much and wanted to discuss it with Howser. He knew that if he didn't get to show that he could still play, a new contract would not be in his future. The name "Piniella" was not on the list of the team's twenty-five most important players. Casey Stengel had once explained how a team is divided up.

"You don't have to bother with the first fifteen guys on a team," the Old Professor once said. "They are playing a lot and don't need any conversation. The next five guys on the team you might need, so you have to talk to them. The last five guys you almost never need, so you have to keep them away from the next five above them if you want a peaceful team."

Piniella had complained to several sportswriters about his lack of playing time, always a sore point with aging players. Howser overheard a few of these comments but said nothing. The Yankees were in Boston for a Series against the Red Sox when Howser struck. As the team moved out of the airport toward the bus that would take them to the team hotel, Howser moved to Piniella's side, looked at him for an instant, and then shouted, "Why don't you just brick it?"

Piniella was puzzled. As Howser moved on toward the waiting bus, Piniella went up to Nettles, repeated what Howser has just said, and asked him to explain it. Nettles was noted for his quips. He had once missed a Yankee hotel fan banquet and was fined by the club. "If they want a third baseman they have me," he said. "If they want an entertainer they should get George Jessel." The next day Nettles received a telegram from the legendary show business personality thanking him for the free publicity.

Now Nettles was the wordsmith who could explain Howser's crack to Piniella.

"Why don't you 'brick it'? Why don't you quit and get a job. Why don't you lay some bricks." Then Nettles laughed, "Are you going to 'brick it,' Lou?"

Piniella was not about to "brick it" since he could see the Yankees were on their way to another title and another chance at the World Series.

The season ended on October 5 against the Tigers with a remarkable 103-59 record under Howser. That gave him the distinction of becoming only the fourth manager in baseball history to win 100 or more games in his first year. Mickey Cochrane had won 101 with the 1934 Detroit Tigers, Ralph Houk had won 109 with the 1961 New York Yankees, and

Sparky Anderson had won 102 games with the 1970 Cincinnati Reds.

Now it was on to the playoffs again against the Kansas City Royals. This had become a bitterly contested series each year, with the Royals falling to the Yankees in the playoffs in 1976 to Chris Chambliss's homer and in 1977 and 1978 to overall Yankee depth. Another loss was anticipated by the stronger Yankees under Howser, against Jim Frey's Royals.

If one single play, one small baseball incident could describe an entire career, that occurred in the second game of the 1980 playoffs for the American League pennant between the Yankees and the Royals.

Run, Willie, run. That about summed it up.

Ron Guidry, surprisingly, had been hit hard in the first playoff game and the Royals won 7-2. Piniella, back in hitting form and not even remotely considering "bricking it," homered for the Yankees in the losing game.

The Yankees trailed 3-2 in the eighth inning. Willie Randolph, a fine base runner, was on first with two out, and Bob Watson, later to be a Yankee general manager in their 1996 pennant-winning year, was at bat. Watson crushed a long drive off the left center-field wall. The ball got out there quickly as Randolph took off around the bases. He made an awkward step around second base and picked up third base coach Mike Ferraro, a longtime buddy of Howser's, waving his arms. Run, Willie, run. Willie Wilson was the Kansas City outfielder and he had a weak arm. Ferraro knew that and he knew Randolph could run. He sent him home with the tying run. It never happened.

George Brett, the future Hall of Fame third baseman, picked off Wilson's weak throw toward the infield and fired a bullet to catcher Darrell Porter at the plate. A close play at the plate is one of baseball's most thrilling moments. Randolf came in hard, the throw was on the mark, and Porter's tag was perfect. Randolph was out.

George Steinbrenner was sitting in the lower stands during the game in a section reserved for Yankee wives and staff. He was standing as Randolph raced around third. Gene Michael, his general manager, was standing next to him. As Randolph was tagged out, a brilliant television director switched to the sight of Steinbrenner in the stands. He pulled his sweater off his body and waved derisively at the play at the plate.

At that instant, Dick Howser was gone as Yankees manager.

George reacted the way many fans reacted at the disappointment of the play. The only difference was simply that Steinbrenner's reaction was caught on national television with, oh, maybe seventy-five million people watching him wave derisively. George never really cared about embarrassing anybody publicly. He had embarrassed himself enough times to make that part of his routine.

Steinbrenner never quite explained what he had expected to happen on the play. Even a great runner can get thrown out on a close play. Babe Ruth was thrown out trying to steal—the last play of the 1926 Yankee Series loss to the St. Louis Cardinals. Miller Huggins was never seen waving at the Babe. Of course, Huggins was never seen. Big brother television, putting every player in a fan's living room, had not yet arrived.

The Yankees now had to beat the Royals three straight in Yankee Stadium for a chance at the World Series. This was not an impossible task. Tommy John had a 2-1 lead in the seventh inning of the third game. Willie Wilson doubled with two out and Howser walked slowly to the mound. He wanted Gossage.

It was a little early for Goose but this was playoff time. The big guy only had to get out weak-hitting U. L. Washington for the third out, get through the eighth and ninth, and bring the Yankees to within a game of tying. Few of us sitting in the press box thought it an impossible task. After all, the Yankees had been steadily pulling off miracles for about half a dozen years by now.

Washington was a fast runner, so fast that anything hit on the ground resulted in a close play. Washington hit a ball on the ground. Run, Willie, run. Willie Randolph ran hard again as the ball bounced over the mound, fielded it cleanly, fired it to first, and, shockingly, saw the safe sign from the first base umpire.

Now the Royals had the tying run and the lead run on first base. But the Yankees had Goose Gossage. For one of the rare big moments in his career, Goose was not equal to the challenge. The batter was George Brett. Brett had just missed a .400 season with a late slump that dropped him to .390. Ted Williams, with his 1941 .406 average, was safe again. Brett was having one of those miracle seasons great ballplayers occasionally have. The ball appears bigger. The bloops drop in. The line drives escape the outfielders. The long balls carry against or over the wall in all directions.

Gossage fired a fastball. Brett exploded at the plate. The ball went into the third deck at Yankee Stadium. End of story. Kansas City won 4-2 as Dan Quisenberry, a submarine right-hander, pitched three strong innings for the victory. Kansas City went to the World Series. The Yankees went home.

Jim Frey took his team to Philadelphia for the series. The Phillies were able to beat the Royals with ex-Mets left-hander Tug McGraw getting the final out at Veterans Stadium. Mounted Philadelphia policemen circled the field against any possible fan invasion, and a dozen angry dogs strained against police leashes in case the horses couldn't handle the job. Willie Wilson was the final Kansas City batter and McGraw later said, "With the dogs and horses out there I had to get him out or be eaten."

Steinbrenner was still emotional about the loss. He admitted he had talked to former Boston manager Don Zimmer, an old baseball friend, about coming to the Yankees to wave Randolph home next time—only if he knew for sure Randolph would score. Howser read about this in the Florida papers and was quoted as saying, "Managers should have the final say on who the third base coach is."

Uh-uh. Not on the Boss's team. No way. Steinbrenner always understood this kind of statement as a threat. Within a few days the papers were filled with stories about the managerial situation around the Yankees. Nobody was ever safe in that job.

Larry Wahl, the new publicity director, called me early on the morning of November 21 for a press conference in George Steinbrenner's Stadium office. It was always fun to sit in that soft fielder's chair, eat Steinbrenner's luncheons, talk about the shipbuilding business with the Boss, and analyze what really was being said and done.

The discussion seemed to bounce around a lot of topics for a while until it became clear that Howser would not be back as manager in 1981. Gene Michael would be the field manager, Cedric Tallis would be the general manager, and Bill Bergesch would be the assistant. Bergesch, a man of imposing size and girth, had been in baseball a long time, working for many years with the Cardinals and Yankees. He survived because he never rocked a boat. All he ever did out of the ordinary was eat a few extra hamburgers in the press room for dinner before games, earning the enduring nickname of Wimpy, comic strip character Popeye the Sailor Man's pal.

With Michael, Tallis, and Bergesch in attendance, Steinbrenner described how much Howser wanted to enjoy the real estate business in 1981. "Enjoy the real estate business in 1981," I wrote in my notebook. Then I looked at it. Why in hell would I write something like that about a man who had spent his entire adult life in baseball as a player, coach, manager, college coach, and division-winning Yankee skipper? George said it so I wrote it. I knew it didn't make any sense. While Steinbrenner was talking, Howser was sitting in the back of George's office, looking out over the quiet Stadium, watching a fall breeze blow the flags around, and thinking of many things. I knew the real estate business was not among them. Why was it so hard for George to say the words, "I fired him." He had fired Billy Martin a couple of times by now, fired coaches, fired publicity directors and Stadium executives. He fired secretaries by the dozens, often reconsidering the next day when they showed up. He would apologize by picking up the college education costs for their kids. He had fired drivers and parking lot attendants.

Anyway, this was the second most embarrassing press conference I had ever attended. The most embarrassing was when the Yankees under Ralph Houk as general manager hired Johnny Keane from the Cardinals after Yogi Berra was fired. Keane and Houk were both asked if there had been contact with Keane about the job while he was still the St. Louis manager the previous August. That would be a baseball illegality. Both denied it. The truth came out the next spring when Keane's daughter, who was dating Yankee first baseman Joe Pepitone during spring training, admitted it to *New York Post* sports columnist Milton Gross.

The man who said, "I did not have sex with that woman, Miss Lewinsky," was not the first public figure caught in a bold lie. Baseball should have a Pinocchio Hall of Fame for the lies told under press questioning.

It was later revealed that Howser *did* have some real estate interest. Steinbrenner had agreed to pay off the mortgage Howser had on his home in Tallahassee, Florida, some $200,000, if he would leave the Yankees quietly. Steinbrenner even admitted that losing the managerial skills of Howser—a knowledgeable, dedicated, intelligent baseball leader—was one of his grand mistakes. Not re-signing Reggie Jackson, when his contract was up after the 1981 season, was another self-admitted Steinbrenner mistake.

Gene Michael, my card playing buddy and as bright a guy as the game has ever introduced, would become the field leader in 1981. He had never been a star but somehow he had become important in the Yankees picture. He was one of George's favorites. George later made Lou Piniella, another favorite, a manager, and Bobby Murcer, the first player he complained about when he popped up in Steinbrenner's first 1973 spring game as Boss in Fort Lauderdale, would become a general manager. It paid well to be one of George's favorites.

Dick Howser went home to his mortgage-free house in Florida, played golf, did some fishing, spent some time with his wife, Nancy, and their two daughters, and waited for another phone call. He was on the managerial wheel now and knew the call would come.

The Royals got off slowly that next season and Howser became the manager of his former team. He rebuilt the club, used players carefully, avoided conflicts with the press, of whom there were almost none, remained on comfortable terms with owner Ewing Kauffman. Kauffman was a classic owner who was almost never around and was hardly ever involved in the team except for parties. The team was ready for a title by 1985.

Howser's Royals beat the St. Louis Cardinals in a tough seven-game Series in 1985 with Bret Saberhagen pitching an 11-0 shutout in the final game for the first Kansas City title. It ended the frustration for all those years of losing the playoffs to the Yankees, finally beating them in 1980, and then losing the championship to the Phillies.

Now Howser was a man about town, a heroic Kansas City figure, a public celebrity who could dine freely in any KC restaurant, get his shoes shined for nothing in the town's best hotels, and have cabdrivers refuse his generous tips.

At the age of forty-nine, he had escaped the stress of working for Steinbrenner, had become ever so comfortable and heroic a figure in Kansas City, and seemed destined to become one of those long-serving baseball managers, admired by his players and deeply loved by the fans.

A year later he started suffering headaches. He thought the headaches were only from the strain of pitching batting practice and so he stopped doing that. His neck hurt and his eyes would water occasionally for no reason. He felt dizzy a few times and even fell a couple of times in hotel rooms. Finally he decided to see a doctor.

The news, after a series of tests, was as bad as it could be. Dick Howser was suffering from a rapidly growing tumor in the brain.

Why him? With all the brilliance of modern day science, why should anyone have to suffer from a brain tumor? With all the available medicines and all the machines, with all the present day knowledge, no one can tell who will be hit with these damaging, destructive ailments. Why should this man be struck down?

The newspapers were filled with optimistic stories about Howser, about his treatment, about his condition. In 1986 he had to leave the club and turn over managerial duties to his old pal, Mike Ferraro, who had gone with him to Kansas City. Then there were several months in 1987 when there were few stories out of Kansas City about Howser. His name was hardly mentioned in New York where the new manager of the Yankees, the new episodes under Steinbrenner, the new heroes and villains filled the back pages of the *Post* and the *News* and the sports pages of the *Times*.

On June 17, 1987, the *Associated Press* moved a story onto the wires across the country. Dick Howser, manager of the 1985 World Champion Kansas City Royals and former manager of the New York Yankees, was dead. He was fifty-one years old.

I wrote a story in the *Post* about him, recalling that afternoon in Yankee Stadium in George Steinbrenner's office. I said, even now, I could not understand why the manager of the New York Yankees would "resign" to go into the real estate business.

Ironically and coincidentally, on September 30, 1998, former Kansas City relief pitcher Dan Quisenberry, Howser's tower of strength in the championship year, also died of a brain tumor. He was fifty-five years old.

Why?

CHAPTER

FOURTEEN

On December 15, 1980, George Steinbrenner signed Dave Winfield as a free agent from San Diego. Steinbrenner spent the next ten years eating out his right *and* left ventricles over that one.

Winfield's agents, business managers, lawyers, and handlers had hookwinked George. It wasn't that Winfield couldn't play; it was that George couldn't count. They slipped a cost-of-living clause into Winfield's contract that changed the worth of the deal from a piddling $21.1 million dollar deal over ten seasons into a $23 million plus deal over that time. Steinbrenner got agitated every time he thought about that and never could escape the feeling that this one player, as good as he was, had embarrassed him. No one embarrasses the Boss without paying.

Winfield paid plenty. He was never accepted as an important Yankee. He was criticized by Steinbrenner and his flunkies every chance they had. They suddenly loved Reggie Jackson. Steinbrenner clearly indicated that Winfield was no Jackson. Jackson had starred in fall playoffs and World Series games and had earned the title of "Mr. October." Steinbrenner labeled Winfield "Mr. May" for his postseason failures. There were constant battles over payments to the David Winfield Foundation, a charity group the outfielder had set up to help underprivileged kids and aid his own financial structure through tax write-offs. There was the 1984 batting race when Winfield hit .340 and teammate Don Mattingly edged him out with a .343 average. Many Yankee teammates and sources close to Steinbrenner whispered that they were happy about that.

There was, finally, the Howard Spira episode at the end of

Winfield's stay in New York, when a sleazeball character from the Bronx ingratiated himself to Steinbrenner with promises he would expose Winfield's wrongdoings.

Spira was a convicted gambler and tax cheat who surfaced one day around the Yankee clubhouse. No one knew who he was or what he did. Somehow he had credentials and would be allowed into the Yankees clubhouse. He was thin, bony-faced, pale in complexion with slicked black hair and an ever-present camel hair overcoat. It could be July and one hundred degrees outside, but Howie Spira wore that camel hair coat. He sat in the Yankees dugout, ate in the press room with members of the press (never me), worked his way upstairs to the press level, talked rapidly, and hung on. He was a professional hanger-on.

Steinbrenner would eventually pay Spira forty thousand dollars to dig up dirt on Winfield. Steinbrenner earned his second baseball suspension for that one, and later Spira earned some time in the slammer.

I never saw Spira on the road with the club but I saw him often around the clubhouse. Sportswriting is a profession where you can have a lot of fun. It's a fine profession, and one of which I'm proud to be a part. Spira just made you feel dirty. Every time I saw him I wanted to rush home and take a long shower.

Winfield was from St. Paul, Minnesota, and had starred in three sports—baseball, basketball, and football at the University of Minnesota. He was a big guy, six feet six inches tall, weighed a lean 220 pounds, could run, hit, and throw. He was handsome, with a full mustache, a wide smile, and a magnificent voice. He played twenty-three big league seasons, batted .283, and hit 465 homers. I will vote for him as a Hall of Famer when he becomes eligible, after the year 2000. It should be interesting to see how many of my colleagues will go along with me.

The Yankees got off well under new manager Gene Michael. More significantly the papers were filled with stories about a possible strike that would shut down baseball. Sure enough, that happened on June 11, when the strike was called and big league ballplayers suddenly had to haul their own suitcases to airports, make their own plane reservations home, pay their own taxi fares, and arrange for their own airport pickups. What was this life coming to, anyway?

In a few days, the out-of-work big league players resorted to golf games at local courses, summer swimming pool time with their own children, barbecues in their own backyards, and fights with their own wives. Baseball families are not used to having the breadwinner around during the season with discussions of transportation for the kids, recreational activities, and giddy gossip on the agenda.

This was best explained in 1961 when George Weiss, the fired general manager of the New York Yankees, spent an entire year at home, the first in his professional career after being in the game more than forty years. Finally the new team in town, the New York Mets, asked him to help build their organization. He started off well by hiring Casey Stengel, guaranteeing space in the newspapers and a few laughs.

At the first Mets press conference announcing the signing of Weiss, his lovely wife, Hazel, was asked what it was like having George around after so many years as a working baseball executive.

"I married him for better or worse," smiled Hazel Weiss, "but not for lunch."

Hazel Weiss became a heroine to many baseball wives after that, and to many wives around the country who stole that classic line. With the growing number of women in the workplace, lunch was out of the question for many stay-at-home men, and dinner wasn't too certain, either.

There was one other factor quietly at play as the strike dragged on. None of the players talked about it. It was their little secret and we sportswriters kept silent on the matter as well. This was the disappointment many women known in the trade as Baseball Annies were suffering around the country. They missed having quiet moments with their baseball-playing friends.

Professional ballplayers are young men, some athletically handsome, certainly wealthy, and desperately in need of friendly faces while in strange cities. There were regulars in lots of towns.

One nut, Ruth Ann Steinhagen, took it to an extreme when she collected photos of Philadelphia Phillies first baseman Eddie Waitkus, invited him to her room, and then shot him as he walked in. Waitkus survived and continued his career. It was a warning to all of them, but it did not slow down the clandestine meetings.

Richie Ashburn, the Philadelphia center fielder when Waitkus was shot and one of the game's wittiest fellows, always kidded that Steinhagen (not Steinbrenner, now) was really after *him*.

"I was Eddie's roommate," said Ashburn. "She just got us mixed up."

Baseball romances—following the code of traveling salesmen, cross-country truck drivers, and, okay—sportswriters—always remained a secret. If a player was ever caught by family or friend, he followed the code of the road: Deny, deny, deny.

A handsome Brooklyn Dodgers right-handed pitcher with the odd name of Kirby Higbe best demonstrated this technique in the 1940s when the Dodgers visited the St. Louis Cardinals at Sportsmen's Park. This was the farthest outpost for big league players before the Brooklyn Dodgers and New York Giants moved out west.

Higbe romanced a lovely lady for several days while the Dodgers were in St. Louis and then moved on to the team's next stop on the road, in Chicago. When the pitcher was out fishing in Brooklyn on an off day, a package arrived at Ebbets Field. Clubhouse man Babe Hamburger accepted it for Higbe and then decided to bring it to the player's home.

Higbe's wife opened the package and saw a pair of his pajamas, scented with his gal pal's perfume, a Brooklyn schedule with the team's next visit to St. Louis circled in lipstick, and a beautifully written note tucked inside. Higbe's wife read the note and fumed as the writer complimented the pitcher on his lovemaking, admitted she was counting the days until the club's next visit, and congratulated him on his last pitching performance.

Some hours passed before the unsuspecting, tired pitcher returned from a day at sea with some teammates and pals. His wife heaved the package at him and demanded he explain the note with its lurid suggestiveness.

Higbe read the note carefully and slowly, turned the paper over, and stared at the Ebbets Field, Brooklyn, address on the outside.

Then he shook his head and confidently announced, "This isn't for *me*. This is for some *other* Kirby Higbe."

The gag line, "It's for some *other* Kirby Higbe," has survived in baseball press boxes across America for half a century.

Now the restless striking players played golf, studied the stock market, went fishing or hunting, drank beer at friendly barbecues, and strongly supported their esteemed leader, lawyer Marvin Miller. He had won free agency for them and now he was about to win another strong contract.

It all ended in early August. The players were back, the sportswriters stopped posing as legal and financial experts, and the fans, their anger lessened, quickly returned to their teams.

The Yankees had won the first half of the race, as the agreement indicated, allowing them into a playoff with the second-half winner. Steinbrenner grew restless as the Yankees moved slowly through their final fifty games. They were saving themselves for the playoffs.

Nobody could convince George that the players knew better than he did how to get ready for postseason play. Instead of remaining quiet and calm (George be quiet and calm?) he harassed Gene Michael to distraction, telling the press that the Yankees weren't hustling, weren't serious about the season, and no way would be ready for the playoffs. Michael took it all personally.

"If he wants to fire me, let him get it over with," Stick Michael blurted out to a reporter.

On September 6, 1981, Michael was fired and replaced

again by Bob Lemon. It was George's version of musical chairs.

The Yankees and Milwaukee Brewers would compete in the strike playoff for the right to move on against the west division champion, the Oakland A's, under a manager named Billy Martin.

The Yankees won the first two games of the playoff, lost the next two, and were greeted early before the final game. George Steinbrenner and company marched into the Yankee clubhouse, together with all the Yankee front office personnel, his personal valet, his driver, his pal Bill Fugazy, the limousine king, and assorted public relations people. He looked like General Douglas MacArthur aboard the deck of the *Missouri* in Tokyo Bay.

"I want to tell you guys that if you lose this game today you'll be the laughingstock of New York," Steinbrenner bellowed. "Your neighbors won't talk to you, your families won't talk to you, your friends won't want to talk to you. You'll be embarrassed to leave your houses. You'll be known as losers, the most famous losers in baseball history, the first team to lose a playoff for the division. That's what everybody will remember you for."

George had something there. As a young reporter I once wrote a critical story about the New York Mets, and my teacher, hero, and professor, Casey Stengel, explained why I should be more gentle in print. Stengel pointed out that only ballplayers have their work recorded each day in public. A player who fails to get a hit in four tries sees oh-for-four in the box score clearly registered next to his name. A pitcher who gives up a home run sees that clearly reported in the box score.

"How would you like it if your stories in the paper were measured each day, a good one, a bad one, oh-for-four on this reporting day, and all your neighbors knew you wrote horseshit that day?" Stengel demanded.

If doctors, lawyers, writers, engineers, truck drivers, delivery men, and street sweepers had their work recorded publicly each day society's structure might be severely al-tered. Perhaps with better results? Perhaps worse? Different, certainly.

Steinbrenner was trying hard to reach his players, to move them, to motivate them to win the most important game of the year. He moved around the clubhouse, paused in front of the locker of catcher Rick Cerone, and began berating him. Cerone, the Munson successor, had handled that emotional chore in 1980 with style and grace. He hit .277 and led the Yankees pitchers. When he broke a thumb early in 1981 his production fell to a .244 average.

Steinbrenner said Cerone's hitting was weak, his catching stank, and he clearly wasn't the player he had been the year before.

"Go fuck yourself, George," Cerone whispered, loud enough for Steinbrenner and most of the players to hear and all of the sportswriters to learn about after the meeting.

That ended the meeting. Steinbrenner and his entourage stormed out. Cerone was on George's shit list for quite some time after that—even more so when he defeated the Yankees in an arbitration ruling the following year.

Steinbrenner forgets nothing. He forgives most everything. Later, when Cerone was traded to Atlanta, Steinbrenner said how competitive he was. He talked about what a tough kid Cerone was and eventually hired him as a Yankee broadcaster. Cerone went on to buy a minor league baseball team in Newark, New Jersey, not far from where he grew up and not far from Seton Hall University, where he spent his days of college glory. Cerone's team, the Newark Bears, brought minor league baseball back to his hometown in 1999, fifty years after it had disappeared. Typically, George Steinbrenner gave plenty of support to Cerone for his team.

The Yankees beat Milwaukee that day for the Eastern title, swept Billy Martin's Oakland A's for the pennant, and celebrated the triumph at Vincent's Restaurant in downtown Oakland. It was a raucous party with players and their wives joining for a wonderful evening.

Wise old Casey Stengel, in the game for over sixty years, also had a theory about baseball wives. "Keep them apart,"

Stengel always said. One or two wives together at a game is a social event. Six or eight together could lead to wars, the pitcher's wife complaining about the shortstop's play and the third baseman's wife suggesting the first baseman had bad hands on his low throw.

Add a couple of drinks to a party and anything is possible. At the victory party in Oakland, the beautiful wife of third baseman Graig Nettles, Ginger, put her purse on a chair and moved to the food line for the buffet. When she returned her purse was gone and one of Reggie Jackson's guests was in the chair.

Reggie Jackson had been married as a young college student to a beautiful Mexican American lady named Jennie Campos. She was long gone from his life now and Jackson consistently replaced her with dozens and dozens of attractive women, most of them blond and beautiful. Graig Nettles didn't like the idea that his wife had to search for her purse—later discovered nearby on the floor—while Reggie's friends took over the area.

There were words between the two stars and soon punches. Jackson got the worst of it. End of party.

The Yankees played hard and fought harder. This was not always the case with baseball teams. The Mets once had a field fight with the San Francisco Giants. Willie Mays, Willie McCovey, and Juan Marichal knocked over half a dozen young Mets. The *New York Post* headline the next day read, "They Can't Fight, Either."

The Yankees could fight on and off the field.

The Yankees won the first two World Series games against Tommy Lasorda's Dodgers and lost the next three in Los Angeles. George Steinbrenner took some of the pressure off his losing team by showing up in the hotel lobby prior to the flight from Los Angeles back to New York with a bandaged hand. He told the press he had gotten into an argument with two guys in the hotel elevator and had hurt his hand punching them out.

"I clocked them," Steinbrenner said. "There are two guys in this town looking for their teeth."

Lou Piniella was standing outside the crowd of reporters as Steinbrenner told his story to the press. He turned to teammate Bobby Murcer and in a loud voice asked Murcer, "Did you find the teeth?" Murcer became hysterical. Reporters searched the grounds for guys without teeth. They couldn't be found. Despite insistent questioning, Steinbrenner stuck by his tale. Maybe George will devote a chapter to the episode in his memoirs.

The Yankees were beaten 9-2 in the final Series game in New York. Relief pitcher George Frazier lost for the third time, an unheard of World Series feat for a relief pitcher, and Dave Winfield went one for twenty-two, an .045 Series average. It irritated many of his teammates when he asked the umpires to save the baseball for him after his first Series hit.

After the Series ended, Steinbrenner was unavailable to the press. He was busy drafting a concession speech, apologizing for what he had put the city of New York through.

It did not rank in eloquence with the Gettysburg Address or Washington's Farewell at Fraunces Tavern. It was simply a statement in which he apologized for the play of his team in the Series and promised that it would not happen again.

It certainly wouldn't. The Yankees would not get into another World Series for fifteen years.

CHAPTER

FIFTEEN

Baseball players are very competitive individuals. They have, in most cases, been involved in sports competition ever since they were children. They star and win at Little League, at American Legion baseball, at Babe Ruth ball, in high school and college, and in every form of amateur sport until they are signed as professionals. They do not take defeat easily.

The Yankees finished fifth in 1982. It was not a pleasant year to be around them.

Ralph Kiner, the Mets broadcaster and former Pittsburgh Pirate home run slugger and later Hall of Famer, best explained the competitive fire that rages inside a professional athlete.

Kiner was once married to Nancy Chaffee, a national tennis champion. They lived in a beautiful home outside of Palm Springs with a tennis court on their property and a golf course just outside their front gate. During the quiet winter off-seasons away from the home run race, Kiner and Chaffee often played tennis in the backyard of their sprawling home. It did not mean either forgot the essence of competition.

"I could never beat Nancy," Kiner once explained. "She was a wonderful player, of course, but I was a pro baseball player. I couldn't beat my own wife in tennis. I would not give up until I did."

One morning Kiner played well and had Nancy in trouble. It actually got to match point for the baseball star. Kiner was serving to his wife. He held the tennis ball in his hand, threw it up carefully, and followed through hard with a strong serve. The ball landed clearly inside the serving line, bounced off Nancy's racquet, and dribbled to the outside of the court. Kiner had won the match, finally won, finally defeated his wife at her own game. He leaped joyously into the air.

"The next morning," Kiner continued, "she delivered our first son."

Maybe that tennis defeat had something to do with the breakup of the marriage between Kiner and Nancy Chaffee. Years later, Kiner was traveling in France on his first vacation trip overseas when a French vineyard owner spotted him in a tourist crowd. The winery man had lived in Pittsburgh, where his father worked in international trade, during those years when Kiner was winning home run titles. He asked Kiner to wait a few moments while he went down into his cave for a bottle of wine.

He brought up a dusty bottle and presented it to Kiner saying, "This bottle, on the open market, would be worth two thousand dollars."

"When will I ever have the occasion to open a bottle of wine worth two thousand dollars?" questioned Kiner.

"When your former wife, Nancy Chaffee, remarries," the winery man said.

It took more than thirty years before Kiner could take that advice and pop the cork on that expensive wine. Eventually he celebrated his former wife's remarriage to another broadcaster, Jack Whitaker.

Professional athletes of every sport understand the elements and significance of competition. Green Bay Packers coach Vince Lombardi said winning wasn't everything, "It was," he said, "the *only* thing."

The Yankees didn't win much in 1982. They finished fifth with a 79-82 record, went through three managers, saw new players such as Ken Griffey (Junior's dad), Dave Collins, Roy Smalley, and Butch Wynegar join the team, and watched Reggie Jackson sign with California. He hit thirty-nine homers and knocked in 101 runs for the Angels, showing no signs of slowing down.

Jackson was a complicated human being. True, he had a

massive ego but as Muhammad Ali once said, "It ain't brag-
gin' if you can do it." Jackson could almost always do it—
and he did it with a flair not seen around the Stadium since
Babe Ruth. No player since Jackson has been able to match
either his triumphs or his style.

Winfield was having some fine seasons for the Yankees in
the early 1980s, six out of seven years with a hundred or
more runs batted in, the almost batting title in 1984, and
strong home run seasons, including thirty-seven in his peak
1982 power year. There was never any of the Jackson
charisma around him.

Most of the off-field stories about Winfield had to do with
the Winfield Foundation, what Steinbrenner was supposed
to contribute, how the money was controlled, where the
money would be spent, who would eventually profit from
this group. It became far too tangled for most sportswriters
to deal with and we left it to the *Times* to explain it to the rest
of us.

While the reporters from the *News,* the *Post,* and Long Island's *Newsday* seemed to concentrate on the new pitcher
for the Yankees, the new second baseman, the new funny
guy coming to the clubhouse, the *Times* saw baseball as another business aspect of the American economy. The *Times'*
coverage of the Yankees read the same as their coverage of
General Motors.

While the players were deep in heated competition, certainly recognized by the public, the sportswriters competed
in a more subtle way. My idea was to write the lighter,
brighter stuff with as much humanity as possible. After all,
these were guys with wives, kids, families, and mortgages.
That's what I hoped readers would be more interested in
than the complicated details of their free-agent contracts.

My wife, Janet, once came up with an Oscar Wilde quote
out of Bartlett's that about summed up the relationship I had
with the other sportswriters, the relationship most sportswriters seemed to have with each other.

"It is not enough that I succeed," Wilde wrote, "my enemies must also fail."

Gene Michael had replaced Bob Lemon early in 1982 after Steinbrenner decided Lemon was too tired to continue and Michael had been replaced late in the season by longtime Yankees front office aide Clyde King.

King, a dead ringer for Superman's alter ego Clark Kent, had broken in as a pitcher for the Brooklyn Dodgers in 1944 as an eighteen-year-old right-hander out of Goldsboro, North Carolina. He had been a teammate of Jackie Robinson's in 1947 when Robinson broke into big league baseball as the game's first black player. King, a southern gentleman, had gotten along well with Robinson. King was a God-fearing man and believed strongly that all men were the children of God. King was more determined to establish himself as a Dodger pitcher than he was to combat any social turmoil imposed by Dodgers owner Branch Rickey with the Robinson signing.

He had his best year with the Dodgers when he was 14-7 in 1951, a year that will live in infamy for all Brooklyn fans—me among them. I had grown up in Brooklyn, rooted madly for the Dodgers, spent many thrilling afternoons in the bleachers in Ebbets Field, and dreamed of one day becoming Pee Wee Reese's successor as Dodgers shortstop. I always kissed Pee Wee's 1955 Brooklyn World Series ring when I saw him each summer in Cooperstown at the Baseball Hall of Fame weekend.

I was saddened in July 1999 when Pee Wee's pal, Rex Bradley, a Hillerich and Bradsby Bat Company executive from Louisville, told me Pee Wee wasn't well enough to make the Hall of Fame weekend trip to Cooperstown, New York.

"Send him my love," I told Bradley.

He said that he would talk to Pee Wee as soon as he got home to Louisville.

On August 14, 1999, the Captain of the Brooklyn Dodgers, Harold (Pee Wee) Reese died after a long, brave fight against lung cancer. He was only eighty-one. The famous Brooklyn Dodgers infield of Gil Hodges, Jackie Robinson, Reese, and Billy Cox was now gone. But never,

ever forgotten, especially among those who remember their deeds in Ebbets Field at Bedford Avenue and Sullivan Place in Brooklyn.

Clyde King was probably better known in New York for his doings with the Dodgers than he was for his executive time with the Yankees.

King never threw very hard but he had a good curve ball, excellent control, and was a smart pitcher. He maximized his limited baseball skills with an abundance of baseball intelligence. He was smart enough to be injured on October 3, 1951, when the Dodgers played the New York Giants in the third game of the 1951 National League pennant playoff.

When manager Charlie Dressen replaced starter Don Newcombe, who had grown tired in the ninth with starter Ralph Branca, who had pitched in the first game, King was on the bullpen bench. He simply couldn't pitch because of an arm injury. Bullpen coach Clyde Sukeforth made the fatal response to Dressen's phone call about which of the two pitchers warming up, Branca or Carl Erskine, he should bring in; Sukeforth replied, "Erskine just bounced his curve ball." That meant he did not have control of his best pitch, a sinking curveball to a right-handed hitter such as Bobby Thomson, waiting to bat, and the next scheduled hitter, a rookie named Willie Mays.

Branca came in, Thomson hit the Shot Heard Round the World, and King sat stoically on the bench.

"Ralph and I were the closest of friends," King said recently. "I felt more pain for him giving up that homer than if I had done it myself."

History little notes nor long remembers pitchers who don't get into historic games. Ralph Branca's obituary will make the front page of the *New York Times*. Clyde King's won't.

King was a student of the game and studied the Yankees the last few weeks as manager. Nobody expected him to stay on and the managerial chairs moved again on January 11, 1983, when Billy Martin, of all people, was named manager of the Yankees for the third time.

Steinbrenner had this strange fascination with Billy Martin. It was a wonderful love-hate relationship. When Billy won, as he did in 1977, Steinbrenner couldn't stop falling over himself in admiration of Billy. When he didn't win, he second-guessed him in the press, called him constantly in the clubhouse, belittled him publicly, and threatened constantly to fire him.

Billy, for his part, was far too emotional, too attached, too dependent on his connection with the Yankees. It was the weapon Steinbrenner used constantly against him.

The Yankees bounced around most of the 1983 season but couldn't really threaten the hot Baltimore Orioles of manager Earl Weaver. There seems to be an ebb and flow to baseball seasons and once a team establishes its position it is difficult to catch them. Unless they happen to be the Red Sox.

Nobody was catching Baltimore that year.

The highlight of the year came on July 4, 1983. It happened to be Steinbrenner's birthday and he had a little gathering in his office prior to the game. A few friends toasted the Boss, congratulated him on some recent moves in improving the club, and thanked him for allowing them to enjoy the status of the owner's box.

Then Dave Righetti went out to pitch.

Righetti was a handsome kid from San Jose, California, twenty-four years old that summer, a hard-throwing left-handed pitcher. Indications of greatness often showed in his appearances. He won fourteen games that year and lasted sixteen years in the big leagues. He would never have a better season than he did in 1983.

Righetti had a blazing fastball that day, a crackling curve and excellent control. He pitched a no-hitter against the Red Sox as Steinbrenner partied upstairs. It was the first Stadium no-hitter since Allie Reynolds had done it in 1951.

When the game was over Righetti was aglow in the Yankee clubhouse, reminiscing about his days as a young pitcher in California, talking about how he had always followed the Yankees as a kid, and hoping the no-hitter would lead to a steadier, more successful career.

In a few minutes a magnum of champagne arrived in the clubhouse. It had been sent down from Steinbrenner's office and was placed in Righetti's locker as he talked to the press. The note with it simply read, "Congratulations. I knew you could do it. Have a nice dinner tonight." Wrapped around the bottle was an envelope with a one thousand dollar check in it signed by George M. Steinbrenner.

Not much changed for the Yankees after the Righetti no-hitter. The team—changed again with the addition of a high-quality player, Don Baylor, and a low-quality ball player, Steve Kemp—was not a serious factor in the pennant race.

Billy Martin seemed to have lost his fire. He was more concerned with what Steinbrenner might be saying to us about him each day than he seemed to be in winning. When Billy's buddy Art Fowler was fired as pitching coach it was clear that Billy's days as Yankee skipper were numbered again.

Martin could be tense and angry one afternoon and calm and thoughtful the next. Here he was—the Civil War buff, who read many histories and was always willing to discuss the moves of Grant, Sherman, and McClellen as a diversion from the moves of Steinbrenner. It always amazed me that a man of such intensity could show that poised, calm, historic side at any moment.

Billy Martin got really mad at me only once that year. I had accepted a $3,000 magazine assignment from Larry Flynt's *Hustler* magazine to do a profile on Billy. I was off the day the magazine came out, and Billy screamed about me to the other members of the press covering the club. He wasn't mad that I had written about him in a magazine that touched the edges of pornography. He was angry that I had written about one of his romantic interludes when he was a single man.

He was now happily married and when I arrived at the park the next day he screamed, "Are you trying to ruin my marriage?"

I told him I hoped his marriage to his wife, Gretchen, would last forever. I was only describing his full life in the article. He finally calmed down and said of the girl I had described in the article, "Well, she *was* good-looking. Mickey (Mantle) had her later on."

My garage mechanic made me a hero in my own neighborhood. When I pulled in to have my gas tank filled he pulled out the *Hustler* magazine from behind a counter, asked me to sign the article, and wondered if I could get Billy to sign it, too.

"Boy, they have great articles like yours in here all the time," he said, as he held open a page to a photograph of a naked woman. "I never miss an issue."

On July 24, only twenty days after the Righetti no-hitter, one of the strangest occurrences in baseball history transpired at the Stadium. George Brett of the Kansas City Royals hit a huge homer off Goose Gossage to put the Royals up in the ninth, 5-4. Billy Martin asked the umpires to examine the bat, and when they did, they discovered that pine tar, the sticky stuff that helps hitters hold on to bats while swinging with sweaty hands, was above the eighteen-inch mark on the bat. This was a rule violation. No one in the park, except maybe for Martin, had ever heard of such a technicality.

Brett was suddenly called out and the homer nullified. Enraged, Brett came charging out of the Kansas City dugout at the home plate umpire. Only quick action by other umpires and several players saved Brett from a physical confrontation that might have caused him to be banned from baseball.

When Brett was inducted into baseball's Hall of Fame in Cooperstown on July 25, 1999, more fans in the audience recalled *that* incident than his run at .400. He finished with a .390 average in 1980.

Many baseball players get ten or fifteen years in the game, play quietly, retire or are released when no longer useful to the club. They disappear forever from the public scene. No baseball fan ever forgets Ralph Branca, Bobby Thomson, Chris Chambliss, Bucky Dent, or George Brett for one memorable instant incident.

The Kansas City protest was upheld by League president

Lee MacPhail, the home run stood, and the game was ordered finished with the Royals ahead 5-4. Billy Martin emphasized his protest by playing pitcher Ron Guidry in center field in the top of the ninth, putting left-handed throwing first baseman Don Mattingly at second, and having his team walk through the bottom of the ninth.

Kansas City reliever Dan Quisenberry, later the victim of a fatal brain tumor, retired the Yankees in the bottom of the ninth without effort in an uncaring finale to the weird event.

Dave Winfield may or may not make the Hall of Fame, yet no Yankee fan will ever forget when he was arrested in Toronto during a warmup for knocking a seagull out of the sky with an errant throw.

Winfield later played for the Blue Jays, and one Toronto paper suggested all was forgiven. The gulls could come back to the Stadium. Winfield's record had been wiped clean.

The fans quickly forgot the 1983 season. The Yankees had won the World Series in 1977 and 1978, got close in 1981, and now were ready to rebuild again for another shot at the October Classic.

They wouldn't rebuild with Martin. Yogi Berra was named manager of the team on December 16, 1983, for his second tour as Yankees skipper and Martin was assigned to scouting duties.

Another future Hall of Famer, Phil Niekro, the former Atlanta Braves knuckleballer, was signed as a free agent while two Yankees who had done so much for the team, third baseman Graig Nettles and relief pitcher Goose Gossage, moved on to finish out their declining careers elsewhere.

What was evident to baseball executives and baseball fans alike was that the loyalty and dedication to teams, so significant in baseball history, was now being destroyed by free agency. Almost ever successful player was motivated by a new contract with another team. If the old line for detectives had been *Cherchez la femme,* look for the woman in solving their most difficult cases, the new line for baseball had quickly become, in Watergate words, *Follow the money.*

Marvin Miller, executive director of the Major League

Baseball Players Association, had revolutionized the game as players sought free agency, huge contracts, greater security, and better playing conditions. Ballplayers were now acting like industrial management CEOs. They were chasing big contracts, and loyalty be damned.

This would be a factor in taking some of the romance out of the game in the final years of the twentieth century.

CHAPTER

SIXTEEN

In the early 1950s half a dozen Yankees—Mickey Mantle, Whitey Ford, Billy Martin, Hank Bauer, Tom Sturdivant, and Yogi Berra—bought property together in central Florida.

The idea was to keep the inexpensive property, about $1,000 an acre, and build retirement homes on it when they were finished with baseball. That would put all of these players, and friends who visited, close together for hunting and fishing trips, family retirement barbecues, wonderful reminiscences, and lifelong friendships.

The purchase of the property, whatever happened to it in the future, appealed to all of the players, none making more than fifty or sixty thousand dollars a year at the time.

A relief pitcher named John Wyatt, famed for a Vaseline ball, with the greasy stuff coming out of a large jar he kept in his locker, played for Kansas City in the 1960s and for the Yankees for a short while. He always talked about the property he owned and was constantly buying.

When I asked him one day why he owned and purchased so much property, he replied, "The only thing on God's earth that always goes up in value is God's earth."

While so many players bought property, and later made profit on the purchase, as developments and shopping centers sprung up over ground they once expected to use for private homes, the Yankees talked of their companionship in retirement.

One thing led to another and they began selling off—for $5,000 an acre for the three or four acres they owned, or $10,000 an acre, or even $15,000 for the players who held out the longest. Wyatt seemed to be right. "God's earth" never went down in value.

All the players had sold off their property by the late 1950s except for Lawrence Peter Berra. Then came the phone calls.

Every day for several weeks Berra's lawyer was called about a deal for the property. Berra refused to sell. The price continued to rise. Berra refused to sell. The price continued to rise.

One day Berra's lawyer received a phone call. "We *must* have that property," the lawyer representing the proposed buyer said. "Just name a price, any price, just name it. We want to close the deal."

Berra's lawyer named a price, a ridiculous price, a price so huge it sounded as though, if the prospective buyer wanted it, he must be purchasing all of Florida.

The buyer wanted it. He paid the price. Yogi would only laugh later and say, "Ask my lawyer" when the price was being questioned. The buyer *had* to have that property in central Florida.

The land once owned by Mantle, Ford, Martin, Bauer, and Sturdivant, purchased modestly, plus the parcel owned by Berra, purchased extravagantly, is now part of Disney World.

Lucky Yogi.

This land deal was typical of Yogi. Players often said that whatever Yogi touched turned to gold. As a player he almost always won. As a hitter he almost always got the big hit. He won three MVP titles. He played on more Yankee pennant winners than anyone.

He managed the Yankees to a pennant in 1964 despite losing his shortstop, Tony Kubek, and his great star, Mickey Mantle, who missed a good part of the pennant run with injuries.

General manager Ralph Houk then fired Berra because he thought he had lost control of the club, made up mostly of former teammates.

I visited him that night in his handsome, sprawling Tudor home in Montclair, New Jersey, in 1964. He wasn't upset. Comforted by his wife, Carmen, and three strong sons, he knew life would go on.

The next day Casey Stengel called and hired him to coach the New York Mets.

When Gil Hodges died of a massive heart attack in 1972, Berra was picked as the next Mets manager.

He won a pennant in 1973 for the Mets and lost the seventh game of the Series. Yogi became a more sympathetic figure when it was leaked that owner M. Donald Grant had forced Berra to switch pitchers to get Tom Seaver and Jon Matlack into the final rotation instead of a journeyman having a big year named George Stone.

When Berra was the manager of the Yankees in 1964 a scary airplane flight forced shortstop Tony Kubek to visit a card store in Minneapolis. Fake newspaper headlines could be made up there. Kubek brought a sheet of newspapers with the fake headline to the next trip.

Kubek's headline read, "Yankees Crash: Berra Only Survivor."

If Berra's good fortune became legendary, his face was even more legendary. Could there possibly be a more recognizable person in a crowd in America than Yogi Berra?

In the 1970s, while he managed the Mets, Berra and wife Carmen hosted a party for the press during spring training. This was an annual ritual in which the manager, the coaches, and the press had a chance to relax together for an evening, trade off-the-record stories, and get a little closer to each other.

I have always told young sportswriters that the most important part of any season is spring training. That is when the manager, coaches, and players are most relaxed and most cordial. Winning does not matter. It is a time to prepare for the season and build contacts. A spring training beer together may be the opportunity for a big late season story.

Yogi and Carmen Berra sat at the head of a large table in the St. Petersburg Yacht Club. The other coaches and their wives were nearby and the press members sat with their wives at the opposite end.

A middle-aged woman, wearing a flowered dress, coiffed hair, and a stupid smile, walked up to Yogi with a huge menu in her hand.

"Sign this," she demanded.

Yogi, almost always pleasant about these constant interruptions, was upset at her pushy manner. He simply said to her, "I'll sign it after I've finished dinner."

She growled and walked away. Another round of drinks was served. She was back again. Yogi repeated what he had said before. She left again. The first appetizer was served. Now she was back for a third time, a little more obnoxious, a little louder, and far more drunk.

"Please, Yogi, sign it for her," implored Carmen Berra. Translation: Let's get rid of her.

The fan thrust the large menu in Berra's face. Yogi took a pen out of his jacket pocket and held up the menu.

"Sign it to my son, Donnie, with best regards and congratulations from your best pal, Yogi Berra," she demanded.

"I won't do that," said Berra, terribly annoyed now at the interruption.

"You won't? Then, the hell with you," she shouted.

The woman then took the huge menu and began tearing it up, throwing several of the pieces in front of Berra, as the coaches ushered her away from the table. Being famous and recognizable, as Yogi is, may not always be the most pleasant life experience.

My favorite autograph story for famous baseball players came from Hank Greenberg, the great slugger of the Detroit Tigers who challenged the Babe Ruth home run record of sixty with fifty-eight in 1938.

Greenberg was a handsome Jewish kid from the Bronx, extremely popular in New York even though he played for the enemy Tigers. He was always pleasant with the fans.

"I was outside Yankee Stadium after a game one day, standing on the street across from the parking lot," Greenberg once told me. "I was wearing a white summer suit and was on my way downtown to Manhattan for a dinner date. I started signing and the crowd of kids just seemed to grow, maybe fifty or a hundred kids before I realized I had to rush off."

Greenberg told the fans he had to leave, and one autograph hunter refused to give up and get out of the way. As Greenberg walked away from him the fan lifted a fountain pen filled with ink, held it a foot from Greenberg, and shook it at him ferociously.

"The ink ran all over my white suit," Greenberg recalled. "I had to go back to the hotel for a change of outfit. I was pretty late for my date. I don't think I signed autographs for a good long while at Yankee Stadium after that."

Yogi had won a pennant for the Yankees in 1964 and again with the Mets in 1973. He had lost the World Series each time. He was determined to bring the Yankees another pennant and win his first World Series.

One season and sixteen games into his second season in 1985 as manager ended that dream.

Berra's Yankee teams this time were different from the ones he managed in 1964. That club had old stars—Mickey Mantle, Whitey Ford, Elston Howard, Roger Maris, Bobby Richardson, Tony Kubek, and Clete Boyer—still capable of playing quality ball. This 1984 team—except for Dave Winfield, and Don Mattingly emerging as a star—was short of talent.

When Casey Stengel won his first pennant as Yankee manager in 1949 he shouted in the clubhouse, "I never coulda won it without my players."

Yogi just didn't have the players.

The team bounced around the middle of the pack most of the year, never made a serious charge, and ended the season seventeen games out of first place. Steinbrenner was grouchy most of the way, criticizing Yogi's handling of the team and indicating changes might have to be made again.

The only drama on the field came with the wonderful batting race between Dave Winfield and Don Mattingly, not settled until the last day of the season. Mattingly caught Winfield in the final days and Winfield suggested it might have been fixed. He thought opposing pitchers were giving in to Mattingly while bearing down harder against him. There *was* open opposition to Winfield around the team. Winfield would suggest occasionally and privately that some of the antagonism toward him was racial bias, a premise hard to prove. Mattingly, a likeable kid from Indiana, was a dedicated worker. Winfield had little show business in him (no Reggie here) and seemed to irritate some of his teammates with all the Winfield Foundation talk.

Mattingly's batting title later motivated Steinbrenner to name him captain of the team, an honor that had stayed vacant after the 1979 death of Thurman Munson.

For many Yankee fans, especially older ones who remembered the glory days of the 1960s, the highlight of the season came on Old Timers Day, July 21, 1984. Roger Maris was honored.

Maris had hit sixty-one home runs in 1961 in the greatest home run race of all time, far more thrilling if the truth be known, than the Mark McGwire chase at the Maris record with Sammy Sosa finishing at sixty-six to McGwire's seventy in 1998.

Maris had to beat the record set by the most famous player of all, Babe Ruth, do it within 154 games in a 162-game season—due to Commissioner Ford Frick's stupid ruling—and do it in a race against teammate Mickey Mantle, the most beloved Yankee of his time.

Maris was tough to talk to in those days—introverted, stubborn, and almost always angry. All of that changed years later when Roger received much public recognition.

A sportswriter named Frank Graham had written of Yankee outfielder Bob Meusel in the late 1920s, "He learned to say hello when it was time to say good-bye."

That line suited Maris perfectly. He was a hard interview in New York, became much easier when he moved on to St. Louis in his final two seasons, and was warm and open when he returned to Yankee Stadium after his playing days.

George Steinbrenner, with a great sense of Yankee history, brought Maris and Mickey Mantle back to New York to raise the 1977 Series flag on Opening Day, April 12, 1978. It was the first time in ten years that Maris had come to New York from his Florida home.

Maris was concerned about the fan reaction. He dined

with old pal Julie Isaacson, a union organizer who had be-friended him when Maris first came to New York in 1960. They had remained close friends.

"I picked him up when he first arrived here," Isaacson re-membered. "He was wearing a sports jacket and white shoes. I told him, 'Roger, this is New York. You have to dress like a Yankee.' After that he was all right."

Now, in 1978, Maris came back to Yankee Stadium as 44,667 people watched the scoreboard screen showing Boston pitcher Tracy Stallard throwing that final home run ball to Maris in 1961. The cheers were huge.

Roger was later asked if he was surprised at the warmth and depth of the feeling of the fans.

"No, I expected it," Maris said. "It's like obituaries. When you die they always give you good reviews."

Maris returned again to the Stadium on July 21, 1984. George Steinbrenner, that old softy, had arranged for Maris to be immortalized in the Yankee Memorial Park. His plaque would join those for Elston Howard, who had recently died; Thurman Munson, killed in a 1979 plane crash; along with Miller Huggins, Lou Gehrig, Babe Ruth, Jake Ruppert, Ed Barrow, Joe DiMaggio, Mickey Mantle, Joe McCarthy, and Casey Stengel.

Maris had been diagnosed with lymphoma, cancer of the lymph glands, and was undergoing experimental treatment in hopes of prolonging his life. Roger returned to New York one more time when Steinbrenner gave him the Lou Gehrig Pride of the Yankees award at a huge dinner the night before the 1985 season began. The M and M Boys, Mantle and Maris, took the field together, again to huge cheers.

Maris soon returned to his home in Gainesville, Florida, and the beer distributing business he had been awarded by St. Louis owner Gussie Busch for his services with the Car-dinals. He grew weaker. Through the efforts of his pal, Julie Isaacson, Maris agreed to see me in his offices in March for an interview. We both knew it would be the last time.

"I just spoke to [Mike] Shannon [a former Cardinal team-mate and friend] and he said you want to interview me now before the twenty-fifth anniversary of the home run year in case I die," Maris said, with a weak smile.

"That's not it," I lied. "It's the twenty-fifth anniversary of your arrival in New York."

We spent the day together, talked of the old days in New York and reminisced about mutual baseball friends. We finally got to the subject of his health.

"I'm prepared for whatever happens," he said.

In December Maris was admitted to the famed M. D. Anderson Hospital and Tumor Institute in Houston. He received intense treatment. He had massive blood transfusions, mostly from three of his sons. The fourth cried bitterly when told his blood type was not compatible with his father's.

Yogi Berra had been named a Houston coach. He was in town for meetings and drove to the hospital. He was denied admission to Roger's room. He left the hospital in tears.

"It tore me up not to be able to see him that one last time," Berra later said. "I wanted to see him badly. They told me he was too sick."

At 1:45 P.M. on Saturday, December 14, 1985, the greatest single-season home run hitter of his time died peacefully.

A few days later his old teammates gathered together again in Roger's hometown of Fargo, North Dakota, for a final farewell. I had arrived earlier in the day, and a Maris family friend, Don Gooselaw, asked me if I wanted to ride out to the airport with him to pick up Mickey Mantle and Whitey Ford, who were arriving together from a golf tournament in Florida. Mantle walked off the plane. He was wearing a black leather jacket, a cowboy shirt, a string tie, and cowboy boots. He asked me how cold it was in Fargo. When I said it was seventeen degrees below zero during the night he let out a long obscenity and turned to Gooselaw. "You got a drink in your van?"

They were all there, the 1961 home-run year teammates—Mantle, Ford, John Blanchard, Moose Skowron, Tony Kubek, Bob Cerv, Bobby Richardson, Ryne Duren, and Clete Boyer. Boyer was the only Yankee to talk at Saint

Mary's Church in Fargo in a memorial service the night before the funeral. He told some funny stories about Roger's huge appetite and made the audience chuckle.

"That was the most nervous I had ever been in my life," Boyer said later.

A week later on December 23, 1985, with New York City bathed in Christmas glow, Roger Maris was remembered at St. Patrick's Cathedral in a Mass celebrated by John Cardinal O'Connor, leader of the New York Archdiocese. Former president Richard Nixon sat in a front pew next to New York City mayor Edward Koch, limousine magnate Bill Fugazy, Yankee owner George Steinbrenner, and baseball commissioner Peter Ueberroth.

More than 2,500 people filled the church. Opera star Robert Merrill sang the Lord's Prayer. Broadcaster Howard Cosell delivered a touching eulogy. Ex-Yankee shortstop and broadcaster, Phil Rizzuto, who had called the home run with his distinctive, "Holy Cow," in 1961, delivered a touching prayer.

In death, Roger Maris had had a day in New York more splendid than any he had ever experienced in life.

CHAPTER

SEVENTEEN

The baseball season of 1986 in New York was all about the Mets. Davey Johnson led his gritty team to its first World Series title since 1969 with a little help from the Curse of the Bambino.

The Boston Red Sox had the Mets beaten in the sixth game of the Series until Mookie Wilson hit a ground ball deep behind first base. First baseman Bill Buckner surrounded it with his open legs as the ball trickled into short right field with as famous an error as the game has seen. The Mets won that game and won the final game the next day. It all led to a massive city celebration.

Billy Martin had a couple more barroom fights in 1985, one with a Yankees pitcher named Ed Whitson and one with a fan.

Whitson was a strange case. He had won fourteen games for San Diego in 1984 and been signed as an expensive Yankee free agent. He was a quiet fellow from Johnson City, Tennessee, and he gasped when he saw several dozen sportswriters surrounding him when he reported to spring training. Frank Sinatra sang in *New York, New York* that "if you could make it here, you could make it anywhere." A lot of baseball players simply couldn't make it in New York. Whitson had a fifteen-year career, had won 126 big league games, and hated every day he played in New York.

After Billy Martin took over for Yogi Berra again in April of 1986, he rode Whitson hard, called him gutless, demeaned his pitching style, and challenged his masculinity. Whitson, not a very articulate guy, never knew quite how to respond to Martin's attacks. It all came to a rousing finale in September, at the Cross Keys Inn, where the Yankees stayed in Baltimore. A drunken Billy Martin and an unsteady Ed Whitson started fighting in the bar, moved into the lobby, spilled over into the parking lot, and continued at a third-floor elevator bank. Billy's right arm was broken, his face was smashed, and his legs were bruised.

"Billy's like one of those old-fashioned gunslingers in the Westerns," said old pal Phil Rizzuto. "There is always some young guy wanting to take him on."

Soon Billy Martin was fired again and Lou Piniella, then a Yankee coach, would become the manager of the team for the 1986 season.

Of course, this would not be the last of Billy Martin for Yankee fans. Despite the barroom fights, the firings, the confrontations with Steinbrenner, the antisocial conduct he had shown for many years, there was still room for Billy Martin in the Yankee picture.

On August 10, 1986, his uniform number 1 was retired, only to be recycled again by Billy when he returned as the team's manager for the fifth and last time in 1988, and permanently retired after his death in 1989.

George Steinbrenner never could quite make up his mind about Martin. He wanted him . . . and he didn't want him. He wanted Lou Piniella and then he didn't. He wanted Gene Michael and kept him.

Piniella was clearly George Steinbrenner's favorite player. Steinbrenner respected Piniella's competitiveness, his dedication to excellence, and his determination to win. They had some raging arguments over the years but somehow each one ended with a peace pact.

Piniella reported to spring training one year with long, flowing hair. Nothing made George angrier than seeing his players, especially his favorite players, looking shaggy and unkempt.

On the right occasion, a banquet, an outing in public with his beautiful wife, Anita, a team event in a Manhattan hotel, Piniella, a ruggedly handsome guy, always looked splendid in tie and tux.

In the clubhouse, especially on the road after a few beers

with teammates and some strategy sessions, Piniella might appear with a worn look to his pants and shirt, a pair of old sneakers, and a scraggly beard of two or three days growth.

Steinbrenner, trained in military school as a kid, always dressed neatly, had his hair cut weekly, and seemed never to sweat, even on the hottest days. One of his tricks was the pile of fresh shirts he kept available for changing in his office or in the hotel closet on the road. He always tried to get his team to conform to his standard of dress.

Piniella showed up once at spring training with long, unkempt hair. Clubhouse man Pete Sheehy approached him carefully. He told Piniella, "You can't suit up."

"Why not?" asked Piniella.

"You have long hair. George told me to send anyone with long hair directly to him," Sheehy said.

Piniella marched across the clubhouse to the large trailer parked outside. Steinbrenner had his spring training office inside that trailer.

Piniella was forced to sit in his office for half an hour while Steinbrenner talked on the phone. Steinbrenner always talked on the phone. Piniella thought he would never get off the phone and this silly disagreement over hair would never be resolved. Steinbrenner's secretary was buzzed and Piniella was allowed inside the Boss's Fort Lauderdale office.

"Lou," said Steinbrenner in his best father-to-son voice, "you can't dress with hair that long."

"Why not? What has long hair got to do with my ability to play?"

"It's a matter of discipline," Steinbrenner said. "I just won't have it."

The voices of Steinbrenner and Piniella were both getting louder. The tension in the room was growing thicker as Piniella, always a tough verbal opponent for the Boss, refused to give in. Piniella decided to go with his big ammunition.

"If our Lord Jesus Christ came back down with his long hair," shouted Piniella. "You wouldn't let him play on this team."

Steinbrenner got up from his thick leather chair, walked out from behind his desk, and motioned to Piniella. "Come with me," he said.

Piniella followed Steinbrenner across the parking lot of the Fort Lauderdale Stadium where the trailer was parked, across a wide street, and into the lobby of the nearby motel. The Boss did not say a word. Piniella was silent. Steinbrenner opened a door of the hotel lobby and walked into the motel swimming pool. A couple of bathers looked up without a word.

"If you can walk across the water in that pool," said Steinbrenner, matter-of-factly, "you don't have to get a haircut."

The next day Piniella reported to the park with his thick black hair cut short.

"George always loves those kinds of verbal challenges," said Piniella in a 1999 conversation about the Boss. "If he can get the last word in, he feels so wonderful."

Piniella had started his career with Cleveland. He spent some time in Baltimore under feisty Earl Weaver, went back to Cleveland for a while, and then was drafted by the one-year expansion team, the Seattle Pilots. He was traded immediately to another expansion team, the Kansas City Royals, and won Rookie of the Year honors in 1969.

He spent five years in Kansas City before being traded to the Yankees for the next eleven seasons of his career. He had five seasons over .300 and seemed to be in the middle of every rally the Yankees staged in all those seasons. He was a wonderful hitter, a strong outfielder with a good arm, and an inspirational leader.

His last couple of seasons on the field, he was a player-coach with the Yankees and was given a day at Yankee Stadium on August 5, 1984. With his wife, his three children, and his parents on hand from their home in Tampa, Florida, Piniella was cheered by a full house of fans who yelled his name in rhythmic chants, "Lou, Lou, Lou." The press had called him "Sweet Lou" in tribute to his warm personality and sweet swing. No pitcher ever seemed to intimidate him and no sportswriter was ever turned away.

Piniella stood at home plate, in front of a bank of microphones, with Steinbrenner standing in his Stadium box in the loge level, smiling and clapping at every word. Piniella later said he remembered the historic retirement of Lou Gehrig on that same field on July 4, 1939, when Gehrig called himself the "luckiest man on the face of the earth," despite a fatal illness. Piniella said he felt so lucky for his marvelous career, his grand family, and the devotion and dedication of so many fans and baseball officials, including the beaming Boss upstairs.

"For the past ten years, every time I came up to home plate you people supported me with chants of 'Lou, Lou, Lou.' I can only tell you how the adrenaline flowed when I heard that, and the desire welled up in my body to do well for you," he told the crowd. "I am forever grateful for that. I thank you for all your warmth, all your kindness, all your support. I love you all. The way I feel today, this is not a farewell, this is only a hello."

The crowd stood on its feet for several minutes and Piniella, as tough a player as the Yankees had in that time, stood at home plate, his head down, his eyes tearing, his heart pumping rapidly.

The Yankees starting winning shortly after Piniella joined the team in 1974 and stopped completely after he left as a player in 1984. Piniella played on a Yankee pennant winner in 1981. There would not be another Yankees pennant for fifteen years, until Joe Torre led the team back to success in 1996.

Piniella was named the Yankees manager on October 27, 1985, as the Kansas City Royals, Piniella's old team, was beating the St. Louis Cardinals for the World Series title. Dick Howser, a teammate and friend of Piniella's, was the winning manager. Howser would be dead of a brain tumor in less than two years, another example of the creeping reality of the game in contrast to its eternal romance.

Piniella's first Yankee team, in 1986, finished second behind the Boston Red Sox. The Mets took care of the Red Sox in the 1986 World Series, which made it a little easier for Piniella.

As soon as he began managing the 1986 Yankees, Piniella knew his relationship with the Boss would not be the same. He was treated as a Steinbrenner pet during his years as a player and now he was being treated as a Steinbrenner project. The Boss wanted to teach him how to manage, and the constant clubhouse phone calls proved irritating. Piniella's personality, usually carefree and light, became hard and tense. It would not be long before Steinbrenner would have another victim. Billy Martin was warming up in the managerial bullpen again.

Steinbrenner would give us sportswriters off-the-record interviews criticizing Piniella every time there was a losing game or a small losing streak. It wasn't that George didn't love Piniella as much as always. It was more that he doubted his own decision in hiring Piniella for his first managerial position without minor league training as a field boss.

One of Piniella's toughest critics that year was broadcaster Howard Cosell. Cosell had a regular radio show on ABC and was seen frequently on interview programs and doing commentary on ABC television. Cosell had become close to Steinbrenner through the years and always bragged that he was the first person Steinbrenner dined with at "21" after buying the Yankees.

As mentioned earlier, Cosell had been born and raised in Brooklyn and had become a lawyer after World War II service and represented a Brooklyn Little League. The Little League led him to events at Brooklyn's Ebbets Field where he was involved in a pregame show for youngsters called *Happy Felton's Knothole Gang*.

Cosell decided he could do Felton's show better than Felton and began with the Dodger players, whose interviews he sold on a freelance basis. It took several years before he could establish himself as a broadcaster. Felton remained the fans' favorite.

In those days players would be selected by the kids to go on the *Knothole Gang Show* with them. Felton gave each player who was a guest fifty dollars, a meaningful sum for a player making five thousand dollars a year in the late 1940s or early 1950s. One player, outfielder Cal Abrams, had never been on the show.

"I always wanted to be picked by the kids," said Abrams during a New York visit shortly before his death in 1997. "It was sort of a status thing. This one time I cornered one of the kids who was on the show and told him to ask for me when Happy came to him. I told him I would give him an autograph. He fielded a couple of ground balls with Pee Wee Reese as his instructor. Then Felton asks him what player he wants to go on the show with him. I'm standing right off to the side with a big smile on my face, knowing I'll be picked and make that extra fifty. The kid looks at Felton and says, 'Carl Furillo.' I almost fell over."

Cosell got his first radio experience with Felton and then moved on, creating his own style of broadcasting—loud, pompous, .controversial, and outrageous. He befriended boxer Muhammad Ali when Ali refused to step forward for his draft induction. The national furor over Ali's refusal to fight "them Viet Cong," and Cosell's support of his stand, elevated Cosell to national status.

By the 1980s he was a household name. He might be loved or hated—but never ignored—in every home in America, especially a home in which sports was a subject of conversation.

We played a party game in our house (not leading to a wife swapping) in which we kept score of how much time it took for guests to mention Cosell's name. It never took more than twenty minutes.

Cosell dined often with Steinbrenner in the 1980s, put him on his radio and television shows, mentioned his name frequently on Monday Night Football asides and helped the Boss manage the Yankees.

Piniella, who could smell a phony a block away, never warmed to Cosell. As Cosell had done fifteen years earlier when he constantly criticized Casey Stengel—then managing the Mets—because Stengel would not give Cosell exclusive interviews, he began criticizing Piniella. He suggested Piniella was inexperienced, didn't use his players properly, knew little about handling a pitching rotation, and had no sense of the game's strategy. What Cosell had a sense of was the second-guessing element in baseball, one of the game's major attractions.

Baseball is a simple game—three outs, three strikes and you are out, four balls and a walk and most runs win. Everybody is an expert after a few games. George Steinbrenner was a Cleveland Indians fan as a kid. That qualified him to second-guess every manager he ever hired. That, and the fact that he owned the team. When he fired Gene Michael as the team's manager in 1981 and moved him into the front office, Steinbrenner summed up his baseball philosophy. "Why would you want to be the manager and be second-guessed by me when you can come upstairs into the front office and be one of the second-guessers?" Michael quickly got the idea.

Cosell, always complaining about the ignorance of the print media and especially his most serious rival, columnist Dick Young of the *New York Daily News*, put a lot of ideas in Steinbrenner's head. He seemed to be pushing for a Piniella firing with only Billy Martin in sight.

Piniella survived his first season as a manager with a second-place finish, and Cosell went on to attack others. One afternoon we attended the same press conference at "21" and we both wanted to attend another press conference later at the nearby Hotel Americana. We walked out the door together and Cosell began talking to me very quietly and interestingly. He spoke of his Brooklyn youth, his struggles as a lawyer, and the joys he found with his family. He lived in Pound Ridge in northern Westchester County in New York and talked about the pleasures that property provided for his family.

We were almost at the hotel now, walking toward the press conference ballroom together. A large group of sportswriters, Young included, stood outside the room waiting for the summons that the press conference room was ready. Cosell did an immediate about-face, bellowing, "The Fourth Estate is here, ready to distort the story, make up some lies, and seek big headlines."

I could hardly believe that this was the same guy I had quietly walked a few blocks with, listening to him talk so sweetly about his family.

Broadcasters had always been a large part of the Yankee scene—from Arch McDonald and Mel Allen in 1939 to Bobby Murcer, Tim McCarver, Ken Singleton, and Jim Kaat in 1999.

I traveled for many years with Mel Allen. We often got hotel phone call mix-ups, with a drawling southern voice asking for Cousin Mel. He was from Birmingham, Alabama. He had also studied law, and when he came to New York, he secured a job with CBS and became the Voice of the Yankees from 1939–64. His calls of a "White Owl Wallop and a Ballantine Blast" for home runs and sponsor advertising became known by every Yankee fan.

Mel Allen was with the Yankees through 1964. He was fired by general manager Ralph Houk. It all happened because Allen became too loud and too boring in the press rooms around the league. All of his stories began with, "When Joe DiMaggio hit in fifty-six straight games . . ." Houk traveled with the club that year, while Yogi Berra served as the rookie manager. Houk was talking to the attractive waitress in the Minnesota press room when Mel Allen's voice, broadcast level, overwhelmed the room. The decision was made. Houk simply didn't want Mel Allen around anymore.

Mel Allen was a wonderful storyteller if you had the time—a sweet man, a generous person, and a broadcasting legend worthy of his Hall of Fame status. He could also get a little hard to take on a daily basis. He did well when he was brought back to the Stadium by Steinbrenner for special events and when he served on occasional cable television broadcasts.

Allen was a lifelong bachelor and upon his death a few years ago I could still hear his marvelous voice, enjoy the stories he told of DiMaggio and the early Yankees, and recall his kindness.

I also recalled a line written about him in a *Sports Illustrated* magazine profile when I worked at the magazine. His elderly mother was interviewed about her famous son. One of the questions she was asked was whether she was incredibly thrilled about his broadcasting success.

"I wish he was a shoemaker," his mother said. "A married shoemaker."

The Yankees won ninety games under Piniella in 1986, finished in second place five and a half games behind the Boston Red Sox, moved a lot of players in and out of the lineup, and seemed ready to challenge for the top again in 1987.

One of the additions to the team in 1987 was a big left-handed pitcher by the name of Steve Trout. His father, Paul (Dizzy) Trout had pitched for the Detroit Tigers and helped them to the pennant in 1945 in a pitching tandem with future Hall of Famer Hal Newhouser. They won the pennant on the last day of the season, the first after World War II ended, when home run slugger Hank Greenberg, back from four years of service, hit a grand-slam home run.

Detroit beat the Chicago Cubs in that 1945 World Series, the last time the Cubs have made it to the October Classic.

Trout, bigger than his father at six feet four and two hundred pounds, seemed just the right addition to the team, a hard-throwing left-hander in Yankee Stadium.

Steinbrenner had no doubts about Trout's value to the team when he joined the Yankees. "I just won you the pennant," he told Piniella.

Trout turned out to be one of the biggest busts around the Yankees in many years. He had every pitching ailment that could be imagined, he really didn't throw very hard, he was terribly introverted, he had poor eyesight, and he hated being in New York with the Yankees. He finished the 1987 season without a victory, was 0-4 in fourteen games, was soon shipped west to Seattle, and was out of baseball in two more years.

Steinbrenner pushed for a lot of wonderful deals for the Yankees. He also came up with a lot of clinkers. The trade for Steve Trout, hardly his father's son once he walked onto the mound, was an albatross George had to wear for a long, long time.

The Yankees had last won a World Series in 1978 and had last won a pennant in 1981. Soon all these comings and goings of players and managers, without pennants, might start reflecting on George Steinbrenner.

Sportswriting changed forever in New York on August 31, 1987. After a month-long battle with a stomach ailment, Dick Young died. He was sixty-nine.

The first thing most young reporters write is an obituary. The last thing written about them is an obituary. That's the way we come into the business and that's the way we all go out.

My obituary of Dick Young in the *Post* was about the hardest thing I ever had to write, a fair report of the life and career of a man who was my hero as a young reporter and my hated enemy as an older one.

He had influenced the profession tremendously by chasing after tough stories, gaining valuable access for sportswriters, and showing up sham. He called Dodger GM Branch Rickey "El Cheapo," for low salaries paid to his players. He wrote controversial stories about Jackie Robinson, Duke Snider, Carl Furillo, and other Brooklyn Dodger heroes. He was kind and helpful to young sportswriters such as myself when we broke in, and hateful, selfish, and bitter when he envisioned us as threats to his media power. He was one man as a young Young and a completely different, nasty, vain, and arrogant man as an old Young. He talked about honor among ballplayers and then jumped a contract with the *Daily News* to come to the *Post* for more money. He was small in build, a dapper dresser who favored colorful bow ties, and a Napoleonic sportswriter with a huge following. I stood on a Brooklyn street corner as a kid to read the first edition of Dick Young's Clubhouse Confidential in the *Daily News*.

I wrote his obituary in the *Post* with a cheer and a tear.

CHAPTER

EIGHTEEN

It is the link from generation to generation, father to son, grandfather to grandson or granddaughter that defines baseball. The game's history is known by those who watch a game on television or get out to the ball park once or twice a year.

When I was a kid we had all the numbers memorized. Babe Ruth hit 60 homers in 1927 and had 714 for his career. Lou Gehrig played in 2,130 consecutive games. Joe DiMaggio hit in 56 straight games. Ted Williams hit .406 in 1941, Ty Cobb had a lifetime average of .366, and Cy Young won 511 games.

These numbers stood the test of time. Only a few were passed—the sixty-one homers of Roger Maris in 1961 and seventy home runs for Mark McGwire with sixty-six for Sammy Sosa in 1998. Cal Ripken passed Lou Gehrig with 2,632 games played in a row. Many of the memorable records in baseball remain forty, fifty, or sixty years after they were set.

In 1966 New York University economics professor Lawrence Ritter wrote what may be the best book ever on the game with, *The Glory of Their Times,* a collection of sweet visits at their homes with old-time players discussing their distinguished careers. He gave readers a personal look at these elderly men—Rube Marquard, Sam Crawford, Fred Snodgrass, Stanley Covelski, Bill Wambsganss, Lefty O'Doul, Paul Waner, and many others as they revisited their youth.

The back cover of his book shows a 1903 photograph of Christy Mathewson, maybe the game's greatest pitcher; John McGraw, regarded by most observers as the game's greatest manager; and Iron Man Joe McGinnity, a giant among the New York Giants pitchers in the early years of the twentieth century.

Above the photograph in Ritter's book are the words of French-born naturalized American history professor and philosopher Jacques Barzun, a dean at Columbia University in New York City who wrote, in the 1930s, "Whoever wants to know the heart and mind of America had better learn baseball."

Immigrant sons such as Joe DiMaggio, whose first language was Italian, and Lou Gehrig, whose first language was German, became true Americans after neighborhood games. There were arguments about Cobb and Ruth, Walter Johnson and Smoky Joe Wood, Rogers Hornsby and the famed Chicago Cubs infield of shortstop Joe Tinker, second baseman Johnny Evers and first baseman Frank Chance. Tinkers to Evers to Chance was made famous by the F. P. Adams poem. The third baseman on those World Series champions of 1907 and 1908 was Harry Steinfeldt. Winning the World Series more than ninety years ago is a feat not duplicated since for intense Cubs fans like Hillary Clinton and Ernie Banks. In his poem, Adams didn't bother mentioning Steinfeldt but baseball trivia fans have answered the question, "Who was the third baseman on the Tinker-to-Evers-to-Chance Cubs infield" with the name Steinfeldt for many years.

As Ritter's book brought to life again these old baseball warriors, dozens of sportswriters across the country, including me, began writing about local heroes of past generations. Newspaper reporters may have some creative ideas. They almost always have a sense of what is good that they might steal from others. My column in the New York Post was called "Yesterday."

For the price of a phone call I could interview old heroes across the country.

I started the weekly column using conversations with old Dodgers I had worshiped as a kid growing up in Brooklyn, many of whom I had met later on as a sportswriter.

Brooklyn Dodgers shortstop Pee Wee Reese was my hero as a boy. He had played for the Dodgers from 1940 through their move to Los Angeles in 1958. I met him for the first time when he was coaching the Dodgers in Los Angeles. We chatted for a bit about his days in Brooklyn, threw around some old Ebbets Field names he played with, and I remembered and smiled about the only Brooklyn Dodgers World Series victory over the Yankees in 1955. Suddenly, in the clubhouse of the Dodgers in the Los Angeles Coliseum, Reese said, "Wait a minute, let me show you something."

He walked over to a huge floor trunk where the Dodger players and coaches stored their valuables under lock and key during the game. Bending over, he pulled out a large ring, wet his finger, and placed it on his left hand. Then he held up his hand to show me. It was a huge diamond-studded ring. It read "Brooklyn Dodgers World Champions 1955."

"Did you ever see one of these?" he asked.

"Never," I said.

I grabbed Pee Wee Reese's left hand, held it with my two hands, bent down, and kissed his 1955 World Series ring. I managed to kiss it once a year for the next forty years as he continued his career in baseball as a coach, a broadcaster, and a member of Baseball's Hall of Fame. It became a joke—a ritual between the two of us, a link between a great Dodger player, my boyhood hero, and a worshiping sportswriter.

Reese told me a story once that locked the final out of the 1955 Series into my memory permanently.

The Mets were driving for the pennant in 1969 under the leadership of Gil Hodges—the former first baseman of the Brooklyn Dodgers, a longtime teammate and pal of Pee Wee Reese's—as manager. The Mets were playing in San Francisco while Reese and another Brooklyn teammate, third baseman Don Hoak, were together in Pittsburgh at a public appearance. It was late at night now and the two old Dodger teammates had downed a few in the hotel bar when Hoak began kidding Reese about the last out of the 1955 World Series.

Elston Howard, a Yankee rookie that year, had hit a routine ground ball to shortstop for the final out in a shutout pitched by Dodger left-hander Johnny Podres, a twenty-three-year-old left-hander. The low throw went from Reese to Hodges at first as Howard moved slowly down the line.

"The ball bounced," Hoak said to Reese. "You choked."

"It did not bounce," said Reese. "It was just low where Gilly liked it."

While film exists of the final throw, it does not clearly show whether that ball bounced in the dirt in front of Hodges—or whether it didn't. Only one man really knew. They bet another round of drinks on the outcome. Then they dialed the Mets team hotel in San Francisco.

Hodges was in bed in his San Francisco hotel room when the phone rang. Hoak waited, looked at Reese, and finally heard a sleepy voice.

"Yes."

"Did it bounce?" asked Hoak, without any other greeting.

"It bounced," said Hodges. Immediately he hung up the phone.

Reese argued with Hoak for a few minutes and finally paid up. Hoak died shortly thereafter, October 9, 1969, and it was only then that Hodges finally admitted to Pee Wee that he had this gag going with Hoak about that famous last throw to first base. Hodges would say it bounced if any Dodger 1955 teammate asked about the game's last throw. It never bounced.

"Of course not," said Podres, years later. "That was Pee Wee Reese out there."

The captain of the Brooklyn Dodgers was one of the most admired and respected players of his time. His only baseball frustration was losing to the Yankees in the World Series time after time, 1941, 1947, 1949, 1952, and 1953. Finally, under Walter Alston, the Dodgers beat the Yankees in the 1955 World Series.

So Pee Wee Reese became my first interview for my new weekly "Yesterday" column. It became very popular, and dozens of old Brooklyn Dodgers, New York Yankees, and

New York Giants got their Andy Warhol fifteen minutes of fame again as they relived their careers. Stars—Reese and Duke Snider, Allie Reynolds and Tommy Henrich, Larry Jansen and Whitey Lockman—were interviewed for the column. Journeymen players such as Gene Hermanski, Eddie Basinski, Cliff Mapes, Bob Grim, Sal Yvars, and Danny Gardella got some long-needed attention.

A discussion in the ballpark one afternoon led me to interview a player named Dale Long. A few young fans had come to the press box at Yankee Stadium for a school project. They were writing about baseball oddities and had come across the name of Dale Long as baseball's only left-handed catcher. Long had caught a couple of games in 1958 for the Chicago Cubs. They wanted to know how all this had happened. Yankee backup catcher and manager Ralph Houk had explained it to me years earlier by jumping over the technicalities and emphasizing that it was simply against custom.

Long had played for the Pirates, Giants, Cubs, Senators, and even the Yankees for a bit as a first baseman and excellent pinch hitter. He had hit eight home runs in eight straight games for the Pirates in 1956, a record that had not been threatened since. He was a good hitter on the Yankees in 1960 and 1962, and was sent to the expansion Washington Senators in 1961 before coming back to New York.

He asked about Mickey Mantle, Whitey Ford, Yogi Berra, and some of his other Yankee teammates when I called in the early 1980s, and he was happy to discuss his home run record. I told him everybody connected his name in baseball with that but that the left-handed catching was something else.

"Well, at least I'm still remembered for something," he said.

His name probably did not come up again until the middle of July 1987.

A young Yankees first baseman named Don Mattingly was on a home run tear that would link him forever in baseball history books with Dale Long.

Mattingly was twenty-six years old that summer of 1987.

He was from Evansville, Indiana, and while the Yankees seemed to be going nowhere under Lou Piniella, Mattingly was saving the season. He had won the American League batting title in a bitter race down to the last day against Dave Winfield in his first full Yankee season of 1984. He batted .324, .352, and would finish at .327 in 1987. His first four seasons as a Yankee resulted in a .337 average with only Babe Ruth (.350), Lou Gehrig (.341), and Joe DiMaggio (.341) doing better in their first four Yankee years.

Mattingly had hit twenty-three, thirty-five, and thirty-one home runs in his first three seasons at Yankee Stadium with a grooved left-handed swing very similar to that of Roger Maris in his two wonderful Yankee years of 1960 and the record breaking homer season of 1961.

Mattingly was six feet tall, weighed about 175 pounds, was an all-around graceful athlete, had a wonderful glove at first base, ran well, and was a very tough, competitive player.

With one of the game's greatest leadoff hitters ever, Ricky Henderson, topping the Yankees lineup, Mattingly drove in 100 or more runs in his first four full seasons with a high of 145 in 1985, the league leading figure.

In each of eight straight Yankee games from July 8–18, 1987, Mattingly hit a homer. Only Long had accomplished that remarkable feat as a Pittsburgh Pirate first baseman in 1956.

When he hit his eighth homer off Carl Erskine of the Brooklyn Dodgers (Ebbets Field's Oisk), the Forbes Field crowd demanded that Long come out of the dugout to take a bow.

Long later recalled a conversation with Pulitzer-prize-winning sportswriter Dave Anderson of the *New York Times*. He referred to the Pirates general manager who gained baseball immortality—the man who signed Jackie Robinson in Brooklyn to break the color line. "Branch Rickey told me it was the first curtain call he'd ever seen in baseball."

Mattingly got a little break during the streak as he traveled to Oakland for the All Star Game, as the Yankees were out of action from July 13–15. He hit five homers in five games prior to the break and three more in three games after the break, including the second grand slam in six days.

As the Yankees were being clubbed 20-3 by the Texas Rangers, with catcher Rick Cerone forced to pitch an inning, Mattingly had a single and a double in four chances at the plate but did not drive a ball out of the park. It was the first Yankee game since July 7 in which Mattingly did not homer for the team. He had hit ten home runs in his previous eight Yankee games.

He remained tied with Dale Long, a fact that was noted in all stories about Long's death in 1991.

"There's no disappointment in me at all," Mattingly told the assembled press in Arlington, Texas, shortly after the game. "I don't feel relief. It was no big thing."

Mattingly was a wonderful player and a fine gentleman. He was not an extraordinary personality. He seemed, at that moment, to be following the Yankee company line for modesty and respect perhaps established by Lou Gehrig during his consecutive game streak and exaggerated by Joe DiMaggio when his consecutive game hitting streak ended in Cleveland in 1941 after fifty-six straight games. Two fine fielding plays by Cleveland third baseman Ken Keltner helped Cleveland end the streak.

"The press made a big deal out of Keltner's fielding those balls over the bag," said Harry Eisenstat, a Brooklyn native who was a relief pitcher for the Indians in 1941 in a 1999 conversation about that game. "Kenny used to make those plays every day. DiMag had been thrown out a couple of other times that year on plays like that."

What made the Mattingly moment so dramatic was not only the attempt to pass the Long record but the poise he showed throughout the chase. Mattingly was completely in control of himself. Never once in the streak did he show any signs of pressure as he grew nearer the mark each day.

"I really enjoyed myself," Mattingly quietly told reporters. "*You* hit ten home runs in eight games and see how *you* feel."

All the reporters laughed. They consider one home run story in a week cause for celebration. Much of Mattingly's success could be attributed to his professional work ethic, his devotion to excellence, and his pride.

"I just enjoy this so much," he said.

Dale Long said over the phone from his home in Palm Coast, Florida, that he followed the chase intently and was actually rooting for Mattingly to pass his mark.

"Everybody knows baseball records are made to be broken," Long said. "I wouldn't have minded being second to Mattingly in that home run streak department."

It was through the efforts of Texas pitchers Greg Harris and Jeff Rusell, who kept Mattingly homerless on July 19, 1987, that Mattingly and Long would remain tied.

"I am happy to go down in baseball history with him," said Long. "Mattingly and Long. That's quite a thrill for me."

Mattingly was pleasant during the entire home streak, comfortable with the press, and happy to share his feelings. There was another left-handed hitter he reminded me of as I watched him drive home runs to right field, occasionally to left field, and once even to center field.

Stan Musial, nicknamed "The Man" in Brooklyn for always destroying the Dodgers, especially in Ebbets Field, played from 1941 through 1963. When I interviewed him once toward the end of his career I kidded him about always smiling. I asked him why. He answered, with a smile of course, and said "If you hit .331 all your life you'd be smiling, too."

Each summer when I visit Cooperstown, New York, for the Baseball Hall of Fame inductions, one of the treats is watching Musial in action. When former greats are introduced on a large stage, Musial steps forward, bends deep in his famous batting stance, and takes a big swing at an imaginary baseball. Then he laughs.

When I catch him later at night in the lounge of the Otesaga Hotel, where the Hall of Famers stay during the induction weekend, Musial is never without his harmonica.

With just the smallest urging, Stan Musial will pull out the harmonica, beep out a few practice notes, and play, "Take Me Out to the Ballgame," to the huge cheers of all in the room.

Mattingly and Musial seemed to have similar styles in their swings and their personalities—happy, heroic gentlemen who could swing the bat efficiently and successfully over many years.

Musial's top salary was $100,000, made in 1963—his final playing year. The Cardinals wanted to retire him for a run at the pennant in 1964. They got him to go and opened up a spot for a young new outfielder named Lou Brock, traded to them from the Chicago Cubs. Brock helped the Cardinals to a 1964 World Series win over the Yankees.

Mattingly had won an arbitration award of $1.975 million for the 1987 season, annoying George Steinbrenner no end.

"Mattingly's like all the rest of 'em now," Steinbrenner said after the arbitrator's award. "He can't play Jack Armstrong of Evansville, Indiana, anymore. He goes into the category of modern players with agents, looking for the bucks. Money means everything to him."

That was Boss owner talking about the bottom line. When the Yankees returned home from the trip, Boss fan had a magnum of champagne delivered to Mattingly's locker.

Mattingly continued to impress the Boss and Yankee fans the rest of that marvelous summer of his. On September 29, 1987, he hit his sixth grand-slam home run of the season off Boston left-hander Bruce Hurst, the pitcher who had failed to hold the Mets in game seven of the 1986 World Series with a 3-0 lead.

Mattingly retired after the 1995 season with a .307 average for fourteen Yankee seasons. He becomes eligible for Baseball's Hall of Fame election in the year 2001, five seasons after his retirement. His support will be strong. The 1987 season, with home runs in eight straight games and six grand slams in that one year, should be a strong enough credential for adding his name to the exalted list of heroes.

The Yankees finished in fourth place in 1987 with an 89-73 mark. Steinbrenner was clearly restless with the result and wanted to fire all his players. He settled for his manager and general manager.

Woody Woodward allegedly resigned as general manager on October 19, 1987, with Lou Piniella, of all people, named general manager after being relieved of his managerial duties in Steinbrenner's great game of musical Yankee office chairs.

Piniella was always a Steinbrenner favorite but lost favor one afternoon when he happened to be in the hotel coffee shop instead of his hotel room, a Steinbrenner no-no, when the Boss called.

Piniella had become angry at Steinbrenner's treatment and was thinking of resigning along with Woodward when he was promoted. This was not a case of the Peter Principle in which people are promoted to the level of their inadequacy. This was a simple case of a guy who liked the dugout action being hidden upstairs in the office. It would not work.

On that October day Steinbrenner hired and fired just about everybody around him. Woody Woodward left, Piniella became the general manager, and a guy named Billy Martin was named manager of the Yankees for the fifth time. Can't live with him, can't live without him.

CHAPTER

NINETEEN

Hammy. That's what the Yankees called Rickey Henderson. He seemed to sit out games on a regular basis during the almost five years he spent with the Yankees from 1985 through 1989. It was always the same thing—pulls in the upper portion of his right or left legs, the hamstring area. He would turn his leg slightly in the clubhouse and pull down the huge bandages that covered his thighs.

"This hammy is giving me more trouble now than the other hammy," he would say.

He would discuss his hamstring pulls for several minutes, take a seat on the bench for another day, and cause the manager of the moment—Yogi Berra, Billy Martin, Lou Piniella, or Dallas Green—more heartache as they battled to get him out on the field.

The reason was obvious. Rickey Henderson was simply the most talented leadoff man in the history of the game, a fine outfielder, a dangerous long-ball hitter, and the greatest base stealer of them all. He made Ty Cobb, Jackie Robinson, and Lou Brock look like slowpokes when he broke every existing stolen base record for one season, 130 in 1980 with Oakland. For his career, he totaled well over 1,300 as he played the 1999 season with the New York Mets at the age of forty.

"My whole game has been my legs," said Henderson, one day in the summer of 1999, as he sat in front of his locker at Shea Stadium. "I've taken care of them. I managed to stay off them as much as possible."

He stayed off them by resting when he felt it was necessary and by sliding head first most of the time, bruising his belly on occasion but saving his legs from further damage from the dirt.

Henderson was pounding second and third base on his steals. He was also pounding first base more times, probably, than anyone in the history of baseball. Pitchers threw over there more often in an attempt to get him out or at least keep him close enough not to steal.

"His body takes such a tremendous pounding," said 1988 Yankee teammate Jack Clark. "If he wasn't built as thickly as he is he wouldn't be able to perform. Look what his legs have had to endure over the years. He's constantly diving back to the bag with guys trying to tag him and hurt him. When he's hurt it's better to take a couple of days to get well than a couple of weeks."

Don Mattingly said he understood Henderson's desire to perform only when he was completely healthy.

"There's a difference in players," Mattingly said. "You have to know what you can do and when you can play. If I feel I'm taking a chance, I'm not going to go out there. If Rickey says he can't play, he can't play. You have to trust the player."

Henderson pointed out in 1988 that he had not been placed on the disabled list when he had a little hammy trouble.

"A lot of guys will pull a muscle and they are on the disabled list. "But the team can't afford to lose me in case I'm ready to come back in five or six days. I like that because I feel I'm a quick healer."

He was closing in on 2,700 big league games played in 1999 as he performed impressively for the Mets.

In the meantime, Billy Martin was sinking fast in 1988. His drinking was no longer amusing. He seemed to be drinking heavily before, after, and during games, a bottle of scotch always in the top drawer of his Yankee office desk. He got into another Billy Brawl in a topless bar in Texas. He battled with umpires in a dirt-kicking incident, causing a three day suspension. He screamed at a female reporter in the clubhouse, got caught up in several verbal wars with Steinbrenner, and finally went down for the count for the fifth time on June 23, 1988. Lou Piniella became the manager again.

A few weeks earlier Murray Chass of the *Times* had interviewed a sports psychologist named Dr. John Silva, past president of the Association for the Advancement of Applied Sports Psychology. He had never met Billy Martin.

He asked Silva why Martin, a sixty-year-old man now, would act so childishly, throwing dirt on umpires.

"I've asked myself that question many times," said Silva, a strong Yankee fan. "What possesses a person to do such a thing and why would a league allow a person who is in such an influential position with fans and youngsters and other people in the game to exhibit such infantile behavior?"

"Kicking dirt and throwing dirt are obvious simple displacements from kicking the person and hitting the person," said Dr. Stanley Cheren, a Boston psychiatrist who works with athletes. "Dirt adds another quality—filth—ultimately meaning contempt. It's an expression of contempt.

"As you get older," Dr. Cheren told Chass, "when you feel that something is being unfairly imposed by authority, you fight back more readily than you would as a younger person. In this situation with Billy it really is an extension of a longstanding conflict with authority. The guy [Martin] is legendary for his conflict with bosses and I'm equating umpires with bosses."

Meanwhile, Boss Steinbrenner had again had enough of Martin. He relieved Billy of his duties and once again appointed his pal Lou Piniella to lead the Yankees.

Piniella had finished second in 1986 with the Yankees and fourth in 1987. Steinbrenner reluctantly went back to Martin again in 1988, because no one knew Billy's track record better than George. All the psychiatrists in all the world could never clearly explain the strange connection between Billy and Boss. Steinbrenner respected Billy's leadership abilities, motivational skills, and knowledge of the game. He hated his conduct. Steinbrenner had been accused of some tricky business practices (convicted felon George Steinbrenner) but he had never been anything personally but a model citizen. He was proud of his family, charitable to an extreme, available for important civic events, gushy at the

Fourth of July national celebrations in conjunction with his July 4, 1930, birthdate.

Steinbrenner was certainly more comfortable with Piniella as his manager again. Lou and his gorgeous wife, Anita, and their three handsome children lived in a beautiful home in suburban Allendale, New Jersey. No baseball couple in those days could possibly be more attractive than Lou and Anita Piniella, wonderful representatives of the Yankees and all the tradition that went with the team.

I sat in Lou's living room one afternoon after he was named manager of the team, discussed his baseball future with him, and asked why he would subject himself to George's doings.

"I think I've learned a lot from the other times," he said. "I don't expect that managing the Yankees now will be as difficult as it was on me the first time around."

When I went back home to write my story about the visit and Piniella's optimistic future, I considered what he had said. I knew it couldn't be so. Steinbrenner was the ultimate bottom-line guy. Winning was absolutely the *only* thing that mattered. Steinbrenner had a true feeling of affection for Piniella. He admired his toughness, his skills as a player, his dedication to excellence, his determination to continue the remarkable Yankee tradition. Piniella stood up to Steinbrenner and Steinbrenner admired him for that.

Billy Martin, always in financial trouble, needed the Yankee job desperately. George could maneuver him through that avenue. Piniella, as much as he craved the Yankee managerial job for the sense of competition, didn't need it financially. He had invested wisely in shopping centers, assorted real estate properties, and a booming Westchester car dealership. It was not unusual to drive through any Westchester, New York, street where I lived and see dozens of cars carrying the advertising logo of the Lou Piniella dealership. He wasn't out there pushing cars. Names sell. Piniella's name was as popular a Yankee brand as there was in the late 1970s and 1980s.

When the Yankees finished fifth in 1989, Piniella was finished. Next up on the wheel, as Joe Torre called it, was Dallas Green, who had managed the Philadelphia Phillies to their only World Series in 1980 and then became the general manager of the Chicago Cubs. He did not lead them to a World Series win, as no one had since Frank Chance (Tinker to Evers to him) in 1908. As the Cubs were still trying more than ninety years later, not even sixty-six homers by outfielder Sammy Sosa could get them a Series win. The Cubs made it as the wild card in 1998 but soon faded from Series potential.

General manager Clyde King had been instructed to scour baseball for the strongest managerial candidate possible. Green had been fired from the top executive position on the Cubs. King decided he was the best man for the job and recommended him highly to Steinbrenner.

Green had been a big, strong, right-handed pitcher for the Phillies in the early 1960s, but he couldn't throw very hard. He hung on for eight years, including four games for the 1966 New York Mets, one of baseball's all time worst teams.

He was soon scouting and into management, brought Philadelphia that glorious 1980 victory, and was hired away by the Cubs for the same chore. He didn't have the players and could not obtain that triumph in Chicago.

Green developed a no-nonsense reputation for toughness; he was demanding of his players and willing to criticize them publicly to the press, something most managers avoid if they want to retain player loyalty. Green had decided sometime during his career that ballplayers could be treated as adults, subject to criticism when necessary and appreciative of praise when called for. Not all players responded well to that mature attitude.

Future Phillies Hall of Famer Richie Ashburn had moved on to Chicago by the time Green came along as a Philadelphia pitcher, but he knew him well from his broadcasting days selling Tasty kakes, the major Phillies sponsor.

"Dallas is a very strong personality," Ashburn told me shortly after Green was hired by Steinbrenner. "He knows the game, he's very smart, and he doesn't need the job. His wife's family has DuPont money."

The Greens lived on a large farm in Delaware in the off-season. Dallas Green always said he enjoyed getting his hands dirty.

Ashburn was one of the wisest and wittiest men in the game. He would have made a marvelous manager but never wanted it. He liked broadcasting too much. It was a sad loss for baseball fans in general and me, personally, when he died suddenly of a heart attack in a New York hotel room while in town to broadcast a Phillies-Mets series. He was seventy years old, the youngest seventy-year-old man I could ever remember.

"I played the game because it was so much fun," he once said. "It beat working."

So many ballplayers go through their careers with their heads down and their tension level continually on high. Ashburn always had his head up and the next funny line ready at a moment's notice.

There had been a journeyman first baseman in the Yankees organization in the late 1950s named Marv Throneberry of Collierville, Tennessee. Throneberrry was built well, had left-handed power, and played first base. He didn't play it well but he could stand there as good as anybody.

The *Daily News* sportswriter Joe Trimble labeled Throneberry "Marvelous Marv" in derision after he pulled a few bonehead plays and missed a couple of ground balls. Throneberry hated the name, knowing that Trimble and all the other copycat sportswriters were making fun of him.

Throneberry had a hard swing and imitated the great Mickey Mantle in his stance, his walk, and his night life. It just didn't work. Throneberry drifted off to the Kansas City A's, the Washington Senators, and in 1962 the New York Mets under manager Casey Stengel who had him for several years with the Yankees.

He lockered next to Ashburn, who immediately welcomed him to the team by shouting, "Marvelous Marv is here. We'll win the pennant."

The Mets were 40–120 in 1962, baseball's worst record ever, with the team finishing 60 1/2 games out of first place.

The season ended with catcher Joe Pignatano hitting into a triple play.

While Dick Young popularized Casey Stengel's label for the team—"The Amazin's"—and produced witty copy about them instead of criticism, Ashburn provided most of the humor inside the clubhouse. He got Throneberry to relax, enjoy his rare successes, and appreciate the humor of failures of "Marvelous Marv." One day Ashburn made an error in the outfield and Throneberry marched up to him and asked, "You trying to steal my fans?"

"What I remembered most about those early days dressing next to Marv," Ashburn once told me, "was the photograph of this gorgeous girl in a tight bathing suit with lots showing hung inside his locker. I kept looking at that locker picture and thinking I knew the girl. The next afternoon I recognized that a person who might be that girl was sitting behind our dugout. I tapped Marv on the shoulder and asked him to look at her and see if he knew her. He moved his head over the dugout roof, looked up, and said, 'Sure I know her. That's my wife.' It really was."

Yankee coach Don Zimmer told a story once about Yogi Berra's inability to identify someone on the field.

"We were playing a game and all of a sudden a streaker raced on the field," recalled Zimmer. "There was a paper bag over the streaker's face but the rest of the streaker was completely nude. The cops rushed on the field to remove the streaker. Someone turned to Yogi and asked, 'Was it a male or a female?' Yogi answered, 'How should I know? The streaker had a bag on over the face.' That was beautiful."

Ashburn and Throneberry made for a wonderful team throughout the 1962 season as the Mets entertained their new fans. Ashburn hit .306, Throneberry actually hit sixteen homers and gave back about sixty runs with his gloves, and the Mets became the darlings of New York, a significant rival to the Yankees for fan affection.

Throneberry was released after a salary dispute with GM George Weiss and went back home to Collierville a famous man. Before he left, the press gathered around his locker in the Polo Grounds in New York, and Throneberry announced, "I ain't gave up yet."

Throneberry died in 1994 and Ashburn was still telling funny Throneberry tales a day before his unfortunate death in 1997. Throneberry had become a famous folk figure after doing Miller Lite ads, with most of the attention generated by Ashburn in those 1962 days.

Publicity in the press can make the names of some baseball players live forever.

Moonlight Graham played in one game for the 1905 New York Giants. His full name was Archibald Wright Graham. He died in 1965 in Chisholm, Minnesota, completely unknown except to his family. Writer W. A. Kinsella used his name and character in *Field of Dreams* with Burt Lancaster playing the part in the film. Baseball fans rushed to the record books. Casey Stengel always said, "You could look it up." When anyone did, there was Moonlight Graham, one game, 1905 New York Giants.

Another one-gamer was Walter Alston, 1936 St. Louis Cardinals. He became my favorite manager when he led the Brooklyn Dodgers to their only World Series title in 1955. He became my most unfavorite manager early in 1964.

Alston's Dodgers, now in Los Angeles, had tied the Giants for the pennant in 1962. The Giants won the pennant in a playoff. Many of the Dodgers on that team—Duke Snider, Tim Harkness, and Larry Burright—played for the Mets in 1963. As the Dodgers were involved in another tight pennant race in 1963, I asked each of them if they thought the Dodgers would win. They said they did not, because Alston would tighten up under the pressure.

"Late in 1962," Snider recalled, "Alston called a team meeting. We thought he was going to discuss the next opponent. Instead he discussed the shortage of checkmarks on the list of cokes taken from the cooler."

This seemed like the drama of Captain Queeg in *The Caine Mutiny*. I jumped on it as a hot story.

The Dodgers won in 1963 and swept the Yankees in the World Series.

The next spring, 1964, a newspaper reporter pal named Barney Kremenko of the *Journal American* told me Walter Alston was looking for me. When a manager is looking for a sportswriter it is good news—if he is about to give you a news story, a scoop for past favors—or bad news, for something you wrote he didn't like.

I walked into Alston's Dodger office in their spring training home at Vero Beach, Florida. Alston was sitting in a chair. He rose slowly, the blood reddening the skin of his neck, his eyes growing wider, his huge hands reaching out for my throat. He was six feet two, about 200 pounds, baldheaded, and angry. I was five feet eight, 170 pounds, grayhaired by that time, and nervous as hell.

"What kind of shit is this?" he bellowed.

He threw the old *Post* clipping on the ground and turned around to close the office door. I could feel my knees shake. I thought about the tragedy of my new, beautiful young wife being an early widow.

"That's what those players said," I moaned.

He moved closer, screamed a couple of curse words I had never heard before, and reached for my throat.

Then came the most blessed event in my sportswriting career. Lee Scott, the dapper, handsome, wonderful, kind, saintly traveling secretary of the Los Angeles Dodgers suddenly appeared in the room between Alston and me. He said nothing, just pushed me gently out of the room. I moved quickly past Sandy Koufax, Don Drysdale, John Roseboro, and Maury Wills to the Florida sunshine.

I walked rapidly over to the Mets' side of the field, spotted my pal Barney Kremenko, told him what had happened, and asked if he knew Walter Alston could get that angry.

"I was mad because I thought he was giving you a scoop," he said.

Alston was a fine manager, deserved his Hall of Fame recognition, but had a smoldering volcanic side to his personality that few knew. I stayed far from him most of the rest of his career.

I thought of that when Dallas Green became the manager

of the Yankees. He was a big guy, very tough, outspoken, quick to explode at the press when he felt he had been wronged. I decided I would never write a story about him that quoted former players.

Green said he thought he knew Steinbrenner better than anyone would expect.

"When I was a minor leaguer in Buffalo, I ran into him in a lot of my favorite haunts," he said.

Steinbrenner would often dine in popular sports hangouts when he was in Buffalo on Great Lakes shipping business.

"I attended a lot of meetings on behalf of the Cubs [Green had served as general manager and team president] that Mr. Steinbrenner was at. I've listened to him talk. I've been in conversation with him. I think I know him and I think he, in turn, knows me."

Green recognized the job he was assuming.

"What I intend to do is instill in this team the discipline I think is necessary to win. If that doesn't work I'll probably go the way of all Yankee managers."

Dallas Green was manager number sixteen in Steinbrenner's sixteen years with the club.

"They're in such a hurry to win that it seems like they do things spur-of-the-moment," said Yankee slugger Jack Clark, unhappy ever since he joined the club for the 1988 season. "The result is a lot of confusion. It's tough to get consistency on the field that way."

The Yankees had finished fifth in 1988 under Billy Martin and Lou Piniella. They finished fifth again in 1989 under Dallas Green and after August 18, 1989, under the managerial direction of Boston playoff home-run hero Bucky Dent.

Where had all the heroes gone?

CHAPTER

TWENTY

Ralph Kiner, the home-run hitting star of the Pittsburgh Pirates in the 1940s and 1950s and later the Mets broadcaster from their first season of 1962, loved to tell the story of the day he was eating dinner in a fashionable Pittsburgh restaurant years after his playing career ended.

"This woman stared at me from another table for a long time," Kiner recalled. "She just kept staring and staring. She finally got her courage up and walked over to where I was sitting. Then she said, 'Didn't you used to be Ralph Kiner?' I just smiled and admitted I used to be."

The story always got a big laugh when Kiner told it. I had heard it so many times, it became a gag line for all players, especially around Old Timers Day when I would use it on Yogi Berra, Mickey Mantle, or Whitey Ford—always with a laugh. I never used it on Joe DiMaggio. Nobody used funny lines on Joe DiMaggio.

Ballplayers come along from small towns and big cities, from farm communities and industrial centers, from the deep south and the far north and now from Japan, Australia, Canada, and Cuba.

They play the game for ten or twelve or fifteen years. Most are never heard from again. A few are seen occasionally at special events such as Old Timers Day or a baseball-card show, an autograph signing session or a special banquet. Very few cross that line from playing idol to icon—always honored, recognized, worshiped, and admired. DiMaggio led that list until his 1999 death. Ted Williams is the present leader of that group with Hank Aaron, Willie Mays, Bob Feller, Stan Musial, maybe Reggie Jackson and Nolan Ryan falling into the group. Reclusive Sandy Koufax, as good as he was, never made it because his public appearances were too infrequent.

There was a skinny, left-handed kid pitcher from Lafayette, Louisiana, who joined the Yankees in 1976. He was five feet eleven inches tall, weighed maybe 150 or 155 pounds, had bony cheeks and a thin neck, and could throw very, very hard. No matter how good a pitcher he became, he never became a baseball icon.

He talked with a strange accent, consistent with the Cajun country of Louisiana where he grew up, but sounding offbeat to this Brooklyn-born ear. He spoke softly and gently and it was fun to talk to him because of that unusual accent.

Billy Martin thought he threw hard enough, even with that smallish body, to be an effective relief pitcher. Gabe Paul and the other Yankee executives convinced George Steinbrenner the kid wasn't ready for the big leagues despite more than five years of minor league training.

Ron Guidry became the object of a tug-of-war between Martin, who wanted him now, and the Yankee brass, certain he could only be useful if he stayed in Syracuse for more training. The Yankees finally brought him around.

He sat on the outside of an aisle seat on the Yankee charter on his first trip with the Yankees. I walked down the aisle, hoping there was an empty seat next to him, where I might sit and interview him for the next day's *Post*. There was a seat and we began talking. I asked him how big a town Lafayette, Louisiana, was—always a terrific in-depth interview question—and he said about eighty thousand. We chatted about his track career in high school. His high school had no baseball team. His baseball beginnings were at Southwestern Louisiana State University, where he studied architecture before the Yankees discovered his fastball.

Then he looked at me and in perfect Cajun asked, "Do you play chess?"

I had played the game a lot as a kid with my own father and had played a few times through the years with my own kids. My chess was about as good as my tennis, my favorite participation sport now. I was known in my local tennis club not for my backhand, my serve, or my forehand. I was known for showing up anytime anybody called me for a game.

Guidry reached into his attaché case under the seat and pulled out a chess set. He quickly set up the board, got me to put down my notebook, and had me tied up in that game for the next hour or so.

Guidry played chess through the years with an occasional teammate, with myself or other sportswriters, with club officials on the Yankees charter flights.

In the meantime he pitched brilliantly.

He won sixteen games in 1977 after Martin made him a starter and was 25-3 with a 1.74 ERA in his Cy Young season of 1978. He won the Boston playoff game in 1978 in a 5-4 game with a little help from Goose Gossage, Reggie Jackson, and the Boston Back Bay Boy, Bucky (Bleeping) Dent and his Fenway Park screen homer. Guidry won twenty-one games in 1983 and twenty-two in 1985. Then his arm went south, about as far south as Lafayette, Louisiana.

Dallas Green really didn't want him around anymore in 1989 as he struggled to rebuild the team, but George Steinbrenner, again revealing his softness of spirit, ordered Green to accept Guidry in camp. Steinbrenner wanted to be sure about Guidry before he bid farewell.

As he closed in on the age of thirty-nine in the first days of spring training, he was throwing hard fastballs, that famed biting slider that upended the Red Sox in the 1978 playoff game, and had his usual excellent control.

Then his elbow began hurting more and more, the almost certain indication that his arm was finished. Whitey Ford had to quit with a bad arm in 1967 and said it best. "If you pitch in the big leagues, not one day will go by when you're arm won't hurt. If God wanted to make pitchers, he would have given us arms that hang up instead of down," Ford said.

Ford also understood retirement for a baseball player. "I used to think golf was a great game," Ford said, "until I was forced to play it every day."

Guidry tried rest, surgery, every treatment known by trainer Gene Monahan. Nothing worked. He got up one morning in July 1989, looked at his wife, Bonnie, and simply said, "I'm done."

The Yankees gave him a star's sendoff with a Stadium press conference.

How does a reporter know if a press conference is important? He looks at the buffet table. A few daintily sliced sandwiches, a couple of beers, and a clubhouse worker handling the table means it isn't much. When the guy behind the table is in a tuxedo, the meat is being sliced by a chef in white uniform and big hat, and the hard drinks are filled without ice, it's big. This was big.

There were a few sobs and a few tears from Bonnie Guidry, sitting in the front row. (Remember—"I married him for better or worse but not for lunch," courtesy of Hazel Weiss). There were some expressions of sadness from Yankee executives and there were some laughs provided by Guidry.

He talked about a game he pitched against the California Angels in 1978. He struck out eighteen batters.

"I had nothing in the bullpen when I was warming up," Guidry recalled. " I struggled through the first inning and a line drive off the bat of one of the Angels almost killed me."

Guidry walked up to his catcher, Thurman Munson, as they reached the dugout after the Angels were retired in the first inning.

"Whattaya think?" Guidry asked his catcher.

" I think you ought to say a prayer," Munson said.

The press laughed heartily as Guidry told the story. I could only think, then, ten years after Munson's death, "Why couldn't Munson have been funny around us?"

Guidry struggled for another inning or so in that game against California and then it all came together in the next inning. California batters couldn't keep up with his fastball, couldn't find his slider, and were lost when he eased up with a changeup.

"I got my first indication something was up when I overheard Thurman say to the trainer, Gene Monahan, that he needed another pad to protect his hand," Guidry said.

Guidry reminisced about the glory days of the late seventies, the characters he played with—Goose Gossage, Munson, Lou Piniella, Reggie Jackson, Sparky Lyle, Graig Nettles, and the rest of the players under the direction of Billy Martin, Bob Lemon, and the rest of the managers.

He seemed to be always on the side in those wonderful days, pitching great games every fifth day, answering questions from the press afterward in that high Cajun, as long as sportswriters from Brooklyn, Manhattan, the Bronx, and Long Island wanted to ask them. But he was never deeply involved in the turmoil of the moment. He would go home to Bonnie and the kids after each home game, look for a chess partner on the road, talk about the hunting sessions he had scheduled for late October when the Series was finished, and look forward to the next season.

Now it was over.

In a year or two, as is his style, George Steinbrenner brought that thin, mustachioed left-hander back to spring training in Fort Lauderdale and then in Tampa for a couple of weeks. Guidry worked with some kids, showed them a little about his slider, encouraged them to challenge hitters even when behind on the count. They would drift away, these nineteen-, twenty-, twenty-one-year-old pitchers wearing Yankee uniforms, not quite certain who this soft-spoken guy with the funny accent and the number forty-nine on his back really was. These young pitchers were interested in their own fastballs, their own sliders, their own careers, their own possibilities of that two-, or four-, or ten-million-dollar contract down the line.

Guidry would go home again, as he did in late March of 1999, work on his farm, stay out of Bonnie's way, help the kids with their sports programs, play a little chess with them, thumb through the papers at the latest standings and the latest doings of the Yankees.

Ron Guidry will be fifty years old on August 28, 2000. He has never done well in the Baseball Hall of Fame voting despite a 170-91 mark, a .651 winning percentage—one of the best in the game's history. He was always quiet and professional. He never drew much attention to himself. Winning games, it seems, is not enough for the highest honors.

"I don't miss it," he said during spring training of 1999. "The family is doing well. I'm busy, I'm happy. I still get a kick when I get to put the uniform on again in spring training or at the Old Timers Day."

I forgot to ask him if he was playing much chess.

In 1989 the Yankees won only seventy-four games. They finished in fifth place. Dallas Green, combative with George Steinbrenner almost from the beginning, was gone by August 18. Bucky Dent, yes *that* Bucky (Bleeping) Dent, was the new manager in a move no one could understand. Dent was far too gentle and sweet a man to be a manager of the Yankees under the aegis of George M. Steinbrenner.

That move would hold up only until June 6, 1990, about as long as a Liz Taylor marriage.

Bob Quinn, who could trace his family baseball history back to the turn of the century, nineteenth into twentieth had been elevated and quickly disposed of as general manager. Harding Peterson was next in line, a guy who had been successful in Pittsburgh.

The bad season, the turmoil in personnel, and the lack of exciting names forced attendance down about half a million. Steve Sax, a decent hitter and a nervous fielder, led the club in batting average in 1989 with a .315 mark, and Andy Hawkins, who would pitch a no-hitter in 1990 against Chicago, led the club in pitching with a 15-15 mark.

The Yankees, sad to say, had become dull.

George Steinbrenner's changing act (managers, general managers, coaches, players, front office executives, farm directors) had become wearisome. Steinbrenner was unimportant as far as fans were concerned when the team was winning pennants and World Series games in the late 1970s.

In the 1980s, without the apologetic 1981 event against the Dodgers, the Series had gone on without them.

Bucky Dent was not the kind of inspirational figure

Steinbrenner needed to rally the team again, bring heroics back to the Stadium, and dramatize the improvement projected for the decade of the 1990s.

Only one guy could do that. His name was Alfred Manuel Martin.

Martin had stayed on the payroll after Steinbrenner fired him in 1988, made an occasional Stadium appearance, talked to the Boss by phone about certain players, scouted a promising kid in a small town, and waited for the next call.

All he wanted to do was manage again.

Martin had married the former Jilluan Guiver, a fan he saw in the stands one time and liked immediately, in January of 1988. When he was fired, Jill and Billy Martin bought a farm near Binghamton, New York, in the tiny community of Fenton, off Potter Hill Road. They raised a few head of cattle, kept a few horses on the farm, walked the fields together as they looked at the corn and the hay. They had a couple of hired hands to do the serious work and they often sat together at night in the large living room watching a late-night movie or talking about the phone call from George they soon expected.

A few days before Christmas in 1989, Billy Martin called an old pal from Detroit named William Reedy. He had run a restaurant in Detroit when Billy managed there, was a devoted admirer of Billy's, and would drop everything if Billy needed him by his side. Billy needed him.

There is a small collection of men and women devoted to professional athletes. They will sacrifice their own lives for the chance to be with a sports star. They love to dine with him protectively in a popular restaurant, and they offer any services needed by their hero. They glory in the closeness.

Joe DiMaggio had a stable of these men and women in almost every major city in America. Someone was always available to pick DiMaggio up at the local airport, drive him back for a large Italian family meal, and stand unobtrusively nearby in worshipful poses, never asking for anything other than his presence. Asking the Yankee Clipper for an autograph—he only did that for paying customers—was always forbidden. When DiMaggio died in 1999, dozens of photographs appeared in dozens of newspapers across the country of DiMaggio and local friends enjoying a good meal. Joe was America's Guest, never one to buy a meal, pay for a hotel room, or struggle for an airline reservation.

Billy Martin wasn't quite in Joe's class. Who was? But Billy Martin had many friends across America thrilled to be in his company. That was the service Bill Reedy provided the five-time Yankee manager.

Reedy arrived on Christmas Eve at Martin's farmhouse. They spent most of the night talking and drinking. They slept late on Christmas morning. Shortly before noon, Martin and Reedy took off together as Jill Martin worked on an elegant Christmas dinner for her husband and his friend. She finished about 3:00 P.M. and waited for Billy's arrival home.

A light snow fell on the winding road outside the house, and the falling late-afternoon temperatures put an icy glow on the highway.

Martin and Reedy had been drinking all afternoon. They left a local bar at about five-thirty and drove a few miles to the Martin farm. At about 5:45 P.M., with Reedy driving, according to a report later filed by Sheriff Anthony Ruffo of Broome County, though disputed by others who said no one ever drove Billy's new pickup truck but Billy, the vehicle went into a skid. It slid down an embankment some three hundred feet, bounced wildly through the icy brush, and came to rest at the approach to Martin's driveway.

Jill Martin heard the noise of the crash from the house, ran outside, saw her husband on the ground outside the car, cradled his head, and quickly ran back inside to dial 911 for help. An ambulance arrived within three minutes. Martin and Reedy, suffering a broken hip and broken ribs, were both taken to Wilson Memorial Hospital in nearby Johnson City, New York.

Hospital spokesman Michael Doll said Martin was pronounced dead at 6:56 P.M. of severe internal injuries and traumatic head injuries. Billy Martin was sixty-one years old.

He had been born poor, lived in a broken home, made it into baseball on limited talent and limitless fire, roared through life, and died hard.

George Steinbrenner was at home with his family in Tampa Christmas night when he was notified by the Broome County sheriff's office. He was told that Billy Martin was dead and that his friend, Bill Reedy, supposedly driving the pickup, would be charged with driving while intoxicated.

Steinbrenner insisted that he had not been about to hire Martin again for a sixth tour of duty if new skipper Bucky Dent didn't get off to a 162-0 season.

"No way," said Steinbrenner. "He was too happy doing what he was doing. He was coming upstairs. He was going to be there more than ever before. He was enthused about the coming season. I must have talked to him twenty times in the last month and a half."

Steinbrenner said he saw Martin a week earlier when the two men appeared at the Tampa Performing Arts Center in a musical program for underprivileged children.

"He was excited about it," Steinbrenner said of the Tampa event. "He talked about how when he was a kid at Christmas he didn't do much."

I was at my family Christmas that night. My wife and I listened to tapes of holiday music as we drove back to Westchester from New Jersey. There was a light snow falling, a perfect holiday setting, as we carried some gifts into the living room. I went downstairs to my office and put on the telephone answering machine. There were several breathless calls from editors with one screeching, "Billy Martin's dead. Come in as soon as you can."

I played the call over again to be sure of the information. Then I went upstairs, told my wife the news, and turned on an all-news radio station. Steinbrenner's statement was already being read.

Sportswriting is a joyous profession. It is mostly about games and heroic performances by athletes, and large celebrations of triumph. Once in a while it is about death. Some player's child dies young. A mother, a father, sometimes a wife dies during the season and the player rushes home. Thurman Munson dies. Roger Maris dies. Billy Martin dies. Mostly, the profession is fun and games. Occasionally, it is about real life.

George Steinbrenner arranged another magnificent send-off for Billy Martin. Martin had been the most saddened, it seemed, at the 1979 death of Thurman Munson. Now it was Mickey Mantle who sat stone-faced in the front row of St. Patrick's Cathedral, as John Cardinal O'Connor celebrated the Mass. Former president Richard Nixon sat silently again between Mantle and Steinbrenner.

Mantle and Whitey Ford stood outside the historic cathedral on a clear, crisp winter afternoon after it was all over. They were telling stories about Billy Martin now, loosening up the atmosphere, bringing Billy back in this way after his tragic end.

Those of us who had been around Billy and Mickey and Whitey a long time had by now heard most of these tales. The young television and radio reporters had heard few of them and were thrilled to get a piece of this Yankee history, thrilled to be around Mantle and Ford. Many of them had been around Billy Martin a few times.

"I'm not surprised he died this way," said Ford. "I'm surprised he lived this long."

Now it was up to Bucky Dent, and those expected to follow, to lead the Yankees back in the 1990s to their previous glory. Billy Martin was gone. An era had ended. Yankee fans were hopeful that the decade of the 1990s would not be as disappointing as that of the 1980s had been.

CHAPTER

TWENTY-ONE

If 1927, the Babe Ruth home-run year; 1961, the Roger Maris home-run year; and 1998, the World Series record-breaking year, 114 regular season wins, and a Series sweep over San Diego were the Yankee peak seasons, then 1990 had to be near the bottom.

The Yankees lost 103 games in 1908, finished tenth in 1966, and won only 67 games in a seventh-place finish in 1990.

The Yankees changed managers, of course. In the middle of 1990, June 6, Stump Merrill replaced Bucky Dent. They changed general managers with old pal Gene Michael taking over for Harding Peterson. They changed managing general partners with Robert E. Nederlander, the theater magnate, replacing none other than George M. Steinbrenner III on September 13, 1990. Not by choice.

Steinbrenner contributed illegally to Richard Nixon's re-election campaign in 1972 and was suspended for it after buying the Yankees.

He contributed $40,000 to Howard Spira, the gambler and con man who hung around the Yankees for no known reason, and he was suspended from daily operation of the club. He was not forced to sell, and he was back after two years, the original amount of time Commissioner Fay Vincent had proposed.

Steinbrenner never really explained his dealings with Spira. He had told Commissioner Fay Vincent that the payment to Spira was extortion and made because he was "scared stiff" for himself and his family. Steinbrenner later denied at a court hearing during Spira's trial that he saw the payment as extortion.

"He was harassing my children, my family, my friends with phone calls," Steinbrenner said. "Second, I was told his mother was sick with cancer. His father had borrowed money from people in his building and couldn't face them. I felt sorry for his parents."

How Steinbrenner ever sat in the same room with someone like Howard Spira or ever took a phone call from him remains a major mystery regarding the psyche of the Boss. After he was sentenced to two and a half years in prison on the extortion conviction, Spira talked to the press outside the Manhattan Federal Court building.

"I sure hope George Steinbrenner never gets the team back," said Spira. "And I sure hope God knows what he did to me."

With Spira's value system, Cain would have pleaded no contest in the Abel killing, citing his brother's constant harassment of him.

Gregory Kehoe, the assistant United States attorney who prosecuted the Spira trial, said after it was over, "The tragedy here is that Mr. Spira has not taken responsibility for what happened. At this particular time, at this particular place, this particular defendant must pay a price for what he has done."

Spira had one last thing to say to reporters after he was ordered to jail.

"My father really should have worn a condom," Spira said. "He did not deserve Howard Spira as a son."

It is simply a strange quirk of the Boss that when he loves, he loves all out and when he hates, watch out. Steinbrenner could never get Dave Winfield to accept his edicts. So Steinbrenner could never accept Winfield as a productive Yankee. He would dig into a garbage can and come up with Howard Spira in his feud with Winfield. Probably one of the Boss's happiest days in his more than a quarter of a century as Yankee owner was when Winfield left for California.

It will be fascinating to see what occurs if and when Winfield makes the Hall of Fame in 2001.

The Yankees finished seventh in 1990 and fifth in 1991

without George Steinbrenner, now suspended, to kick them around anymore. It was the players, stupid.

Don Mattingly's back was acting up and he never again was the player he had been for the Yankees in the 1980s. He had only one more .300 season with a .304 mark in 1994 in ninety-seven troubled games. Ron Guidry was gone, with Andy Hawkins, Tim Leary, and Dave Righetti, aging now, supplying most of the pitching depth. The switch of Righetti—from a starter who could pitch a 1983 no-hitter on July 4 to a reliever—was always a questionable Yankee move.

Tommy John had also left the Yankee scene in 1989, as much of a loss for reporters as it was for the Yankees.

John, a left-hander with a hard curve, a sinker, and just enough of a big league fastball, had come out of Terre Haute, Indiana, to join the Cleveland Indians in 1963. He moved on to the White Sox, the Dodgers, and then the Yankees in 1979. He was a rare baseball artist with his left-handed pitching, someone who could beat the Yankees for the Dodgers in 1978 and turn around to even the favor by beating the Dodgers for the Yankees in 1981.

John was forty-six years old and had won 288 games when the Yankees pushed him away in 1989. They didn't actually release him (a baseball player dies twice), but they told him they would if he couldn't make a deal with another club. At the age of forty-six, he could not.

John was remarkable because he was still pitching winning baseball almost fifteen years after a tendon from his right forearm was removed and used to reconstruct his left elbow.

He called himself the Bionic Man after the machine-constructed television character and would often say, "I'm thirty-five years old but my arm is only three years old."

John gained much attention and much sympathy in 1981 when his son, Travis, three years old, fell twenty-seven feet out of an apartment window to the ground after bouncing on the bed. He survived a fourteen-day coma and a one-month hospital stay. Travis John is now a healthy, handsome young man finishing college playing sports, and looking forward to a future in television broadcasting.

Tommy John had a severe stutter when we first met in the early 1960s. Sportswriters are usually A-type personalities—interested in quick conversations, much detail, and colorful stories.

John could do all that if you waited around long enough for the stutter to stop. In his and my earliest days, I wasn't patient enough for that. Once I realized John had more interesting things to say than most players who talked without a pause, it all became worthwhile.

We would often sit together on the Yankee bench before games in which John was not scheduled to pitch. He wore his baseball cap back on his head with small strands of dark hair peeking out from the front edges.

He talked often about his early youth in Indiana, his high school and college days at Indiana State, his deep Christian faith, his devoted family life, and his miraculous recovery from surgery. He was always upbeat, interesting, funny and well worth putting in time listening to any day.

Did the stutter bother him? Never. He was so self-confident that he talked about a broadcasting career and made it for a while with the Yankees and the Minnesota Twins before turning to other business pursuits.

Tommy John was an exceptional pitcher, an exceptional man, and a personal favorite of mine through the years. He deserves more Hall of Fame consideration.

Some Yankee fans would put Bucky Dent in the Hall of Fame for his Fenway Park shot off the screen on October 2, 1978, in the famed playoff game for the Yankees against the Red Sox.

It just doesn't work that way.

Dent, a native of Savannah, Georgia, broke in with the Chicago White Sox in 1973 and made it to the Yankees in 1977. He was a handsome kid with a dimpled chin and a ready smile. He became a Yankee favorite, especially with the teenage girls, even though he had a wife as cute as himself.

After October 2, 1978, and the playoff homer against the Red Sox, he became a legendary Yankee. One big hit, one great game, one spectacular play and the life of a baseball player changes dramatically.

In reality, Dent was a good field, no-hit shortstop, a label as difficult to shake as his legendary status. Not even the most famous home run in modern Yankee history could change that.

The team didn't do much before Dent was named manager on August 18, 1989, and didn't do much while he was manager. Of course, the Yankees didn't do much after he was replaced by Stump Merrill on June 6, 1990.

It wasn't Dent's slow style. It was a collection of journeymen players in the early 1990s that kept the Yankees down and the House That Ruth Built quiet.

Don Mattingly couldn't carry the load alone. Roberto Kelly and Pat Kelly proved to be journeymen players, and Andy Hawkins could pitch a no-hitter but couldn't carry a pitching staff.

Mattingly, usually affable and easy with the press, was withdrawn for several days after Dent was named field manager.

"It's nothing special," he said, when asked if the managerial change had changed his mood. "It's hard not to be affected. I'm a human being. Change affects you. You just can't pin it down to one thing. Maybe it's just things in general."

Steinbrenner would be gone with his suspension at the end of the 1990 season. Even that hardly seemed to change Mattingly's overall sense that the raging controversies, politics, and tension around the Yankees impacted on him. He may simply have been one of those guys who would have been better off playing in Cleveland, Kansas City, or Texas.

The Yankees kept insisting they were close to being competitive again in the early 1990s even though they had not won ninety games or finished as high as second place since 1986.

This all reminded me of the conflict I had for many years

with M. Donald Grant, Chairman of the Board of the New York Mets and their stuffy senior executive handling owner Joan Payson's money and team. Yes, some owners in baseball have others handling their money and team.

As the nosy sportswriters like myself kept asking when the downtrodden Mets would improve in their earliest years, Grant became more and more outraged at the suggestion that it was simply the desire not to spend more money that kept the Mets down.

"We're only two players away from being a contender," Grant announced at one press conference.

My story about the team the next day began, "The Mets are only two players away from being a contender," M. Donald Grant insisted yesterday, "Babe Ruth and Walter Johnson."

Grant wouldn't take my calls for about three years after that one.

Steinbrenner was gone now in 1991 so there was really no one around to blame as the Yankees struggled on.

Someone named Carl Harrison Merrill became the Yankees manager in June of 1990, made it through that season, and even finished out a full year in 1991. He was known in baseball circles and back home in Brunswick, Maine, as Stump Merrill because he was a little bit of a kid as a kid and not much bigger as an adult man.

"Is it true that for a long time George Steinbrenner thought your name was Lump," he was asked.

"I thought he thought it was Bump," Stump said. "Are you sure it wasn't Lump?" a reporter asked.

"Bump," Stump said. "At least I don't think it was Lump."

The disagreement continued between the reporters and the new manager of the Yankees about whether he was called Bump or Lump by the Boss but no one could call the ousted Boss to find out.

Merrill managed and coached in the Yankee organization for fourteen years, the kind of good soldier every team needs by the time he became Steinbrenner's latest field boss. He was still around the Yankee organization ten years later, still ready to move anywhere Steinbrenner asked, still ready to serve in any position the organization needed.

On his first day on the job, Merrill sat in a new chair—not the same one Dent, Green, and Billy Martin had warmed—and worked over his lineup card. He wore a dirty undershirt, seemed stuffed into his chair, and his desk was filled with packages of Red Man chewing tobacco. He stuffed his right cheek with a chaw just before he addressed the assembled press.

"Right now, as I sit here," he told the reporters, "I'm honored, pleased, proud, whatever adjective you choose. It's been a long road."

"He looks just the way a manager is supposed to look," said pitching coach Billy Connors, who looked the way a pitching coach should look—overweight, overtired, and overimportant. "Just the way he spits the chew, you know—there's a baseball guy."

At the age of forty-six, Merrill had his lifelong professional dream realized. He was the manager of the Yankees and he was forever on the same managerial lists in baseball record books with Miller Huggins, Casey Stengel, Billy Martin, and, well, Dallas Green.

Merrill became the eighteenth managerial change in the eighteen seasons George Steinbrenner owned the Yankees

Don Mattingly, now the captain of the Yankees, the best since Thurman Munson's death in 1979, was asked how the latest change would impact on the team.

"I said last year that we need to get some consistency and I felt Bucky was as good as anybody," Mattingly said. "At some point this has to happen. One guy has to stay for a while. I hope Stumpy is the guy."

There was no way a guy called Stumpy by his players would lead the Yankees anywhere but to more confusion.

Amateur hour around the Yankees managerial picture ended on October 29, 1991, when someone named William Nathanial Showalter III became number nineteen in Steinbrenner's hit parade.

Showalter had a humorless persona, a strong face, a determined appearance, and an emotional dedication to excellence around the Yankees. Billy Martin had pushed him forward among other Yankee coaches.

When Merrill was fired, Showalter was also ousted from the third-base coaching lines. If the big desk and the office near the boss are positions of power in business, third base is the position of power on baseball teams.

After the manager himself, no one has more authority than the third-base coach. He is by tradition the heir apparent to the managerial job and the person who agrees most with the manager to his face and behind his back. Showalter was schooled by Martin in lots of baseball politics, infighting, behavior, and communication. He learned never to tell reporters anything.

Martin always disobeyed his own advice, because he was a compulsive complainer. Showalter learned his lessons well. He said little to anybody, and before long his dedication, determination, and steely personality was working to his distinct advantage. He was considered an important manager, a man with a bright future, and certainly a possible winner as he took over the team at the age of thirty-five.

"I never wanted to do anything else," he said. "If I didn't make it in baseball I would have been a very unhappy man."

He said he was now a happy man but it was always difficult to tell, as his early press conferences were short and not so sweet, less informative than most others had been, and filled with the kind of practiced tension Billy Martin had made famous after losing games.

What became clear early on in Showalter's career was that he was a no-nonsense guy. The laughter in the clubhouse was gone now and the intensity level was raised. The Yankees, for the first time in about ten years, seemed to go about their business in a very professional way.

There were rumblings now that Steinbrenner had some lawyers working hard on his suspension and that the commissioner, Fay Vincent, might soon see that the second year of Steinbrenner's absence from running the team could be his last.

Most reporters who had complained about Steinbrenner's absence now honestly missed him. The Yankees had become tiresome and dull. Mattingly was wearing down. Jesse Barfield and Danny Tartabull were not the kind of players or personalities that had given the Yankees an exciting edge only ten years earlier. Melido Perez was the best pitcher on the team, a losing pitcher in Showalter's first year.

If the Boss was to be back on top of things in 1993, and he was, he would have to unloosen his wallet for new talent.

That was never Steinbrenner's problem. It was nice to make money, and the Yankees always did with television contracts and properties. More important, the idea was to be on top.

Yankee fans could hardly guess in 1993 just how good the next seven years would be.

CHAPTER

TWENTY-TWO

George Steinbrenner returned to the Yankees after his suspension was lifted, on a gorgeous spring morning in March 1993. It was only seventy years after Babe Ruth had opened the House That Ruth Built with a home run against the Boston Red Sox, his former team. Thus started the Curse of the Bambino.

Steinbrenner would enjoy the historic symbolism as he returned to the team he had built over the last twenty years.

The Boss had walked a little over a mile from a private airport in Fort Lauderdale, just behind the spring training complex down Commercial Boulevard, where he had flown in from his Tampa home. He was accompanied by Howard Rubenstein, one of the most powerful public relations gurus, just in case the waiting press got a little too close with questions about the strange deal sending Steinbrenner back to the baseball trenches.

Yankee officials had advertised that Steinbrenner would show up shortly after ten o'clock in the morning. Everyone there expected his limousine to pull into the parking lot around that time. Steinbrenner was not Marilyn Monroe. He was usually on time for his press conferences.

Suddenly, he appeared on foot, casually walking alongside Rubenstein, a huge smile on his face, warm handshakes and greetings for most of us who had known him now for twenty years. He had arrived for the first time fifty years after Ruth became a Yankee. Now he had his second postsuspension return—as dramatic as Douglas MacArthur's return to the Philippines.

Was is that important to Yankee fans? Well, the 1990s, after Steinbrenner's return, would prove even more successful for the Yankees than the 1920s.

He wore a sports shirt without a tie that March day, a Florida outfit seen everywhere. His dark slacks were neatly pressed. His shoes were brightly shined. His hair was freshly cut. The click, click, click of waiting cameras continued as he walked slowly into the crowd of print press, television cameras, radio interviewers, and uncertain Yankee officials.

"I'll have a press conference later," he told the press.

Then he began answering all the shouted questions, describing his absence from the daily running of his team as bitter for himself and his family. He announced that he was enormously pleased to be back, certain he was on the right path in seeing the return of the Yankees to their former days of glory, and anxious to get on with the job.

No one could really explain Steinbrenner's electricity. Other baseball owners have been suspended. Others have been successful. Others have fought with players, officials, and fans. None seem to do it with the flair and attention Steinbrenner mustered every time he shows up in a public place.

Many years earlier baseball owners had attended a meeting in Chicago to discuss the latest conflagration with players' leader Marvin Miller. The owners included such famed celebrities as former cowboy movie star Gene Autry, owner of the California Angels; Bill Veeck of the Chicago White Sox; Walter O'Malley of the Los Angeles Dodgers; John McMullen of the Houston Astros; Charles O. Finley of the Oakland Athletics; and Tom Yawkey of the Boston Red Sox. Gabe Paul, jammed into the entrance of an elevator by the hungry press, had represented the Yankees at the meeting. Paul, upset at the crowd pushing closer to him, was growing angry.

"There's George," a reporter yelled.

The press departed instantly for the spot being pointed to by one of the horde.

Paul quickly entered the elevator and disappeared into his

room. Steinbrenner was not found. Some New York sportswriter had saved Paul from such harassment. He would be repaid later with a story about a trade.

Steinbrenner never understated his own magnetic powers. A high school kid named John Elway showed up at Yankee Stadium one day early in 1982. He had been a tremendous football player and a capable baseball player. He wanted a college education and then a professional sports career. Steinbrenner thought he could make a personal appeal and get the kid with the Yankees.

Elway signed with the Yankees after Steinbrenner entertained him in his Yankee offices. He played a season at Oneonta, New York, batted .318 in forty-two games, entered Stanford University in the fall, starred as a college quarterback, and went on to two Super Bowl wins with the Denver Broncos in his Hall of Fame career.

With Steinbrenner back in power, the 1993 Yankees took on a more serious look. They had acquired Paul O'Neill from Cincinnati and had Bernie Williams about ready for stardom. They had signed Boston Red Sox star Wade Boggs to play third base and left-hander Jim Abbott as a pitcher. Abbott, of course, was one of the game's most dramatic stories ever since he proved that being born without a right hand would not keep him from a sparkling college career and a big league pitching job.

Second-year manager Buck Showalter could also look ahead to the improvement of the team, with highly regarded minor league players including a talented shortstop named Derek Jeter and a left-handed pitcher named Andy Pettitte.

What had really changed around the Yankees under Showalter's leadership was the team attitude. They had finished fourth in 1992 but had played hard every game. They finished second in 1993, drew well over two million fans, and proved to all that they were heading back into contention.

Showalter was an intense man. He studied every aspect of the game, analyzed every opponent, considered every option.

The tomfoolery of earlier years was gone. Showalter's teams were run in a businesslike manner. Early Yankee teams won but they also had more fun doing it. The Yankees of the late 1950s and 1960s, the Yankees of Mickey Mantle, Whitey Ford, and Tom Tresh, enjoyed their days on and off the field.

Beautiful women, known in the trade as Baseball Annies, followed these players everywhere, often offering their services just to be close to a sports hero. Ballplayers are almost always young, athletic, and rich, a rather attractive combination for most females.

The Yankees of the 1970s, the winning Yankees of Reggie Jackson, Lou Piniella, Thurman Munson, Catfish Hunter, Goose Gossage, Chris Chambliss, Willie Randolph, also played hard on and off the baseball field.

So did the losing Yankees of the 1980s. All of that seemed to change dramatically under Showalter in the early 1990s.

When riding a team bus once with the Yankees in the 1960s I learned their value system with one small experience. The bus moved toward a downtown hotel, and a beautiful girl stood outside the entrance. Almost every player got up from his seat to howl his childish greeting at the young lady.

A veteran sportswriter, Harold Rosenthal of the *New York Herald Tribune,* sitting next to me on the team bus, never moved from his seat. He simply turned to me and quietly said, "The road will make a bum out of the best of them."

Showalter seemed able to motivate his players more strongly, to inspire them more purposefully. Their raison d'être was the winning of baseball games.

The player most in Showalter's image in his earliest managerial days was Paul O'Neill. He came to the Yankees in a trade for Roberto Kelly on November 3, 1992. O'Neill would hit over .300 for the Yankees in the next six seasons, a remarkable feat. He became this Yankee generation's Old Reliable, the nickname put on rightfielder Tommy Henrich of the Yankees who played alongside Joe DiMaggio for so many years. Tommy Henrich was famous for hitting in the clutch, a skill O'Neill, brother of famed *New York Times* food critic Molly O'Neill, would show often. He might throw a bat or kick a water cooler if he didn't deliver with men on bases but most often he was the key man in starting or building a rally.

"He's very demanding of himself," Showalter once said. "He hit a homer into the upper deck and it bounced on the field. He was mad because it didn't stay in the seats."

"Sometimes people say there might have been a kid watching you after you do something," O'Neill said. "There probably was. But through the course of 162 games, there's going to be times when this game gets to you. Some people keep it in. Some people don't. I guess I don't."

The most emotional event of the 1993 season, since the Yankees didn't win, occurred on September 4, 1993. Jim Abbott pitched a no-hitter against the Cleveland Indians. The score was 4-0. It was the eighth no-hitter in the ninety-year history of the Yankees and the first since Dave Righetti beat the Boston Red Sox on George Steinbrenner's birthday, July 4, 1983.

"So many things have been nice in my career and this is certainly at the top of them," Abbott said after the game.

What was more amazing was simply the fact that Abbott was in the big leagues at all. He had been born without a right hand. That did not prevent him from being a high school baseball and football star, a baseball star for the University of Michigan, a member of the 1988 gold-medal-winning United States Olympic baseball team, and a reliable pitcher for the Angels and Yankees.

Abbott was popular with his teammates, a soft spoken, intelligent young man who did nothing to emphasize or diminish his unique physical status. He was not pointed out by teammates or opponents and except for the occasional letter he received and always answered from a youngster who might have lost a hand, he was simply another baseball player.

It was quite different in 1945 when a one-armed outfielder

named Pete Gray (born Peter Wyshner in Nanticoke, Pennsylvania) played for the St. Louis Browns. He batted .218 in seventy-seven games with his left hand. He caught baseballs as an outfielder, flipped the ball in the air, stuck his glove under his right armpit, and fired the ball back into the infield.

His teammates rode him terribly about his disability, called him horrible names, and helped drive him out of baseball quickly. He was a crusty, angry man and soon settled back in his coal mining hometown where he spent most of his off time sitting in local bars. When reporters showed up to interview him years later, including myself, Pete Wyshner would always deny he was the guy named Pete Gray who once played in the big leagues.

Veteran New York sportswriters actually had experience with a one-armed colleague. There was a sportswriter named Tommy Holmes who wrote for the *Brooklyn Eagle* and later the *New York Herald Tribune*. He could type faster with one finger than most sportswriters could with ten. He was a fine writer and a pleasant fellow when he stayed away from the sauce.

One night while I was traveling with the New York Mets to San Francisco in the early 1960s, the team took the sportswriters out to dinner in the fashionable Blue Fox restaurant. I was there for the *New York Post*, Tommy Holmes was there for the *Herald Tribune*, and Jack Lang was there for the *Long Island Press*.

Lang became excited about a huge pepper mill that sat on the table. It was two feet tall with decorative designs cut into the shining wood. The longer the evening went on and the more the alcohol was consumed, the more determined Lang became to snatch the pepper mill from the table and bring it home as a trophy. Lang was asked how he could possibly get something that large out of the restaurant without anyone noticing.

"We're in San Francisco," he said. "I'll put it up Tommy Holmes's sleeve and we'll walk out of here holding hands."

Lang was a guy who was quick with a quip. He could cut people down with a fast phrase. He once sat next to famed columnist Jimmy Cannon, a friend and literary hero of Ernest Hemingway's, on a cross-country flight from Los Angeles to New York during the 1963 World Series between the Dodgers and the Yankees.

Cannon rambled on for several hours during he flight about his past columns, about the famous people such as Hemingway who were pals of his, about how influential he was as a sportswriter in America.

"How many great sportswriters do you think there are in America?" Cannon asked Lang.

"One less than you think, Jimmy," Lang said.

Cannon was truly a great sportswriter. He hung out nightly in Toots Shor's famous restaurant on Fifty-second for many years and mingled with celebrities such as Hemingway when the famed novelist was in town.

Cannon once accompanied Shor, Hemingway, and Joe DiMaggio to a Yankee Stadium fight between Joe Louis and Billy Conn. Fans screamed out the name of the Yankee Clipper and a few even noticed Shor and Cannon, whose pictures were often in the local newspapers, but nobody noticed Hemingway.

A youngster tapped the novelist on the shoulder as he walked down the aisle next to DiMaggio and asked, "Are you anybody?"

"Yeah," answered Hemingway, as he pointed toward DiMaggio, "I'm his doctor."

Sportswriters gain their status as much from their writing as from the players they cover, the celebrities they know, the places they go to, the events they attend, and the teams they are connected to in their coverage.

All the New York sportswriters wanted to be connected to the Yankees in 1994, as the team showed strong signs of coming back to prominence. Wade Boggs, who recorded ten straight seasons over .300 with the Boston Red Sox, was now a prominent Yankee. He had batted only .259 in his final Boston season of 1992. The Red Sox thought he was finished as a player. He shocked them with a .302 mark and a .342 mark in his next two seasons with the Yankees.

The 1994 season gave the Yankees a chance for a return to glory. The Major League Baseball Players Union took it away from them when play was shut down in a labor dispute on August 12, 1994, and the World Series was canceled by the owners on September 14, 1994. The Yankees finished first in an aborted 113-game season.

All the fans soured on baseball, and letters poured into newspapers that the Great American Pastime was finished. Nobody believed it but most everybody was angry at the stoppage.

In November of that year, the Baseball Writers Association of New York met at the group's annual meeting. The main business was to plan for the annual winter dinner, a tradition that went back to 1923. It was decided that the only way to entice the usual crowd of 1,500 fans was to bring in some great old heroes. The greatest still around were Willie Mays, Mickey Mantle, and Duke Snider, heroes of the old New York Giants, the Yankees, and the Brooklyn Dodgers.

To entice each of them to attend the event, a new award was created in their names called the Willie, Mickey, and Duke award. These three middle-aged men were to be the first recipients.

Mantle flew up from Dallas for the dinner late in January 1995. Snider came in from his home in Fallbrook, California, and Mays came east from his San Francisco home.

The dinner was a smashing success. The ballroom of the Sheraton New York was filled to capacity, and the 1,500 fans who attended cheered themselves hoarse as the three great stars of yesterday were introduced again to the crowd.

They each accepted their award with modesty. Willie Mays, most touched, said that he knew now that his name would last forever in New York through this award. Snider said it was wonderful to be remembered in New York after all these years away. Mantle had appeared at the dinner some years earlier, gotten wildly drunk, and filled the room with obscenities as he spoke of his days in New York and the harsh financial treatment he believed he had received from the Yankees.

This 1995 appearance was different. He had been cured of his drinking by a long stay at the Betty Ford clinic in Rancho Mirage, California. He had been frightened by doctors warning him about what his drinking might do to his health, and he had been emotionally battered by the death of Billy Martin in a drinking-related automobile accident.

Now he spoke quietly, quickly, thanking the baseball writers for the award, telling the audience how much he loved playing in New York, reminding all the listeners of his status as an icon of the game.

"I just appreciate this so much," he said. Then he sat down as 1,500 fans in the huge ballroom stood and applauded him.

It was the last time most of them would see him.

He entered a Dallas hospital in June 1995 and received a new liver in a transplant on June 8, 1995. Some critics complained that others on the list were not as successful as Mantle in getting a liver donor and transplant so rapidly. Doctors denied there was any favoritism.

Most people hardly cared. This was Mickey Mantle the doctors were trying to save. Didn't he deserve an edge? Mantle improved, held a press conference in Dallas, reminded all his fans young and old alike to take better care of themselves than he had, and thanked his doctors for helping him. He urged all his fans to sign donor cards.

In a few days doctors discovered that Mantle's cancer had spread to other organs despite the transplant. On August 13, 1995, Mantle died. He was eulogized at Lovers Lane United Methodist Church in Dallas. They rounded up the usual suspects—George Steinbrenner, Reggie Jackson, Whitey Ford, Yogi Berra, Johnny Blanchard, Moose Skowron, and Bobby Murcer. Actor Billy Crystal was there. So was New York governor George Pataki.

Broadcaster Bob Costas handled the eulogies after former teammate Bobby Richardson extolled his baseball leader. Costas told a story Mantle had often told himself.

"Mickey pictured himself at the pearly gates," Costas said, "and he was met by St. Peter who shook his head and said, 'Mick, we checked the record. We know some of what went on. Sorry we can't let you in. But before you go, God wants to know if you'd sign these six dozen baseballs.' Well, there were days when Mickey Mantle was so darn good that we kids would bet that even God would want his autograph."

Mickey Mantle was gone at the age of sixty-three, a lot longer life than he or anyone who had hung around with him for lots of years could have expected.

Mantle had dominated the Yankees in the 1950s and 1960s. Steinbrenner had brought in Catfish Hunter and Reggie Jackson and all the rest in the 1970s and had kept the franchise in turmoil in the 1980s without much success.

Now in the 1990s the new era of Yankee glory was approaching. It was the era of Paul O'Neill and Bernie Williams, the era of Wade Boggs and Derek Jeter, of David Cone and Mariano Rivera, of John Wetteland and his battered hat and Tino Martinez and his slugging bat.

Yankee Stadium would once again be a House of Heroes. A kid from Brooklyn would make it happen.

CHAPTER

TWENTY-THREE

The 162-game American League Yankees schedule, in place since the 1961 season of Roger Maris and Mickey Mantle in their thrilling home run race, settled for all of 144 games in 1995.

The game that was supposed to die with labor disruption emerged alive and reasonably well again in the spring of 1995 when the owners cleverly pitched camp with replacement players.

People named Bubba Carpenter, Tremayne Donald, Dave Renteria, and Mike Pitz replaced Don Mattingly, Wade Boggs, Paul O'Neill, and Pat Kelly in the Fort Lauderdale Yankee Stadium.

Some of them were bartenders, truck drivers, computer technicians, and liquor salesmen instead of pitchers, catchers, first basemen, and outfielders. It was the first spring any sportswriter or fan could remember when you couldn't tell the players, even *with* a scorecard.

It would be April 25 before the season really started. The gloom and doom sayers were again proven wrong when fans booed the players early and rooted for them late in all the opening games. As famous sports columnist Jimmy Cannon once said while a colleague named Joe King of the *New York World Telegram and Sun* babbled on in the press box about a football game he had covered, "baseball, gentlemen, baseball."

It was baseball again for the big leaguers, the fans, the press, and the owners. It was the end of a chance at that Field of Dreams for most of the replacement players, but a few did survive to see their names on a big league roster despite union militancy and harassment among many of the players.

Under Buck Showalter's leadership, the Yankees played hustling, exciting, intense baseball. They weren't as good as the Red Sox that year, who won the division, but they were good enough to win the wild card berth, an entry-level position for postseason play.

Mickey Mantle had died on August 13, 1995, and the Yankee pinstripes would carry a black stripe on their sleeves to honor him the rest of their way.

Another event of note occurred in the game that year in Baltimore when one of the historic numbers of baseball was passed. Every kid in New York knew what 2,130 meant when I was growing up. It was the number of consecutive games played by Lou Gehrig.

Gehrig, of course, was one of the Yankee icons. Nearly every fan had seen Gary Cooper play him in *The Pride of the Yankees*. His widow, Eleanor Twitchell, was a frequent visitor to Yankee Stadium events for many years, often sitting alongside Claire Ruth, the Babe's widow.

Marty Appel, former Yankees publicity director, recalled a day when Eleanor Gehrig showed up for a Yankees Old Timers day. When the ceremonies ended and the honored guests were invited upstairs in the Stadium for dinner, Eleanor Gehrig asked if she could be driven home earlier. Barry Halper, a minority Yankee owner and well-known memorabilia collector, volunteered to take Gehrig's widow home to her Manhattan apartment.

"Mrs. Gehrig invited Barry upstairs and they chatted for several minutes," said Appel. "Finally, when it was time to go, Eleanor asked Barry if he could get her 'some hootch.' He went downstairs, checked with the doorman, and found out that Eleanor Gehrig liked scotch whiskey. He walked over to a nearby liquor store, purchased a few bottles of scotch for her, and returned with the 'hootch.' She was so pleased she asked Barry if he wanted an old uniform Gehrig happened to wear on the day he announced his retirement, July 4, 1939."

Halper took the uniform home and added it to his magnificent collection. Years later, when he sold his collection (for tax reasons) it went for nearly half a million dollars when it was auctioned off at Leland's in Manhattan. The rest of Halper's collection was disposed of in a 1999 auction at Sotheby's in Manhattan. The Gehrig uniform earned a lot more for the Halper family than Ty Cobb's dentures. These also were sold at auction, and earned $7,475—part of what turned out to be Halper's $40 million collection.

Actor Billy Crystal, a lifelong Yankee fan from New York, attended the Halper memorabilia auction at Sotheby's in 1999. He sat quietly in a front row of the auction house until a 1960 glove used by his hero of all heroes, Mickey Mantle, was put up for bidding. After spirited bidding Crystal bought the glove for a quarter of a million dollars. He immediately went upstairs to the suite where Halper was sitting, watching his collection go.

Crystal told Halper he wanted to call his mother to inform her of his purchase.

"Mom, I just bought a Mickey Mantle glove," he told her.

"How much did you pay?" she asked.

"A quarter of a million dollars," he said.

There was a long pause on the other end of the phone.

Then Crystal's mother asked, "What was wrong with the glove we bought you at Davega's?"

A few weeks later, Crystal, a quick quipster, attended the HBO screening of a documentary on the life of broadcaster Howard Cosell. He walked into the auditorium of The Equitable Center in Manhattan, spotted former heavyweight champion George Foreman, father of several sons named George, and a Cosell favorite, and introduced him to his nephew John.

"I have four nephews named John," deadpanned the great Yankee fan and new owner of the 1960 Mickey glove.

A couple of days later, Crystal worked out at Yankee Stadium with the team before the Yankees took off for the first 1999 World Series game against the Braves in Atlanta. He wore a Yankee uniform, carried his Mickey Mantle glove, and fielded ground balls around second base with Chuck Knoblauch. He threw a little like Knoblauch.

"Joe Torre let me come out here and work out with the team for luck," Crystal said. "I put my cup on and went right out to second base."

On September 6, 1995 shortstop Cal Ripken of the Baltimore Orioles would break Lou Gehrig's record for consecutive games played, in an emotional setting at Camden Yards. Gehrig teammate Joe DiMaggio was on hand to congratulate him. Ripken continued playing every day until September 20, 1998, when he asked manager Ray Miller to remove him from the starting lineup. He had played in 2,632 consecutive games. This was the first game he had not started since May 29, 1982.

It was an incredible achievement for the future Hall of Famer but it did not have the dramatic, lasting power of Gehrig's retirement speech, which echoed through Yankee Stadium that famous day in 1939. Few youngsters would repeat what Ripken said on *his* famous day (not much), while many have repeated, and still repeat, the echoing Gehrig line in the sold-out Stadium starting out, "Today [with the echo repeating *today . . . today . . . today*] I consider myself [echo repeating *I consider myself . . . myself . . . myself*] . . ." a speech as famous to some as Lincoln's Gettysburg Address.

John Drebinger of the *New York Times* knew Gehrig well. He once told me the only negative thing I had ever heard about this heroic Yankee figure.

"When he didn't want to talk to the press in those days, maybe just five or six of us around, he would go into the trainer's room. It had always been open to the beat reporters. Gehrig made it a private place for players only," said Drebinger.

Howard Cosell always claimed, "I tell it like it is." Sometimes, a sportswriter has to do that, even if he throws a little dirt on an icon. There was one other aspect of Gehrig's Yankee standing that mattered to sportswriters.

The Yankees by tradition had always been close-mouthed about the injuries to their players. Someone in the past, not known to me, created the phrase "Day to day," in explaining how long a player would be out of the lineup. This simply meant nobody—especially paying fans—could be certain if that injured player would be back in the lineup. Gehrig traveled with the Yankees for some time after his announced withdrawal from the lineup. For many reasons it was never stated that he would not play again, so even Gehrig's absence after his famous speech, which clearly showed that he would never play again, had to be explained by the Yankees as "day to day."

Don Mattingly never could quite measure up to Gehrig, but in his final Yankee season of 1995 he did make it to postseason play.

In his final season with the Yankees, the guy the press had come to call "Donnie Baseball" batted .417 with ten hits in twenty-four at bats and a homer against the Seattle Mariners in the 1995 Division series.

Mattingly had lost most of his batting power by then, with a troubling back problem. He fought through in the playoff, starred in a losing cause for the Yankees, and strengthened his credentials for Baseball Hall of Fame consideration. It would be another year, January 22, 1997, before Mattingly officially announced his Yankee retirement. He was only thirty-four years old in his final season.

On October 3, 1995, the Yankees played their first postseason game in fourteen years. The drought had ended. The Yankees were back in contention for baseball honors. The next five years would see the Yankees in postseason play every October.

The five games between the Yankees and the Seattle Mariners, managed by former Yankee outfielder Lou Piniella, were as thrilling a collection of baseball games as ever played. There is something so special, so unique, so gripping about baseball postseason play. Grandmothers who never watch a game all year will skip their sewing to watch these games. Stockbrokers will pass up a big buy order to stay in touch with play. Sanitation workers, truck drivers, and ditch diggers will carry portable radios or jump into a neighborhood bar to stay close to the event.

Even sportswriters get carried away by postseason play.

First of all, there are so many sportswriters. While the Yankees may have eight or ten regular writers on the road during the season, an occasional television reporter, and a few young correspondents with radio microphones, postseason play may include seventy-five or a hundred members of the media.

Some years back, in a Yankee World Series, maybe a hundred sportswriters and television people surrounded Whitey Ford after he pitched a marvelous game. Ford had emerged from the shower room into the mass of media bodies. He turned to Mickey Mantle and asked, "Where the hell did all these guys come from?"

Mantle looked over the crowd and spotted one gawky, unattractive, unfamiliar face.

"I don't know about these other guys," quipped Mantle, as he pointed to the funny-looking fellow, "but this one came from Barnum and Bailey."

While the postseason environment around a clubhouse is certainly larger, it is also much different.

Ralph Terry of the Yankees won the 1962 World Series against the San Francisco Giants when slugger Willie McCovey lined out to second baseman Bobby Richardson.

Several dozen sportswriters surrounded Terry in the clubhouse after the game for his views on his winning performance. Terry was being questioned about his pitching style, his mental attitude about the final out situation, and his feelings about winning the last Series game after losing the last Series game in Pittsburgh two years earlier to Bill Mazeroski's home run.

Suddenly Terry was called away from the crowd by clubhouse man Pete Sheehy for a phone call. He returned after some few minutes and was asked by reporter Stan Isaacs of Long Island's *Newsday* who he was talking to on the phone.

"That was my wife congratulating me," said Terry.

"What was she doing?" inquired Isaacs.

"She was feeding the baby," said Terry.

"Breast or bottle?" asked Isaacs.

The answer is lost to laughter in sportswriting history but

the question has forever remained in press box circles as the definitive "chipmunk" question. The "chipmunks" were a group of new, young sportswriters in the early 1960s, myself included, who asked players more intimate questions than Babe Ruth ever had to answer to John Drebinger of *the New York Times*.

While no historic chipmunk questions were asked in the Yankees battle with the Mariners, the games became memorable.

A six-feet ten-inch left-hander with long hair, blemished skin, and a wicked fastball and slider named Randy Johnson, and the handsome son of former Yankee Ken Griffey, named Ken Griffey, Jr., called Junior, age twenty-five that year, did the Yankees in. Both were brilliant in that playoff, making the big pitch and getting the big hit as Seattle beat the Yankees three games to two.

Edgar Martinez won the final game of the playoff with a two-run double in the eleventh inning off Jack McDowell.

David Cone had won the first game and Mariano Rivera had won the second game in relief after Jim Leyritz enshrined himself forever in Yankee lore with a two-run homer in the bottom of the fifteenth inning.

Randy Johnson won the third game, Yankee reliever John Wetteland, who wore the same sweaty baseball cap all year, lost the fourth game in relief, and Johnson won the final game in the third relief appearance of his career.

Yankee fans probably remembered a game-tying, bases-loaded walk given up by David Cone to journeyman Doug Strange in the bottom of the eighth inning of the final playoff game as the mortal blow for them in the playoff. So does Cone.

For more than a month after he issued that walk to tie the game, Cone remained home in his Manhattan apartment. He thought about the slider he threw low over and over again. He could not shake the depression. He was angry with himself for failing his teammates.

Late in November, Cone appeared at a charity auction at Mickey Mantle's restaurant on Central Park South. Restaurant owner Bill Liederman, who was concerned about the future of the restaurant after Mantle died on August 13, 1995, was surprised when Cone showed up as advertised.

"I know how bad he feels," Liederman said, as we sat in a corner of his place. "I really didn't expect him."

Cone—tall, handsome, well dressed—walked through the revolving doors, shook hands with welcoming fans, signed autographs, smiled for the photographers, and appeared comfortable.

"This is my first time out of the apartment in public," Cone said, as we waited for the program to begin. "I have been so down, so tortured by that pitch."

Cone had come over to the Yankees in July of that year in a trade with Toronto. He finished the season 18-8 and was clearly one of the best pitchers in the game. No matter. It was that one single pitch, that low slider, that called ball, that would identify Cone in the hearts and minds of Yankee fans.

That charity appearance at Mantle's helped Cone escape the trauma. His pitching life went on. Ralph Branca may be remembered for the 1951 home run he gave up to Bobby Thomson as the Giants beat the Dodgers in the Polo Grounds in New York. Mark Littell may be remembered for the home run he gave up to Chris Chambliss for the 1976 Yankees win over Kansas City. Mike Torrez may be remembered for the home run he gave up to Yankee shortstop Bucky Dent in the 1978 playoff against Boston at Fenway Park. Cone may be remembered for that walk though he has been a marvelous Yankee pitcher ever since with so many important wins. Sometimes the Great American Pastime can be a damn painful game.

Cone would finally wipe away the bitter memory forever on July 18, 1999. He pitched a perfect game that day against the Montreal Expos in a 6-0 game with twenty-seven up and twenty-seven batters down. It was Yogi Berra Day with World Series perfect-game-pitcher Don Larsen on hand to watch it. Larsen had also remembered the 1998 perfect game pitched by David Wells.

"It's getting to be a habit, huh?" Larsen said after the Cone gem.

The 1995 playoff defeat had lingered like a dark cloud over New York City for many weeks. George Steinbrenner remained grouchy. Yankee office personnel hid from him as best they could. His telephone calls from Tampa to New York were frequent—and often painful for the receiver on the other end.

Manager Buck Showalter, who had gotten the team to postseason play for the first time in fourteen years, discussed his contract repeatedly with Steinbrenner. The Boss admired what Showalter had done but like Vince Lombardi before him, Steinbrenner was a believer in the theory that winning, winning it all, was the *only* thing. Showalter had gotten the Yankees into the playoff. He did not win. That made Steinbrenner uncomfortable and when Showalter asked for more money and more time on his contract, Steinbrenner backed off.

They started missing each other's phone calls. Their conversations were short and not so sweet. The tension was building. Nothing was happening. Finally, Buck Showalter was gone from the Yankees.

Gene Michael, Steinbrenner's longtime front-office favorite, then decided he would live longer if he lived away from Steinbrenner's daily harangues. He resigned as general manager and was appointed an important scout.

Bob Watson, a former Yankee slugger, became one of the few African Americans to hold an important baseball executive position when he was named general manager of the Yankees on October 23, 1995.

Baseball's racial history is spotty. Jackie Robinson broke the color line as a player with the Brooklyn Dodgers in 1947. Frank Robinson, no relation to Jackie, broke the color line as a manager with Cleveland in 1975. Bill Lucas, a brother-in-law of home-run-king Hank Aaron, broke the color line as GM with the Atlanta Braves under Ted Turner's ownership.

A few other Blacks were named managers and minor executives through the years. This was not an avenue black players or executives saw as having great career opportunities.

One baseball executive explained their consensus thinking on the subject in the early 1970s. "If you won't drink with them at your country club and play golf with them," he said, "you won't hire them."

It is interesting how many times President Bill Clinton made a statement on racism simply by being photographed playing golf with his pal Vernon Jordan, a successful African American businessman, at dozens of snooty country clubs. He may be remembered more for that than for Monica.

Now Watson's first job was to find Steinbrenner a manager for 1996.

Arthur Richman took care of that chore for Watson.

Richman was a newspaper man with a long career on the *New York Daily Mirror*. He had become a baseball fan as a kid growing up in the Bronx. He had connected with the old St. Louis Browns when several of their players signed autographs for him outside the Stadium, chatted for several minutes after games, and finally invited him and his older brother, Milton Richman, into their clubhouse.

Arthur Richman later spent spring trainings with the Browns, stayed close to the retired players through the years, and always attends annual reunions in St. Louis with the decreasing numbers of former St. Louis Browns players. The Browns franchise moved to Baltimore in 1954 and became the Orioles.

After the *Mirror* folded, Richman went to work for the New York Mets as a public relations representative and traveling secretary. He moved to the Yankees in 1989 and became George Steinbrenner's trusted assistant.

Richman simply knows everybody in the game after more than sixty years around baseball as man and boy. He also doesn't *need* the job, because he inherited great wealth from relatives. On top of that, he was awarded a huge sum of money in an-out-of-court settlement after falling on the concrete steps at Pittsburgh's Three Rivers Stadium.

He and Steinbrenner have had some wonderful screaming matches through the years. Steinbrenner threatens to fire
Richman regularly but never does it. He just likes the fights.
Richman always threatens to leave and never does it. He
loves the fights.

He also loves the connection with the game. When he
was married to his lovely wife, Martha, in 1979, he had ten
best men at his Las Vegas wedding, including Willie Mays,
Ralph Kiner, Ernie Banks, Ralph Branca, Dick Williams,
Lee Mazzilli, Joe Pignatano, Ted Sizemore, Doug Flynn,
and Joe Torre. George Brett named a son Richman after him,
and Johnny Bench promised to lead his eulogy at his funeral.

Steinbrenner asked Richman for a list of potential managerial candidates. Richman insisted there was only one
name Steinbrenner should interview. Richman suggested
Joe Torre, the recently ousted manager of the St. Louis Cardinals.

"Torre? He never won anywhere," said Steinbrenner.
"Besides that, could he possibly deal with managing in New
York?"

Richman explained to Steinbrenner. Torre was a New
York kid from the tough streets of Brooklyn. He had managed some terrible Mets teams under enormous financial
pressures, had done reasonably well at Atlanta and St. Louis,
had been an outstanding player for eighteen years, had won
a batting title and been a National League MVP. Torre was
the guy for the job.

"George kept talking about Tony LaRussa and Jim Ley-
land and I kept talking about Torre. Finally he said, 'Call
him.' I immediately went to my office and called. Torre said
he didn't want to be the general manager of the Yankees.
That's what he thought we wanted. 'Joe. George is considering you as manager of the Yankees.' That kind of floored
him."

On November 2, 1995, Joe Torre was named the thirty-
first manager of the Yankees. The press murdered him in
print. Joe Torre had never made it to the World Series as a

player. He had never made it to the World Series as a manager. What made anybody think he could change that negative record with The Boss's Yankees?

I thought it was a hell of a move. I went back a long way with the Torre family—a Brooklyn kid, growing up a few blocks away from their simple residence at 3322 Avenue T in Brooklyn off East Thirty-fourth street in a two-story brick home owned by his family since 1935.

The Torre father, Joseph Torre, was a volatile New York City police detective who slapped the Torre kids around every chance he got. His wife, Rae, the Torre mother, took a few blows in her time, too, when she wasn't cooking up the Italian meals and serving the right wine for papa Joe. They were later divorced, probably because father Joe Torre spent his police vacations in Florida with another lady.

There were two girls, Rae and Josephine. Josephine later became a nun named Sister Marguerite. Of the three boys, Rocco later became a police detective like his father; Frank, a big league ball player; and then there was baby Joe.

Frank Torre was the star of the James Madison High School baseball team in Brooklyn when I attended the same school. I made the junior varsity as a freshman (everybody who came out did) under coach Artie Wunderlich, a New York high school baseball legend. I was certain I would follow Frank to the big leagues. I did. As a sportswriter.

Frank and I would often talk about his kid brother Joe, in the late 1950s when he was finishing with Milwaukee and when he moved on to Philadelphia in 1962.

"He's a much better player than me," Frank Torre would say. "He just has to lose some weight."

Babied by his family, intimidated by his father, and worshipful of his big league brother, Joe Torre swelled up to a bouncy 245 pounds when he was seventeen years old. He once played on a sandlot team managed by Dodgers shortstop Pee Wee Reese. Urged on by Frank, Reese kidded Joe Torre about his baby fat to Joe's horrible embarrassment.

After he switched his position to catcher, a Milwaukee Braves scout named Honey Russell took a chance on Torre, who starred on a Brooklyn sandlot team called the Cadets. Russell had turned Torre down a year before when he was a fat infielder. Torre had worked out with Frank's team, the Milwaukee Braves, at Ebbets Field. The needlers on that team, one of baseball's wittiest, included Warren Spahn, Eddie Mathews, Del Crandall, Johnny Logan, Lew Burdette, and Joe Adcock.

After Torre worked out with them, brother Frank agitated his own teammates to kid the kid. Spahn took it up immediately, "Hey, hide the food," Spahn yelled. "The Torre kid will eat it all up."

"He was the least likely looking baseball player I ever saw when Frank first brought Joe around," Spahn said of Joe Torre at the 1999 Baseball Hall of Fame reunion in Cooperstown. "I only thought he'd lead the league in portions."

Despite his girth but with a quick bat and new skills as a catcher, Joe Torre was signed by the Braves in 1959. He started as a professional player in 1960 in Eau Claire, Wisconsin, where he hit .344. He was brought up to the big league club in September, got into a couple of games, and started his career as a big league star with the Braves in 1961. Torre starred for the Braves until 1969 when he was traded to the Cardinals. By now he had lost the baby fat but was still considered a burly catcher whose career would probably be shortened by the extra weight he carried. The Braves traded him to St. Louis for Orlando Cepeda. They wanted Torre to play third base and ordered him to lose more weight.

"I was determined to save my career," Torre reminisced, as he lounged in the manager's chair in his office at Yankee Stadium one afternoon in 1999. "I knew I had to lose the weight so I did it."

It paid off. In his first year with the Cardinals he hit .289. In his second year he hit .325. In his third year with St. Louis he hit .363, won the batting title, led the league in hits and RBIs, and proved that a svelte body was the quickest way to big league success. He has kept his weight between 200 and 205 pounds over the last thirty years.

Torre was traded to the New York Mets in 1974. He was an aging third baseman when he succeeded Joe Frazier as the team's manager on May 31, 1977.

Fifteen days later the Mets traded their most popular player ever and a future Hall of Famer, Tom Seaver, known as Tom Terrific and sometimes called The Franchise, to Cincinnati after a long, bitter contract dispute with board chairman M. Donald Grant of the Mets.

As free agency was taking hold in baseball, Seaver wanted his contract renewed at more money. Grant was opposed to renegotiations. He was supported in the press by *Daily News* columnist Dick Young. I supported Seaver in the *New York Post,* suggesting that a player known as The Franchise, who had led the Mets to a World Series triumph in 1969 and an unexpected pennant in 1973, deserved special consideration.

The press battle grew as heated as the contract battle. Young wrote a scathing column about Seaver a couple of days before the June 15 trading deadline. He suggested that Seaver's wife, Nancy Seaver, was jealous of the success, fame, and money now being earned by former Mets teammate Nolan Ryan. His wife, Ruth Ryan, my favorite for baseball's best-looking wife ever, was a close friend of Nancy Seaver when the two pitchers were New York teammates.

Young had a son-in-law who worked for the Mets. He had been hired by Grant. I suggested in print that maybe Young's sympathy for Grant's stand had something to do with that family obligation.

All of this came to a head when Seaver was traded away on June 15. Arthur Richman made the announcement in a crowded, steamy, smelly clubhouse in Atlanta.

Joe Torre, fifteen days into his job as Mets manager, stood against a clubhouse wall as dozens of media men (no women yet in those days) grilled the manager about his position on the deal. There had probably never been a bigger in-season trade in the history of New York baseball. Babe Ruth had been traded in the winter of 1919 from Boston to the Yankees (when The Curse of the Bambino was born) and to the Boston Braves from the Yankees in the winter of 1935.

It was clear that Young had forced the hand of the Mets with his vicious columns.

"Dick Young ran Tom Seaver out of town," I wrote the next day in the *Post* to screaming headlines about the deal.

Torre was incredibly poised that day as he dealt with the press. The questions were rough and ugly. They suggested everything from Torre being a puppet of Grant's in allowing this to happen to being a coconspirator because he saw the powerful Seaver as a threat.

I had always respected Joe Torre as a wonderful player, an honest man, a poised competitor and an intelligent baseball figure. I never saw a baseball person handle himself with more confidence and dignity under enormous pressures than Torre did that day. Ernest Hemingway could have written about Torre's "grace under pressure" after Joe's June 15, 1977, performance.

Joe Torre defined the old cliché about being a stand-up guy when I watched him stand up for several hours in Atlanta's blistering heat that June night in 1977.

Arthur Richman remembered it well, too. That is why he told George Steinbrenner that Torre was his man. The Boss was smart enough to listen to his trusted aide.

CHAPTER

TWENTY-FOUR

George Steinbrenner can be mean. As hard as nails, pedantic, tyrannical, cruel, uncaring, verbally violent, narrow, arrogant, abusive, selfish, and pathologically stubborn. He might fire a secretary or a parking lot attendant for a botched phone call or confusion over a parking spot in the reserved Stadium lot. The Boss might dismiss a failed player for a minor infraction on the field that a Little League coach would understand was an expected part of the game.

Then there is the soft Boss.

Steve Howe had six Yankee seasons as a relief pitcher and nine suspensions for violating baseball's drug rules. Steinbrenner kept bringing him back with a basketful of excuses. Most non-drug-using sportswriters wouldn't know an addict if they fell over him. On the off day in the 1981 World Series between the Yankees and the Los Angeles Dodgers, I called half a dozen Dodgers in the team hotel for a phone interview for the next day's paper because I was confined to my suburban home with jet lag. Three were out. Three refused. Would I have to drag my weary bones to Manhattan for a chance at trapping a Dodger in the lobby? My last call was to reliever Steve Howe.

"Sure," Howe said to my request for some of his time over the phone. "What can I tell you?"

The exclusive interview led the *Post* sports section the next day. I owed Howe one. I never made much of a big deal in print over Howe's cocaine habits, later revealed to include his happy days in Manhattan during the 1981 World Series.

Maybe Steinbrenner felt the same way about the thirty-one Yankee victories Howe had saved. The soft Boss kept bringing him back until Howe simply couldn't pitch anymore.

Steinbrenner could be hit for a charity donation at almost anytime by almost anybody. He was soft on charities run by cops and firemen. He loved anything to do with veterans groups, especially around the Fourth of July. He paid college costs for secretaries and burial costs for the widows of old ballplayers. We members of the press get a reserved place for our cars for each game, a Yankee Stadium treasure on a busy game night as valuable as the Hope diamond. It all depended on the day and his mood. Dwight Gooden and Darryl Strawberry caught him on good days.

The New York Mets first signed Strawberry as a draft choice in June of 1980 out of Crenshaw High in Los Angeles for a $200,000 bonus. It was the first signing by the new owners of the Mets, publishing heir Nelson Doubleday and real estate investor Fred Wilpon. Wilpon had been a pitcher for Lafayette High in Brooklyn who kept a kid named Sandy Koufax on first base for that team.

Strawberry, six feet six and 215 pounds, and a left-handed slugger, was being touted as the black Ted Willliams by the Los Angeles press. I wrote in the *Post* that if he was as good as they said in Los Angeles, Williams would soon be known as the white Darryl Strawberry.

At a Shea Stadium press conference in June 1980, Strawberry, eighteen years old, was hardly the star. His mother was. Ruby Strawberry was a striking beauty. She was also thirty-six years old. Sadly, she succumbed to cancer before she reached the age of fifty. Strawberry was assigned to the Mets farm in Kingsport, Tennessee. I was assigned with him. I had never been in Tennessee except for a little car trip to the border town of Bristol, connecting Virginia and Tennessee when I was about Strawberry's age. Now I was flying there via three other cities just after Strawberry took off.

Chuck Hiller was the manager of the Kingsport Mets. Hiller had hit a World Series grand-slam home run against the Yankees in the 1962 World Series in a game that teammate Tom Haller also homered. Entertainer Danny Kaye made them both famous as he sang a ditty called, "The Hiller, Haller, Hallelujah Twist."

I became pals with Hiller when he joined the Mets in 1965, and we often sat together on the team bus entertaining his teammates with a bad version of the Kaye ditty. Now I wanted his opinion on this new kid, Strawberry.

After the first night of batting practice, after seeing that long swing, that quick bat, that rapid shoulder turn, and those bulging muscles in that lean body, Hiller took off his cap, scratched his bald head, stared at my pencil and notebook, and calmly said, "He'll be a great one. Maybe the greatest home-run hitter of his time."

I rode the bouncy buses with Hiller and Strawberry for a week to Norfolk, Virginia; Birmingham, Alabama; and Knoxville, Tennessee. The players wore old Mets uniforms, got five-dollars-a-day meal money, lived mostly in boarding houses in Kingsport, and walked down Main Street to the ballpark. After the couple of home games I saw Strawberry play in, I bought him dinner at the neighborhood diner recommended by Hiller as the place with the best food in town. He ate two cheeseburgers with french fries and drank Coke. How was I to know that he would like another type of coke so much later on?

We talked of his high school days at Crenshaw, the skills he showed in both baseball and basketball, the thrill he felt at having a chance at being a big league baseball player. He also talked of his home life and the discipline imposed on him by Ruby Strawberry, the single mom who had led him carefully to this point in his life.

"I already miss her," he said, quietly.

Strawberry, as Hiller predicted, became a great star with the Mets and helped them to the 1986 World Series title. He also helped himself to an overabundance of alcohol and cocaine. He was suspended by organized baseball and returned to the game with an independent team in St. Paul, Minnesota.

Steinbrenner took a chance on Strawberry. He warned him his behavior would be constantly examined. It was put on a personal level.

"Embarrass me and I'll destroy you," Steinbrenner told him.

Gooden had been the National League Rookie of the Year for the Mets in 1984 and the Cy Young Award winner with a 24-4 mark and a 1.53 ERA. The Hall of Fame had to be his next stop.

Instead, after the Mets won in 1986, he skipped the team parade in which the players were being honored by the city. It was later revealed that he was drunk and high on cocaine. He was suspended for the 1995 season for violating the drug rules. Steinbrenner took a chance on him for the 1996 season.

On May 14, Gooden pitched a no-hitter against Seattle. It was the first of his career and clearly indicated that Steinbrenner's gamble had paid off.

The Gooden no-hitter indicated clearly that the Yankees were now a deep team under Torre. David Cone, known as baseball's Rent-A-Pitcher for his frequent free-agent moves, was the potential ace of the staff. Jimmy Key was the modern Eddie Lopat, a Yankee pitcher who didn't throw hard but could win. Andy Pettitte was maturing as a solid left-handed starter. The bullpen was controlled admirably by John Wetteland and a skinny kid from Panama named Mariano Rivera who weighed 168 pounds and could throw fastballs at one hundred miles an hour.

Tino Martinez had succeeded Don Mattingly at first base and was handling the pressure well. Second base was a little bit of a jumble with Pat Kelly, Andy Fox, and veteran Mariano Duncan being used cleverly by Torre. Derek Jeter, a handsome kid of mixed racial background, was fast emerging as a solid shortstop with surprising poise for one so young and enthusiastic. Wade Boggs, anxious to get three thousand career hits, did most of the work at third base.

Paul O'Neill, a budding superstar, and Bernie Williams, Gerald Williams, Tim Raines, and Ruben Sierra were all significant contributors. A clever catcher named Joe Girardi, who had earned an industrial engineering degree from Northwestern, was the team's best receiver. Jim Leyritz, a rip-roaring kind of guy, was the important backup.

Torre had also accumulated a terrific coaching staff. He

had Don Zimmer as his bench coach with fifty years in the
game; home run hero Chris Chambliss as batting coach; Mel
Stottlemyre, who led the Yankees to the 1964 surprise pennant as pitching coach. Brooklyn kid Willie Randolph, the
smooth second baseman on the Yankee winners in the
1970s, was third base coach; former outfielder Jose Carde-
nal, a Cuban-born dynamo, was first base coach; and Tony
Cloninger, who once hit two grand slams for Atlanta in a
nine RBI game, was bullpen coach.

Torre's team was ready for 1996 success.

By July the Yankees had busted open the East Division
race. They led by twelve games on July 28. The lead would
slip to as low as two and a half games by September 9 but
with the wild card format instituted in 1995, the Yankees
were guaranteed a playoff spot. They won their division by
four games.

They opened the Division series at Yankee Stadium with
the Texas Rangers beating the Yankees 6-2 behind pitcher
John Burkett.

The Texas nightmare would begin the next day at the Stadium when the Rangers blew a 4-1 lead in a 5-4 loss. Texas
would not come close to beating the Yankees again in postseason play for the rest of the twentieth century.

The Yankees flew out by chartered flight to Arlington,
Texas, just between Dallas and Fort Worth about two hours
after the end of the second game. They would arrive at their
Arlington Marriott Hotel headquarters at about five o'clock
in the morning. Most of the players would have a breakfast
sent up to their rooms so they could make the team bus for
the workout at the Ballpark in Arlington late that afternoon.

I no longer traveled with the Yankees out of town and I
hardly missed those rushed flights after late games, the early
morning arrivals, the office wakeup calls, or the lukewarm
coffee arriving with delayed room service. Being a big
league ballplayer, or chasing big league ballplayers around
the country, is not all gold and glory. Players accept the dis-
comfort because they are making five, ten, or twenty million
dollars a year to do it. Sportswriters are making $50,000, or

$75,000, or $100,000 to do it, so they can more easily walk away from traveling with the clubs.

There is only one veteran sportswriter that I can remember who, after about a half century on the road, spoke with regret after being removed by his sports editor and replaced with a younger writer.

"My God," he moaned. "Now I'll have to sleep with my wife."

The Yankees only had to spend a couple more days in Texas as they won game three by a 3-2 score and wrapped up the Series in game four with a 6-4 win. Bernie Williams, fast emerging as the most devastating hitter on the team, had two home runs, and Cecil Fielder, the huge designated hitter who had once hit fifty-one homers for Detroit, knocked in the lead run with a single.

Baltimore was next in the American League Championship Series. The series seemed to turn in the very first game when a twelve-year-old kid from New Jersey named Jeffrey Maier became the most famous Yankee fan since Sal Durante.

Durante was nineteen when he outraced several other fans for Roger Maris's record breaking sixty-first homer in the lower right-field stands at Yankee Stadium. It would be another thirty-eight years before Mark McGwire would make seventy a number to remember in baseball. Durante was brought into the Yankee clubhouse after the game to pose for pictures with Maris. He got a free trip to San Francisco when a restaurateur bought the ball from him and presented it to Maris. Durante outlasted Andy Warhol's budgetary fifteen minutes of fame by thirty-seven years, at least. When McGwire passed Maris, Durante even made it to several television broadcasts to discuss his connection with baseball history.

Maier was leaning over the right-field stands, well-worn glove in hand, when Derek Jeter lofted a fly ball to right. Right-fielder Tony Tarasco of Baltimore had his back against the wall and seemed certain to catch it or, at the worst, keep it from getting into the stands.

Young Master Maier was quicker than Tarasco, who did not jump for the ball. He leaned out about a foot in front of the wall, pulled it into the seats, and picked it up on a bounce.

Right-field umpire Rich Garcia, one of the game's best, ran hard toward the wall, watched the play, and quickly began circling his right arm over his head, the standard umpiring sign for a home run. The game was tied at 4-4.

In the confusion, Bernie Williams went on to hit a huge home run in the eleventh inning for a 5-4 Yankees win.

"In the confusion . . ." was a standard line heard around New York press boxes by sportswriters who had been around the scene for a while. It simply meant that while making a fuss over one fact in the game or seeing that as the angle for a story, something more important probably happened.

Sportswriter John Drebinger of the *Times* brought the phrase into common press box usage when he told an old story about Babe Ruth being in a house of ill repute when it was raided by local police. The establishment was run by an attractive widow, simply working hard to support her family.

Drebinger would describe the furor of people escaping out of windows, cops busting into perfumed rooms, naked men searching for their shoes, while the baseball legend remained calm.

"In the confusion," Drebinger stated, "the Babe did the widow."

In the confusion the Yankees beat the Orioles four games to one and moved into the World Series against the Atlanta Braves.

Joe Torre, labeled a loser by so many sportswriters when he was hired as Yankee manager for never making a Series as a player and never making one before 1996 as a manager, was now facing his biggest challenge.

The Boss had listened to Arthur Richman and Bob Watson, gambled on Torre, and was now on the threshold of a World Series win again, his first opportunity to sit on top of baseball since 1978.

The Atlanta Braves, managed by a former Yankee journeyman third baseman, Bobby Cox, who had proven his excellence as a manager and general manager, was the powerful opponent.

The Stadium was decked out in all its finery. Flags flew everywhere. Well-dressed men and women sat in the lower boxes. The custom of banners in the ballpark was developed into a fine art in Shea Stadium by Mets fans and the Mets organization. They actually encouraged it with a banner day allowing banner carriers in a march onto the field. Now this glorious custom had spilled over to the Bronx. One of the first spotted in the Stadium read in huge letters TORRE ADORERS.

The kid from Brooklyn had become a Bronx hero.

Torre seemed to understand Steinbrenner better than anyone who had ever worked in baseball for the Boss. John Smoltz of the Braves beat the Yankees in game one with Andy Pettitte being slapped around in a 12-1 loss. Greg Maddux topped Jimmy Key in the second game with a 4-0 Atlanta victory. The teams flew off to Atlanta for the third game of the Series. The Yankees were down two games to none in the best of seven Series.

Steinbrenner called Torre in his Atlanta office before the third game. "Let's not get embarrassed," bellowed the Boss.

"We're fine, we're fine," Torre reassured him calmly.

"I hope you're right," Steinbrenner said. "I trust you."

Torre had learned somewhere along the line how to handle the panicky, blustery Steinbrenner, especially in the tense baseball situations when the team was down and all hell was about to burst loose. Stay calm. Keep your voice down. Agree with the Boss. Then do what you think is best.

It also helps if you have David Cone pitching for your side. Cone, one of the grittiest competitors in baseball, held the slugging Braves down for six innings. He gave up one earned run and allowed Torre to move to his bullpen in the seventh with Mariano Rivera, Graeme Lloyd of Geelong, Australia (really), and John Wettleland for the 5-2 win.

The Yankees won the fourth game to tie the Series at 2-2 with an 8-6 win in ten innings. Wettleland got another save but not another cap in that game and saved Pettitte's gem the next night in a 1-0 win.

The Braves had won the first two in New York, and the Yankees had won the next three in Atlanta. Can you say "home field disadvantage?"

Baseball moved back from its romantic aura into a realistic present the next day when Torre received a call at his suburban Westchester, New York, home that his hero and older brother, Frank Torre, was about to receive a heart transplant.

Frank Torre, now sixty-four years old, had worked for many years after his playing days as a sporting goods salesman. He traveled the country constantly, made deals with players for endorsements, stayed up late discussing gloves and bats and baseballs, moved around from place to place with hardly a pause. His heart took a beating. He was finally taken to Columbia Presbyterian Hospital in New York shortly before the Series began to wait for a heart transplant. He was told if he didn't get it soon he would die. Joe Torre knew the score on that one and interrupted several of his baseball conversations and press briefings with phone calls to big brother.

Upon arriving back home after the flight from Atlanta prior to the sixth game, Joe Torre was informed that a heart had been found for his brother. The operation would be performed in the early morning hours, and the surgeon, Dr. Mehmet Oz, soon called Joe Torre with the results. He said Frank Torre had responded well and had a very good chance at life.

Joe Torre, feeling more relaxed now, had a very good chance at his first baseball World Series success as he sat in his Stadium office the next day. He had visited big brother Frank the previous night, seen that he was comfortable, talked about his game the next day, and felt certain that a victory would be as important a medical tool as a scalpel.

The Yankees got three runs off Maddux in the third inning of game six, and the Braves picked up a run off Jimmy Key in the fourth. John Wettleland carried the 3–1 lead into the ninth inning. The Braves got a run but Wetteland got Atlanta second baseman Mark Lemke to hit a foul ball to third base with two out.

The ball curled toward the stands and then back onto the field as foul baseballs so often do for mystical reasons only physicists can truly explain. Charlie Hayes, a journeyman player who had replaced veteran star Wade Boggs at third, moved back for the ball. It came down on a slight slant and Hayes bent with it. He caught it above his head with his glove and his bare hand covering the baseball as he did a strange wiggle. Game over. The New York Yankees had their twenty-third World Series championship.

The bench players raced onto the field and launched themselves on top of the field players. The wrestling, patting, pounding, laughing, screaming, shouting, and squeezing of every other man in Yankee pinstripes went on for several minutes.

Mounted New York City police officers, keeping the crowd of fans away, filled the field. Wade Boggs, exuberant at his team's victory after being on the field in the bitter Boston defeat against the Mets in the 1986 World Series, was helped onto a police horse being ridden by mounted officer Lt. James Higgins of the NYPD. The Lone Ranger never looked better on Silver as Boggs circled the field.

Champagne filled the clubhouse. Television interviewers chased everyone. Players shouted. A few players, notably Bernie Williams, sat away from their teammates in amused separation. After all, these were highly paid professional athletes performing childish acts. Well, it had only been going on for a century or so.

Finally, in his office, covered with champagne, with sweat, and with shaving cream, Joe Torre called his brother at the hospital. His eyes were filled with tears, burning his face slightly when mixed with the bubbly champagne.

"You'll get a ring," little brother told big brother. "You can count on that."

Some months later Frank Torre sat in the press room under the stands at Yankee Stadium before a game. He ap-

peared quite healthy. We talked about a James Madison
High School reunion, something we had both been invited to
as graduates of the Brooklyn school. I asked him if he would
be at the event.

He thrust out his left hand. A diamond ring with a large
NY on top seemed to glow across the table.

"Should I show them this?" he asked.

CHAPTER

TWENTY-FIVE

Legends Field in Tampa, Florida, just along 1 Steinbrenner Drive, is the spring training home of the Yankees. It was opened in 1996 as the Yankees trained there for their first World Series title in eighteen years.

Joe Torre opened up his second spring training as manager of the Yankees there on February 18, 1997. He wasn't wearing his World Series ring or much of anything else as we chatted in his office alongside the bustling clubhouse filled with sixty-two players.

I had last seen him a few weeks earlier at the New York Baseball Writers dinner in Manhattan. He and brother Frank Torre had been awarded the organization's Toast of the Town award for the heroics of 1996, a world championship for the Yankees with Joe Torre as manager and life for Frank.

What seemed most remarkable about Joe Torre that spring was that nothing was remarkable. After some thirty-seven years in professional baseball, he still retained the same calm, cool, collected attitude he had shown throughout his career. A world championship would not change this guy.

We talked mostly that day about his new home in Harrison, in Westchester County, about the joy his new baby daughter had brought to him and his wife, Alice, about the good fortune he felt now with his brother's improved health. We talked about his contentment in achieving this success.

"I'll be sixty years old in three years," said Torre. "I don't expect to be doing this by then. I think it will be enough. I want to see my daughter grow up."

As defending champions the Yankees were favorites to win again in 1997. Nobody knew the Baltimore Orioles would go wire to wire as the first-place team in the East. The Yankees won the wild card spot and would at least make the playoffs for the third straight year.

As I left Legends Field that afternoon I stopped to examine the monuments and plaques to the Yankees of the past. There were beautiful flowers in a garden outside the stadium, and the grass was cut tight. Each plaque—for Babe Ruth, Lou Gehrig, Joe DiMaggio, Mickey Mantle, Roger Maris, Yogi Berra, Phil Rizzuto, Whitey Ford, Casey Stengel, and the rest—seemed to glisten in the Florida sun. Here was a capsule history of the Yankees from their glorious days in the early 1920s reaching to the new success in the 1990s, that linkage that made these players who wore the pinstripes, the managers and coaches included, so very special in the American sports scene.

Yankee fans gloried in the team's new success, while Boston fans and Cleveland fans and Baltimore fans and Seattle fans knew they had no history to match it and, more desperately, no future to prevent it continuing on through the final years of the century.

Two new stars would carry the Yankees forward into the twenty-first century as the team to beat. Again.

Derek Jeter is the son of an African American psychologist and social worker father, and a white mother who is an accountant, and is one of fourteen children. Charles and Dorothy Jeter met while they both served in the U.S. Army in Germany. Derek Jeter was born in Pequannock, New Jersey, and the family, including younger sister Sharlee, soon moved to Kalamazoo, Michigan.

His quick baseball success, three World Series appearances in his first four seasons, and his active New York social life made Jeter a glamorous New York sports figure and the darling of female teenagers.

"The golden child of New York," teammate Bernie Williams told columnist Ian O'Connor of *The Journal News* in a 1999 World Series interview. Female fans waited around Yankee Stadium for hours just to get a smile or a photograph of him as he entered the ballpark. He had a joyous face, almost always showing a warm smile, both on and off the field. He lived in a bachelor apartment in Manhattan and dined in some of the more glamorous New York night spots with teammates and civilian friends. His name appeared constantly in newspaper gossip columns, and when he was discovered leaving the apartment building of singer Mariah Carey, it made for blazing headlines.

"I just like to have fun," explained Jeter.

He had become one of the best shortstops in baseball, an efficient hitter with surprising power, an excellent base runner, and a surprisingly astute player for one so young. He was the regular Yankees shortstop and Rookie of the Year in 1996 at the age of twenty-two. Some sportswriters were already measuring him for Hall of Fame honors.

Bernie Williams (Bernabe Figueroa Williams of San Juan, Puerto Rico) had become a superstar player by 1997. He was a quiet, complex man, often keeping to himself in the clubhouse as rowdy scenes whirled around him. He was a classical guitarist who had actually made it to Carnegie Hall as a performer, a jazz aficionado, a biology student with dreams of becoming a doctor while studying at the University of Puerto Rico, and a devoted family man with three small children.

He was a switch hitter with power from both sides of the plate—not seen around the Stadium since Mickey Mantle—a graceful fielder in the style of Joe DiMaggio, a strong base runner, and a powerful outfield thrower. Superstar. If the proof is a contract that shocks fans, Williams proved it a couple of years later when George Steinbrenner agreed to pay him $87 million over seven years.

The other expensive 1997 player, who proved to be much less than a superstar pitcher, was Hideki Irabu, the chubby-faced, dour right-hander from Japan. Steinbrenner decided he wanted Irabu badly, negotiated a deal with the San Padres for his rights, and signed him on May 29, 1997, to a four-year deal. Irabu wouldn't quite be an Ed Whitson, the pitcher who feared pitching in New York, but he would be a lot less than the Yankees had hoped for in obtaining him.

It was clear in the middle of the 1997 season that the wild card was the best the Yankees could do. Baltimore was having an exceptional season and Cleveland and Seattle were the other league powers.

Cleveland beat the Yankees three games to two in the Division series, then went on to beat Baltimore in the American League Championship Series. They failed in an attempt to win their first World Series since 1948 when the Florida Marlins, in their fifth year of existence, won a bitter eleven-inning seventh game 3-2 for the title.

The game that would mark the 1998 season as one of the most exciting in the long, romantic, beautiful history of the Bronx Bombers occurred on May 17, 1998. David Wells pitched a perfect game in beating the Minnesota Twins 4-0 by retiring all twenty-seven hitters in a row, the first regular season perfect game in Yankee history, the first since Don Larsen had done it against the Brooklyn Dodgers in the 1956 World Series.

Wells was a six feet four inch, 240-pound left-handed pitcher obtained as a free agent after the 1996 season. He was classically un-Yankee-like. The image of the Yankees was set for fans by Joe DiMaggio—quiet, elegant, well dressed, modest, proud to be a Yankee.

Wells was this generation's Babe Ruth. He looked a lot like the Babe in his later years: overweight, hard-drinking, fun-seeking, and hell-raising. He even irritated the Yankees front office once by wearing a grubby Babe Ruth baseball cap he had bought at a baseball-card show

He enjoyed going on Howard Stern's raunchy, raucous radio show and bragged about the amount of beer he could consume in one sitting. He seemed always to be reading letters and signing baseballs in the Yankee clubhouse while others exercised, and he never showed any signs of athleticism on or off the mound. He was a good big league pitcher but hardly an athletic role model with the rolls of fat around his middle.

David Letterman wanted Wells as one of ten Yankees his show was recruiting to do his Top Ten List. Nine other Yankees could not be collected for the appearance so the segment was canceled. Wells was rescheduled on Letterman after his perfect game.

Letterman quipped that Wells celebrated after the perfect game by "retiring twenty-seven Heinekens in a row."

Teammate David Cone, who would pitch his own perfect game a year later, was so nervous he could not watch the final out of the game. He simply pulled a jacket over his face before the final out. A group of hip Wells fans, who would not be so mundane as to place *K*s, the baseball scoring shorthand for strikeouts on the Stadium wall, displayed pictures of beer mugs.

Don Larsen, who enjoyed a drink or ten after a game in his time, heard about Wells's perfect game while watching a golf tournament in the living room of his home in a small, rural location in Idaho. Ironically, Wells and Larsen had both pitched for the same high school, Point Loma, thirty-five years apart in San Diego.

After the game Arthur Richman, the Yankees assistant to George Steinbrenner, who had been close to Larsen since his St. Louis Browns days, called the old pitcher on the phone. He told him about Wells's gem and soon put Wells on the phone to talk to Larsen.

"We've never met," Larsen later told *New York Times* columnist George Vecsey by phone after the game, in reference to Wells. "I'm sure we will—probably at some bar."

The Wells perfect game seemed to trigger an immediate surge in the Yankees. By early June the Yankees had an eleven-game lead. By early July they had fattened that lead to fifteen games, and by September the Yankees led the division by twenty games. They would win by twenty-two games with a 114-48 mark, the best in league history. The 1927 Yankees, regarded as baseball's best team ever, were 110–44 with a .714 percentage in a 154-game season. The Yankees percentage in the 162-game season of 1998 was .704 but their win total was tops.

The pitching was nearly unbeatable. David Cone led the staff with twenty wins, with David Wells collecting eighteen, and Andy Pettitte collecting sixteen. Mariano Rivera, who became the saver after John Wetteland left as a free agent for Texas, had thirty-six saves.

Bernie Williams hit .339, Derek Jeter batted .324, and Paul O'Neill hit .317. Tino Martinez had twenty-eight home runs to lead the team in the year Mark McGwire had seventy homers and runner-up Sammy Sosa, who hit more than anyone else in baseball history except for McGwire, had sixty-six.

Jorge Posada and Joe Girardi handled the catching smoothly, newly obtained Chuck Knoblauch was the solid second baseman, Scott Brosius was a surprise at third base with a .300 mark and a good glove, and the bench players almost always delivered.

A handsome youngster from Panama named Ramiro Mendoza was 10-2 as a valuable spot starter and long relief pitcher, and El Duque, Orlando Hernandez, became the most dramatic personal Yankee story in many years.

Hernandez had been a pitching star in Cuban baseball for many years, until October 1996, at which time authorities banned him from the game because they discovered he had ideas about defecting to the United States to cash in on his skills and get away from Cuban oppression. Fidel Castro, the once and former baseball player from Cuba who had become a revolutionary because his curve ball had failed him, would have none of that. Hernandez's younger half-brother, Livan Hernandez, had already defected. He would help the Florida Marlins win the 1997 World Series.

El Duque worked as a rehabilitation physical therapist at a Havana hospital in 1997 while his brother was pitching and making much money for the Marlins. His escape was being planned.

On December 26, 1997, in the dead of night, under a cloudless Cuban sky, he boarded a small boat with his girlfriend, one of his neighborhood catchers, and five other friends and drifted away from Cuba. In three days the boat, with little water and food still left, landed on the tiny Caribbean island of Anguilla Cay. He established residence in Costa Rica and was granted baseball free agency in January 1998. George Steinbrenner agreed to sign the untried pitcher for over six million dollars in March 1998.

He was assigned to Tampa, moved up to Columbus, and joined the Yankees on June 3, 1998. He was 12-4 in twenty-one starts and contributed mightily to the Yankees 1998 success.

El Duque was listed on the Yankees roster as being born October 11, 1969. That would make him thirty years old on that date in 1999. A few days before the start of the American League Championship Series between the Red Sox and Yankees in 1999, court papers made available in Cuba revealed that Hernandez was thirty-four years old. It was clear he left Cuba for the freedom to pitch, the freedom to make big bucks, and the freedom to lie about his age.

He was not the first, and certainly not the last, baseball player to lie about his age. Satchel Paige joined the Cleveland Indians after a long, brilliant career in the Negro Leagues in 1948. He was anywhere from forty-two to forty-eight when he finally got his chance. The Indians chose age forty-two to make up for the years he was banned from baseball because of the color of his skin rather than the speed of his fastball. He made the record books by pitching at age fifty-nine listed on the baseball rosters, in 1965 for Charlie Finley's A's.

Outfielder Billy Bruton began his 1964 retirement press conference in Detroit by announcing, "Gentlemen, I'm not forty years old, I'm forty-four years old. I want that pension."

Pitcher Roland Sheldon claimed he was twenty-four years old when he broke in with the Yankees in 1961. He won eleven games for the team I always considered the best in baseball history, the Mantle-Maris home run Yankees of that 1961 season. His bubble was burst when high school classmates in Putnam, Connecticut, revealed to the local papers that Sheldon was twenty-eight years old. It happens.

The winningest team in baseball history coasted through the Division series against Texas with three straight wins behind a strong opening start by David (Perfect) Wells, a strong performance by Andy Pettitte in the second game, and a 4-0 third game win behind David Cone and super saver Mariano Rivera.

The League Championship Series put the Cleveland Indians against the Yankees again, with Cleveland taking a 2-1 lead after the first three games. The Yankees had won 114 games in the regular season and swept Texas in the Division series for 117 wins. Before the fourth game, George Steinbrenner entered Joe Torre's office in Jacobs Field in Cleveland.

"You know if we don't win this thing, everybody will forget what we did all season," said Steinbrenner.

"Don't worry, Boss. We got El Duque," Torre said.

Steinbrenner was known to panic every time the Yankees fell behind in any regular season game, any regular season series, certainly any postseason series. Only more so, if it happened in Cleveland.

George was a big man in Cleveland before he bought the Yankees. He felt very emotional about his team showing well in Cleveland. It was that father thing.

In the earliest days of his ownership, the players and the press would be invited to wine and dine at one of the Boss's favorite hangouts in downtown Cleveland, the Theatrical Club. The nights would be long and the drinks would be many. The price would always be right. The bill would always go to George.

Steinbrenner always had strong affection for Cleveland and remained there for many years after taking over the Yankee ownership before moving his business and family to Tampa. He just wanted to make sure his team always beat the Indians and his players and press members were well treated at the Theatrical. He felt the same way about Elaine's in Manhattan. The idea wasn't to taste the smoked salmon or sip the French wine. The idea was simply to be there.

"I remember when I was a kid growing up around Cleveland and I would go to games at the old Municipal Stadium and see Joe DiMaggio facing Bobby Feller," he once said. "There could be no greater thrill."

He found out after 1973 that there was a greater thrill for him—the Yankees beating the Cleveland Indians in Cleveland.

On a bitter cold night, October 10, 1998, just ten months removed from the brave defection from Cuba, El Duque shut down the Indians in a 4-0 game to even the series at two games each. Only in America. Hernandez beat Doc Gooden, the pitcher Steinbrenner rescued from the drug lords.

David Wells won the fifth game with help from designated hitter Chili Davis, who had been out most of the year with an ankle injury. David Cone, with strong offensive help, including a three run homer by Scott Brosius, won the sixth game 9-5.

The Yankees were in the World Series for the thirty-fifth time, all since 1921, after a guy named Babe Ruth joined them. Talk about your Curse of the Bambino. Boston last won a Series in 1918 with Ruth a starting pitcher on that team and would have to go into the twenty-first century before they could possibly get another one.

The San Diego Padres, an expansion team from the 1969 season, was the opposition.

The Padres had one of the game's great hitters and nicest men, Tony Gwynn, in their lineup but not much else to compete with the powerful Yankees. It was an overmatch.

The Yankees exploded for seven runs in the seventh inning of the first Series game at Yankee Stadium and won it 9-6. Wells was the winner again with Tino Martinez hitting a grand slam. It was the first Yankees grand slam Series homer since Joe Pepitone did it on October 14, 1964, against the Cardinals in a Series lost by the Yankees. That Series put the Yankees in a Series slump for the next thirteen years before they could win again.

Pepitone, working for the Yankees now as a community relations representative, had become famous before the homer for his artificial-looking long hair, and for bringing the first hair dryers into a baseball clubhouse. He was also famous for the error he made in the 1963 Series when he lost a ball thrown from third baseman Clete Boyer to first in blinding summer shirts in October. Sic transit gloria.

The Yankees won the second game of the Series behind Hernandez again 9-3. They took the third game 5-4 with Mendoza winning in relief on the strength of two homers by Series MVP Scott Brosius and closed out a Series sweep with a 3-0 victory in the final game on October 21, 1998. It was the twenty-fourth Yankee World Series victory, the most championships by any team in any professional sport.

The usual scene followed.

Champagne was uncorked immediately in the Yankees clubhouse at Qualcomm Stadium in San Diego, street clothes in lockers were protected with plastic, sweating ballplayers and grubby members of the press, males and females now, shouted at each other. Blazing hot television cameras were pressed against almost every open spot in the room.

Great old sportswriters Jimmy Cannon and Dick Young knew how to deal with that common championship scene when the cameras were on their backs. They simply shouted obscenities into the live mikes. That tradition seemed to fade as the press corps became a kinder and gentler group with the addition of females. The famed hyphenated word about family relationships, a baseball standard for so many years in both winning and losing clubhouses, now seemed to disappear.

In the wake of the 1996 victory over Atlanta, George Steinbrenner was calm in the clubhouse and Joe Torre was a man of mush. Torre was overwhelmed emotionally in 1996 by the illness of his brother, his first Series appearance as player or manager and his first Series victory.

Steinbrenner had been on top in 1977 and 1978. The 1996 triumph, a long time in coming, was not a unique experience.

There had been rumors late in 1998 that Steinbrenner's time with the Yankees might be coming to a close. He had his son, Hal Steinbrenner, and son-in-law, Steve Swindal, more involved in the operation. He seemed pleased with new general manager Brian Cashman and vice president of player development Mark Newman. There were several stories that as he sought a new stadium, maybe in downtown Manhattan, maybe in New Jersey, and maybe, lastly, in a restructured area around the current stadium in the Bronx, this would be a fitting time for his Yankee farewell. Cablevision was frequently mentioned as a possible purchaser of the Yankees for, oh, maybe a billion or so. All of these stories filled the newspapers almost daily as the season wound down.

Public relations guru Howard Rubenstein, speaking for Steinbrenner on everything except tomorrow's pitcher, would not clear up the issue.

As the cameras moved closer to Steinbrenner in the winning clubhouse madhouse, tears came to his eyes and he seemed unable to articulate his feelings. He got out a few words about the joy of this victory, but for once, after twenty-five years on the Yankees scene, George M. Steinbrenner III was truly in awe of the Yankee tradition, the tradition he himself had so successfully carried forward for a quarter of a century.

Some few months earlier, after nothing had changed in the management of the Yankees and the last seasons of the century were being planned, Steinbrenner agreed to be honored and roasted by the New York sportswriters. The tradition went back seventy-five years. Thirteen of his former public relations directors (they came and went almost as fast as Steinbrenner's managers) were once honored by the group, and Steinbrenner attended. Mostly, he was ripped for firing them all, one at a time. He just laughed.

His assistant, Arthur Richman, convinced Steinbrenner that the sportswriters would go easy on him in this 1998 event. The party was held in a private dining room in the Stadium on a bitter winter night in January 1998, a month before the opening of his twenty-fifth year as Yankee Boss.

"He was the man who had now owned the storied franchise longer than anyone in history," wrote former PR director Marty Appel in a baseball journal.

A dozen or so sportswriters decided to needle Steinbrenner by wearing turtleneck shirts, his standard outfit for casual winter wear. George fooled them by wearing a suit and tie. The sportswriters needled him by saying he fired managers, public relations directors, and secretaries by the dozens. He stoically sat through the roast. When my turn to talk came, I thanked him for being the kind of baseball owner who called back members of the press when they called him, who was always available to discuss controversial subjects, who never hid from the press, and who gave sportswriters more ego gratification with stories about him than any other figure in sports history in my time. Then I thanked him for allowing me to make a living writing about him for a quarter of a century and helping send my kids to college.

Steinbrenner hugged me when I finished. He likes to do that. Then I sat down. He got up, joked with the sportswriters about having nothing better to do on a winter night than kid him, and sat down.

In a couple of weeks he would be at Legends Field again. In about ten more months he would be crying in public for the first time I could remember, short of the tragic deaths of Thurman Munson, Billy Martin, Roger Maris, Mickey Mantle, and Joe DiMaggio, as he accepted the World Series championship again.

Could the Boss also be made of mush?

CHAPTER

TWENTY-SIX

Not even a perfect game pitcher is safe around the Yankees if the Boss is hungry for more.

On February 19, 1999, George Steinbrenner, determined to repeat the world championship in 1999, traded away David Wells—who had pitched the celebrated perfect game in 1998—for Roger Clemens.

The Yankees included left-handed reliever Graeme Lloyd and infielder Homer Bush (what a wonderful name for a baseball player) in the deal with Toronto.

Clemens was a five-time Cy Young Award winner, a six-time ERA leader, a twenty-strikeout game pitcher, a five time twenty-game winner, and a no-time World Series winner. He had failed the Red Sox in the 1986 World Series against the Mets (thank you, Bill Buckner) and agreed to accept a trade to the Yankees for a chance at a World Series win.

Bartenders all over town hung black mourning bands on their walls as Boomer Wells was shipped to Canada.

Steinbrenner's demanding influence over the Yankees made first place the *only* place. It was Torre's job to integrate Clemens into the rotation and lead the Yankees to their second straight championship. Two in three years would just not do.

Suddenly, the real world stepped in on Torre and the Yankees.

All players, coaches, and the manager take extensive physical examinations in spring training. It cuts into their golf schedule but it must be done. Torre's examination revealed that he had prostate cancer.

He soon left spring training for medical tests in St. Louis

and the Mayo Clinic in Rochester, Minnesota. The options of surgery, radiation, and seed implantation or a combination were considered. Torre opted for surgery. He left the team in the hands of former manager, and his bench coach, Don Zimmer.

Torre's cancer was the second to hit the Yankees in six months. Darryl Strawberry had been diagnosed with colon cancer the previous October, had missed the 1998 World Series, and was attempting a recovery in Tampa in the spring of 1999.

Strawberry was left behind when the Yankees broke camp at the end of March; he grew depressed, started drinking again with so-called friends, and was arrested one night for soliciting an undercover female police officer for prostitution and being found with cocaine in his possession.

He was banned from baseball again and allowed to return in September. All is forgiven if a guy can hit home runs.

On March 8, 1999, Joe DiMaggio died.

He had been ill for many months with lung cancer, a result of years of smoking, even during his playing days.

While I was researching my biography of DiMaggio, called *Where Have You Gone Joe DiMaggio?* whose title came from the line in the popular "Mrs. Robinson" song by Paul Simon and Art Garfunkel, I spoke to clubhouse man Pete Sheehy. "Joe used to come into the clubhouse early," he told me. "He would ask for his Camel cigarettes and half a cup of black coffee. Camel cigarettes and black coffee. Every day."

DiMaggio sat at a center table in the clubhouse, usually alone, well before the other players arrived, and signed boxes of baseballs. He would sign a dozen or two and then say to Sheehy, "Pete, you do the rest." Sheehy signed and signed and signed, capturing DiMaggio's careful handwriting so well that an FBI handwriting expert would be fooled. That is why the autograph collectors of today may well be spending thousands of dollars for an original Pete Sheehy thinking they have purchased an original DiMaggio autograph.

Sheehy got even better with his signing skills when Mickey Mantle joined the Yankees in 1951.

For these reasons plus the fact that he kept the uniforms clean, the clubhouse floors immaculate, and was mostly sworn to secrecy, Yankees of today walk through the Pete Sheehy Clubhouse.

DiMaggio had been a winner, a stylish player, and the husband of a young lady named Marilyn Monroe for all of 274 days. It had made him baseball's twentieth-century icon. He had been ill when Steinbrenner brought him back in September 1998 for another day of honor in Yankee Stadium.

While rumors of ill health moved around him, DiMaggio was able to accept the standing ovation as he always had in the Stadium. His oldtimers agreements commanded the Yankees to introduce him last at all events, even on the day in 1969 when Mickey Mantle was honored after his own retirement.

DiMaggio worked hard on being DiMaggio. He protected his image. He controlled access to media. He seemed to glow when he was out in public. He had presence.

After the September 1998 appearance at the Stadium for his final time, a sign appeared in the ramp between the Pete Sheehy Clubhouse and the field for all Yankees to see. It read, "I thank the good Lord for making me a Yankee," the statement he made when he was first honored on the final Saturday of the 1949 season. The Yankees beat the Red Sox twice that 1949 weekend to clinch Casey Stengel's first Yankee pennant.

After his 1951 retirement, DiMaggio worked hard at the job he knew best: playing Joe DiMaggio. He attended banquets for pay, played golf across the country, stayed in luxury hotels, and flew first class at the sponsor's expense.

He maintained that Greta Garbo mystique, staying away from the press, going near fans only when there was a financial reason, and diligently protecting his image. It may have cost him a lot of friends. Real friends. He led the league in Joe DiMaggio hangers-on friends.

Teammate Eddie Lopat, an unpretentious, gregarious guy who scouted for many years after his pitching career ended, said of DiMaggio, "He was the loneliest man I ever knew. He led the league in room service."

Baseball collector Barry Halper had been a friend of DiMaggio's for many years. Year after year he would pick DiMaggio up in a limousine and keep him happy in his own New Jersey home while Joe awaited a golf tournament. Once, innocently, Halper invited a small weekly newspaper reporter to his home while DiMaggio was there.

DiMaggio took one look at the reporter after he was introduced by Halper, scowled at his host, and left. They never spoke again.

Baseball executive Arthur Richman escorted DiMaggio around Los Angeles prior to a big baseball banquet. They drove through the Westwood section of Los Angeles.

DiMaggio asked Richman to stop the car.

"He got out and walked across the street," said Richman. "He stayed looking across a field at Westwood Memorial Park for a few minutes and then came back to the car with tears in his eyes. I asked him if something was wrong."

DiMaggio said to Richman, "Don't you know? That's where I have Marilyn."

He was married and divorced twice. He married actress Dorothy Arnold in 1939 and divorced her in 1943. He married Marilyn Monroe on January 14, 1954. Miss Monroe, as DiMaggio always referred to the actress, filed for divorce on October 5, 1954, under her legal name of Norma Jeane DiMaggio.

He carried the torch for her the rest of his life. He sent a dozen roses to her Westwood cemetery crypt weekly until late in the 1970s, about fifteen years after her 1962 death. It only stopped when fans began stealing the flowers at Westwood, after the public learned where the roses came from.

Some of his more animated colleagues and friends tried to kid DiMaggio out of his dour persona. Football Hall of Famer Otto Graham was on a bus with DiMaggio and other sport celebrities at an American Airlines golf tournament in Hawaii.

DiMaggio sat alone in the front of the bus, looking as though he had lost his last friend. The ebullient Graham, struggling with cancer at the time, boarded the bus, and spotted the dour DiMaggio. Seeing the look on Joe's face, he grabbed him and kissed him smack on the lips. "For God's sake, Joe," Graham boomed, as his beaming wife looked on, "Cheer up!" DiMaggio's face reddened as the other sports personalities at the tournament got hysterical, but he never cracked so much as a smile.

"Ahh, Joe," said Graham, "have some fun."

Restaurateur Toots Shor had once kidded about the immaculate DiMaggio by saying that when Joe died, a hundred thousand people would line up at St. Patrick's Cathedral in Manhattan for his services, look in his casket, and all say the same thing, "Joe, you look great . . . Joe, you look great."

A few thousand filled St. Patrick's on April 23, 1999, for a memorial prayer service for Joe DiMaggio. John Cardinal O'Connor spoke of DiMaggio slipping into St. Patrick's unobtrusively one day. Mayor Rudy Giuliani, a DiMaggio worshiper, and Yankee teammate Bobby Brown spoke eloquently about the Yankee Clipper. Brother Dom DiMaggio sat quietly in a second-row pew. Henry Kissinger, a regular at these Yankee events of note, sat next to George Steinbrenner. Phil Rizzuto, Yogi Berra, and Ralph Branca were there.

Estranged son Joe DiMaggio, Jr., once an adorable youngster seen on the cover of *Sport* magazine in 1947 with his dad, was not there. The boy, grown now to unhappy manhood, did attend DiMaggio's San Francisco funeral and served as a long-haired pallbearer. He received a meager $20,000 yearly of DiMaggio's $30,000,000 estate, as administered by friend and lawyer Morris Engelberg. Joe DiMaggio, Jr., would never get to use the money. He died of natural causes a few months after the death of his famous father, after a life of drug and alcohol abuse. He was fifty-seven. The weight of carrying the name of Joe DiMaggio, Jr., was too heavy for him.

Steinbrenner often brought the Yankee Clipper back to the stadium for special events. He became an important part of the Yankees nostalgic scene for Oldtimers days, opening days, retirement events for others, and special anniversaries. Steinbrenner clearly understood Yankee tradition, that link of past to present, Ruth to DiMaggio, DiMaggio to Mantle, Mantle to Mattingly, Mattingly to Jeter and Williams and all the rest of the 1990s heroes. Shortly after DiMaggio's death, the number 5, DiMaggio's retired number, was added to the left sleeve of the Yankee uniforms. A black band would later encircle the sleeve after the September death of Catfish Hunter.

Don Zimmer, who played on the Brooklyn Dodgers world championship team of 1955, was the acting manager in Torre's absence. He was bothered by a bad knee, but in his fifty years in baseball, he had learned to survive injuries. He had been hit three times in the head by pitched balls and wore a metal plate inside his skull. He was a backup shortstop to Pee Wee Reese in Brooklyn, which probably kept him from realizing his full playing potential but kept him in the game more years than he might have expected.

Zimmer was an Original Met in 1962 and opened their first season at third base. He went oh for thirty-two. When he finally ended his slump with a hit, manager Casey Stengel sent him off to Cincinnati.

"I had to trade him while he was still hot," Stengel deadpanned.

He managed at San Diego, Texas, Boston, and with the Chicago Cubs before becoming a coach and joining Torre in 1996.

Zimmer was the Red Sox manager in 1978 when Bucky Bleeping Dent hit that famous three-run playoff homer in Fenway off Mike Torrez. Flaky left-hander Bill Lee called him a gerbil. Other Boston players ignored Zimmer's suggestions. Zimmer stayed calm. Fifty years in the game is no accident.

"I don't want the job. I never wanted the job," Zimmer said early in April of the Yankee position after Torre left for surgery. "My knee is bothering me. I can't stand up properly. I can't wait for Joe to get back. I might leave then."

Torre rejoined the Yankees May 19 in Boston. He seemed a little pale when I saw him the next week at his Stadium office before the Boston Red Sox visit to New York.

"I get tired faster," he said. "That's about the only difference I can notice."

Don Zimmer sat on a soft couch. Publicity director Rick Cerrone, often confused with former player Rick Cerone, stood nearby. Cerrone, the son of a Mount Vernon fire chief, looked after Torre carefully. He controlled his schedule and made sure the press never got too intrusive.

Torre had somehow managed to win over all the members of the press with his honesty and his openness. Nobody seemed able to upset him—not even the occasional call from Steinbrenner on his office phone.

"We understand each other," Torre said. "He has been very good and very understanding through all this."

Steinbrenner, approaching his seventieth birthday in the year 2000, seemed to have the same energy he showed more than a quarter of a century earlier when he first purchased the Yankees. It must all be in the genes.

Steinbrenner seemed less combative, less intrusive, and less outspoken in 1999, and he allowed Torre to run the team his own way in 1999. There was only one small Steinbrenner outburst, a spring training popoff that revealed that the old George had not completely disappeared within the new George.

Hideki Irabu, the Japanese pitcher, failed to cover first base on a ball hit to first baseman Tino Martinez in a spring training contest. Steinbrenner exploded at the lack of hustle, called Irabu a "fat, pussy toad," and considered releasing him. He was persuaded otherwise by his "baseball people," the Yankee front office staffers he generally trusted. His patience was rewarded when Irabu recovered his confidence in midseason, put together a modest winning streak, and helped the Yankees pass the Red Sox in the Division race.

The Yankees had won 125 games in 1998. Baseball experts argued most of the winter in print whether or not they were baseball's best team ever. The 1999 team never had to face that challenge. They dropped in and out of first place most of the early season and never could open up in a comfortable ten- or twelve-game lead. They were still good enough to keep the challenging Red Sox away, though, even surviving a late-season Boston sweep.

There were highlights in the 1999 season that equaled the excitement of 1998.

One came on June 10 when the Yankees bused down to Washington from an interleague game in Philadelphia to visit the President of the United States.

Bill Clinton, free now of impeachment problems, requested that the Yankees visit him for a ceremony honoring their 1998 championship. Roger Clemens, who wasn't there in 1998, and Boomer Wells, who was, had exchanged places on the Yankees roster. So it was Clemens, not Wells, who was among the Yankee players at the South Lawn ceremony at 1600 Pennsylvania Avenue.

Hillary Clinton, who would later claim she was a Yankee fan all her life when she wasn't a Chicago Cubs fan, donned a Yankee cap. President Clinton spoke glowingly of the game of baseball and his interest in it.

"Last year was a season—for those of us who loved baseball all our lives—that clearly, irrevocably restored baseball as America's pastime," the President told the appreciative garden crowd.

George Steinbrenner told an amusing story of how he had once coached Donna Shalala, the secretary of Health and Human Services, when she played softball in the Cleveland area. Steinbrenner always enjoyed coaching anybody.

Bernie Williams, born and raised in San Juan, Puerto Rico, and now a resident of Armonk in Westchester County, New York, was thrilled at the visit.

"Once you get inside, you think to yourself, 'Wow, man,

so this is the White House.' You think about everything that has happened here," he later said.

Derek Jeter presented Hillary Clinton with a World Series pendant. David Cone, the veteran pitcher and clubhouse leader, presented the Clintons with a minireplica of the 1998 World Series trophy.

"We missed it in 1996," said Cone of the lack of an invite to the White House that election year. "This counts for two years. If we win again next year, hopefully we can come back."

Cone's presence in The White House that day, his presence in uniform at the Stadium any day, his continued successful career was a major miracle.

David Cone—lean, tall, intelligent—was smart enough as a youngster growing up in Kansas City to think he could be a sportswriter. He was also smart enough to know he might make a few more bucks if he followed a baseball career after being signed by Kansas City. He came to New York in a trade with the Mets, became the night-loving Derek Jeter of his time, was 20-3 in the Mets division winning season of 1988, had a few unpleasant adventures with Baseball Annies around Shea, later was traded to Toronto, signed a free agent contract again with Kansas City, and came to the Yankees in 1996.

After a May 2, 1996, complete game win against the Chicago White Sox with a blue index finger on his right hand, Cone was diagnosed to be suffering from an aneurysm, a debilitating circulation problem sometimes considered life threatening. He had the aneurysm removed from his shoulder in a complicated procedure on May 10, 1996.

He was back pitching in two months and won the vital third game of the World Series against the Braves after the Yankees lost the first two games.

In 1998 Cone won twenty games for the second time in his career.

On July 18, 1999, he was the starter on Yogi Berra Day at the stadium. George Steinbrenner had invited Berra back to receive his full due after fourteen years of estrangement because of the callous 1985 firing. Don Larsen, who had pitched a World Series no-hitter in 1956 and had caught the leaping Berra in his arms after the game, was also invited back to share Berra's joyous moment.

Cone faced the Montreal Expos, a mostly Triple A team posing as big leaguers. No matter. They were getting big league meal money and big league pay. The game counted.

Cone retired all twenty-seven Expos in order. No runs, no hits, no errors, no one on base. A perfect game, the second in Yankee Stadium in two years after David Wells did it in 1998.

When Orlando Carbrera, the Montreal shortstop, hit the last pitch of the game foul to third base where Scott Brosius caught it easily, Cone dropped to his knees and grabbed his forehead. He was soon under a joyous pileup of pinstripes. His Yankee teammates truly liked, respected, and admired the guy. Catcher Joe Girardi, second baseman Chuck Knoblauch, and designated hitter Chili Davis carried Cone from the field. He waved his cap at the crowd of 41,930 roaring fans with his right hand and motioned to all he could see with his gloved left hand.

"I probably have a better chance of winning the lottery than this happening today," Cone said in a raucous clubhouse later. "What an honor. All the Yankee legends here. Don Larsen in the park. Yogi Berra Day. It makes you stop and think about the Yankee magic and the mystique of this ball park."

Cone was soon on the phone in Joe Torre's office being congratulated by the 1998 perfect game pitcher, David Wells, from Toronto. Larsen was soon hugging Cone in the clubhouse for photographers. Three perfect pitchers—Larsen, Wells, and Cone—were now locked together in baseball history, a new version of Willie, Mickey, and the Duke, the honored threesome of New York center fielders of the 1950s: Willie Mays, Mickey Mantle, and Duke Snider.

The rest of the Yankees regular season of 1999 was without much drama. It was the playoffs that mattered now.

Darryl Strawberry returned to the team in September, received a warm reception by teammates, and said all the right things about his troubled life. He could not promise a perfect game but he did promise a perfect effort in beating the twin devils of cocaine and alcohol as he battled back from colon cancer.

"The fans in New York, they love Darryl Strawberry," said Derek Jeter. "I'm sure they'll give him a warm reception. Everyone has a soft spot in their heart for Straw."

On September 9, 1999, Catfish Hunter died and George Steinbrenner issued a statement from his Tampa office expressing his shock at the death and his concern about the family.

"George took care of me," Hunter once said. "He paid me enough money to take care of my family for life."

Steinbrenner believed in performance. Hunter was a Yankee treasure because he performed. When he was clean and sober, Strawberry performed. The moral issues would be left for the philosophers. What do *they* know about the infield fly rule?

Boston made a little run at the Yankees in late September, cutting the Yankees lead in the East to two and a half games at one point. It changed nothing. The Yankees closed out the season in Tampa in a meaningless game with Torre allowing Paul O'Neill to manage the club to a 6-2 loss against the Devil Rays. They won over Boston by four games with a 98-64 record, 16 games under the record win total of 114 in 1998.

The season that started with Torre recovering from prostate cancer and Strawberry battling colon cancer, with Roger Clemens now a Yankee in his twilight years, with Hideki Irabu, a maligned malcontent, with Bernie Williams uncertain if he had made the right move in coming back for huge money, with David Cone pitching on a one-year deal, and with Derek Jeter not possibly getting any better ended in more glory and gold.

Cone pitched the perfect game and Mariano Rivera led the majors in saves with 45. Williams played 158 games, collected 202 hits and 100 walks as the first Yankee to do that since Lou Gehrig in 1937. Paul O'Neill and Tino Martinez each knocked in over 100 runs. Chuck Knoblauch scored 120 runs and Jeter finished second in the batting race to Boston's Nomar Garciaparra with a .349 mark.

Orlando Hernandez, Cuba's and the Bronx's El Duque, won seventeen games as the pitching leader, and Roger Clemens won fourteen games. Cone was 12-9 but ready for postseason play. Torre was after his third World Series title in four seasons, a record only Casey Stengel (five in his first five years) could challenge. Stengel won his first Series in 1949 with the Yankees and proudly announced, "I never coulda done it without my players." Torre was a lot more gracious about his players, simply giving them all the credit for these triumphs.

Now it was on to the winning Division series against Texas again, a bruising battle with Boston for the American League championship, the thirty-sixth pennant in the glorious Yankee history, and the World Series win against Atlanta, successfully completing the Drive for twenty-five. Brooms were at the ready after the second game with fans yelling "Sweep, sweep, sweep."

Chad Curtis hit a dramatic tenth-inning homer in the third game, his second of the contest, for a 6-5 win and a Yankees 3-0 lead.

Roger Clemens, with relief help, of course from Mariano Rivera, won the fourth game 4-1 as the Yankees became the first team in sixty years to sweep back-to-back Series. The Yankees, of course, had done it in 1938 and 1939 when Joe DiMaggio's team beat the Chicago Cubs and the Cincinnati Reds.

Joe Torre had now won three World Series in his four years as Yankee manager. Baseball could start thinking about measuring him for Hall of Fame honors.

George Steinbrenner led this team, The Team of the Century, for more than a quarter of the twentieth century, the longest ownership reign in Yankee history, closing in rapidly on the most successful baseball operation in the game's history.

There had to be Baseball Hall of Fame consideration for Steinbrenner regardless of the stories of a generation of tyranny and terror around that historic Yankee Stadium location at 161st Street and River Avenue in the Bronx. Imagine the Boss as a Cooperstown bust.

They were the Damn Yankees again, loved by their own fans and hated by all others for inordinate success, incredible baseball fortune, and almost uninterrupted triumphs. In the 1990s fans outside New York were forever being consumed with jealousy of the Yankee victories. The Yankees, in humbling the Braves again in four straight, clearly were *the* team of the 90s.

As the millennium passed into history and the year 2000 becomes easier to accept; as George Steinbrenner's seventieth birthday approaches on July 4, 2000; as younger, better players are ready to replace retiring and traded Yankees, the message is clear.

The next Yankee five-year plan will be about the same as the last one. By all odds, the Yankees will win a few more by the year 2004.

The Boss would not have it any other way.

INDEX

ABOUT THE AUTHOR

MAURY ALLEN began his career writing for *Sports Illustrated* and then moved to the *New York Post*, where he covered the Yankees for twenty-seven years. He has written more than thirty books on baseball and his work has appeared extensively in television documentaries.